a step back

St Nicholas

A GLAMORGANSHIRE PARISH

a step back

St Nicholas

A GLAMORGANSHIRE PARISH

Neil Walklate

First impression: 2012

© Copyright Neil Walklate and Y Lolfa Cyf., 2012

Cover painting: L Stone,
by kind permission of Mr and Mrs Richard Harry

ISBN: 978 1847714152

FSC

Published and printed in Wales
on paper from well maintained forests by
Y Lolfa Cyf., Talybont, Ceredigion SY24 5HE
website www.ylolfa.com
e-mail ylolfa@ylolfa.com
tel 01970 832 304
fax 832 782

Explanatory note

Many of the spellings used in the text come directly from old documents and are neither consistent or correct, and some of the names of dwellings strike a precarious balance between Welsh and English reflecting the diversity of backgrounds of the parishioners and more importantly the manner of pronunciation. Scribes wrote what they thought they heard and spelling was not standardised.

The maps are selective, not all-embracing, and are designed to help the reader locate places mentioned in the text.

In the 1841 Census, information is ordered as follows: name, age, occupation. The 1851 to 1901 census returns are more informative giving name, relation to head of family such as married or widowed, and other information, such as age, rank, profession or occupation, and where born.

In the parish Poor Book, money is raised based on the rateable value of land and property listed by occupier, owner, a description of that land or property usually by name, the annual rateable value and the rate payable at 9d. in the pound.

In the parish Rate Book, there is a similar arrangement except the rate is based on area given in acres, roods and perches: 'arp'.

Dates given for an individual's occupation of a particular dwelling are those for which documentary proof exists – tenancy in many cases was probably for a longer period.

Unless otherwise stated all baptisms, marriages and burials took place in St Nicholas parish church.

On family trees the following abbreviations apply: born – b, lived – l, married =, baptised – bap, died – d, circa – c.

Welsh people resident in the Vale of Glamorgan usually referred to the village as Shinicalas or Shini Colas.

Contents

Introduction

"St Nicholas has nothing remarkable about it except some very neat cottages with uncommonly pretty gardens."

Malkin – nineteenth-century traveller and topographer

★

"In the parish are some Druidical remains, and it is said that Oliver Cromwell slept in the manor house."

Slater's Commercial Directory (1880)

★

"The Fairs, for horned Cattle and Sheep, are holden on the 19th of May, 21st of August and 17th of December… There is an House adjoining the church-yard, which is kept in repair at the expense of the Parish, and wherein poor People live: it appears to me, on its first Institution, to have been either a Chantry, or an Alms-house," observes the Rev. David Thomas.

A Topographical Dictionary of the Dominion of Wales (1811)
by Nicholas Carlisle

★

"… the small and untidy notice 'Post Office' over the porch of one of the agricultural workers' cottages near the church" was an aesthetic blot and minor criticism of St Nicholas, according to the adjudicators of the best-kept village in the Vale of Glamorgan competition of 1953. "St Nicholas is deserving of something more dignified to denote its post office." This did not prevent the village from winning the award, however.

★

The church "was shut against me, but we met at a neighbouring house, Mr Deer's, where I offered Christ to all sinners, with much freedom and power." Charles Wesley's comment on St Nicholas on 10th November 1740 as described by him in *First Visit to Wales The Journal of the Rev. Charles Wesley* (1849).

These random observations encompassing just over 200 years in time offer the perceptions and reflect the interests of the authors when visiting and passing through the village.

★

The first and only book relating exclusively to the parish of St Nicholas was published in 1934. It was the work of a local man, Charles Shepherd, who was an enthusiast and a librarian with a passion for discovering the past through painstaking research, active fieldwork and by talking to the people of the parish. He was not originally of the parish but came from another country, Germany. Seeing a village, a locality or a landscape and its people as an outsider, lends objectivity to observations, but through the processes of absorption and osmosis, a gradual integration with the new environment and culture takes place. Mr Shepherd clearly exhibited a formidable affection for and knowledge of his adopted Glamorgan. Since he wrote his book, there has been a change of emphasis in the presentation and content of local historical researches. He deals mainly with the established church and its sphere of influence, the spread of non-conformity, the gentry and some of the antiquities lying within the parish borders. It reflects the hierarchical nature of society, with an emphasis on those at the apex of the social triangle – the few, not the many. Current practice attempts to paint a picture representing all sections of society, as well as taking advantage of newly-available archives and scientific advances which enhance and enrich our levels of understanding.

Below are some of the subjects and topics that have merited inclusion, but the reader will notice that some historical periods in our parish history are still grey areas, unresolved and awaiting discovery, or lost forever.

Many, many generations of people have lived in St Nicholas, for the most part working on the land, and they provide a continuous thread stretching back at least 6,000 years that can be vouched for with certainty. At that time Neolithic or New Stone Age man settled in the area, clearing the dense woodland to establish an organised farming community capable of constructing the massive burial chamber at Tinkinswood. Although it was once postulated that the hillfort Y Gaer was built during the Iron Age, recent research suggests otherwise. Influxes of Romans, Saxons, Vikings, Normans and men and women from the West Country and Ireland among others, have all contributed in their own different ways to the commuting village, yet still farming parish, that we know of today. Use has been made of the most recent information available to help with the dating and diagnosis of the more distant past, and this intelligence has invariably pushed the clock back further, prompting a reappraisal of megalithic tombs and associated earthworks.

Local government, in the form of vestry administration, is dealt with at length using the extensive records of the churchwardens, surveyors of highways and overseers of the poor. The extracts quoted from these largely nineteenth-century documents graphically reveal the structure of parish society from top to bottom, from squire and rector to labourer and pauper, the haves and have-nots, the privileged and the suppressed.

Some chapters are dedicated to everyday country folk who, by their endeavours, have left their mark. They were men and women of resolve who may have designed and built machinery, thatched the local roofs, brewed beer or bent their backs toiling on the roads.

There is a detailed study of the thatched cottages known as Smith's Row, showing the development of this typical Glamorganshire vernacular housing unit as it responded to changing social patterns and needs. All of the old housing blocks in the village – Manor Cottages, The Three Tuns, The Post Office, Church Row – show evidence of extensions and improvements, as do individual houses such as Tŷ-to-gwellt and The School House. Originally the houses of yeomen, tradesmen or craftsmen of the sixteenth, seventeenth and eighteenth centuries, most became overcrowded nineteenth-century farm labourers' cottages subdivided to cope with the rapidly expanding population. These old dwellings have seen thatch replaced by slate, imported brick used to tidy up door and window openings formerly framed by rough dressed local limestone, the rendering of rubble walls or the exposure of the same from beneath many layers of multi-coloured lime-wash. Farms and individual houses of the parish are listed as well as the names and occupations of tenants and owners.

Neil Walklate
July 2012

St Nicholas, the Parish

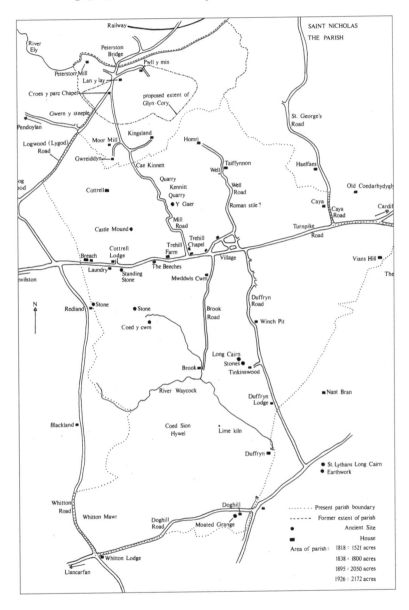

SAINT NICHOLAS
THE PARISH

Railway
River Ely
Peterston Bridge
Peterston Mill
Pwll y min
Lan y lay
Croes y parc Chapel
proposed extent of Glyn-Cory
Gwern y steeple
St. George's Road
Pendoylan
Moor Mill
Kingsland
Homri
Logwood (Lygod) Road
Gwreiddyn
Cae Kinnett
Taiffynnon
Haelfaes
Well
Cottrell
Quarry Kennitt Quarry
Well Road
Old Coedarhydygl
Y Gaer
Roman stile ?
Caya
Caya Road
Cardif
og od
Mill Road
Castle Mound
Turnpike Road
Trehill Chapel
Cottrell Lodge
Trehill Farm
Village
Vians Hill
Breach
The Beeches
The
Laundry
Standing Stone
Mwddwls Cwm
nvilston
Duffryn Road
N
Redland
Stone
Stone
Brook Road
Winch Pit
Coed y cwm
Long Cairn
Stones
Tinkinswood
Brook
Nant Bran
River Waycock
Duffryn Lodge
Blackland
Coed Sion Hywel
Lime kiln
Duffryn
St. Lythans Long Cairn
Earthwork
Whitton Road
Doghill
Whitton Mawr
Doghill Road
Moated Grange

.... Present parish boundary
- - - - - Former extent of parish
●   Ancient Site
■   House

Area of parish: 1818 : 1521 acres
                 1838 : 1800 acres
                 1895 : 2050 acres
                 1926 : 2172 acres

Whitton Lodge
Llancarfan

13

CHAPTER 1

The Parish

HOW MANY TWENTY-FIRST century inhabitants of St Nicholas could accurately describe the houses, farms and lands comprising the parish? To those living here in the nineteenth century the concept of parish was deeply ingrained. There was an identity fostered by the church and by the vestry, with both bodies exercising a considerable degree of control over local matters such as roads, the welfare of the poor, education, the upholding of the law and the levying of rates. The loss of this power in the second half of the nineteenth century meant less parish activity and less emphasis on purely local matters.

The ancient sites of the area include: Tinkinswood burial chamber and related stones; St Lythans burial chamber (not in, but adjacent to the parish, recently scientifically excavated and with a possible circular earthwork to the south); a circular earthwork, Coed y Cwm, above the source of the eponymous brook of Brook Lane; plus a number of standing stones between it and Cottrell Lodge; a circular motte or castle mound in Cottrell Park, Y Gaer hilltop fort or castle; and just south of the parish the relatively recently excavated Iron Age and Roman farm or villa at Whitton and lastly the moated grange at Doghill. This would seem to indicate a sizeable, shifting and organised population in the area over thousands of years which, from available evidence, lived well outside the present village envelope.

Tinkinswood

Dating of ancient sites has always posed problems – Tinkinswood is said to have been constructed by colonists from the continent along the lines of French prototypes of the Loire estuary. Modern radiocarbon dating methods and increased research and investigation might well ascribe new dates and meanings, different from those previously suggested, to some of these old sites. The oldest European megalithic tombs date from well before 4000 BC, with the current forerunner being at Kercado in Brittany and constructed around 4800 BC, while Britain has many examples which are older than 3000 BC.

The latest information reveals that Tinkinswood dates from the fourth millennium, a time not long after the first clearance of the land and the introduction of farming and settlements as opposed to the nomadic hunter-gatherer lifestyle. It can be best described as a megalithic long cairn with a capstone of Triassic mudstone quarried nearby weighing something in the region of 40 tons and being the largest in Britain measuring about 30 feet by 18. This suggests that it is a product of a well-organised and firmly led society or group presumably living nearby. It belongs to the Severn-Cotswold group of megalithic monuments prevalent in those areas. The burial chamber was accessible after the covering mound of earth was raised and was used over a very long period, being reopened and resealed to admit bones or bodies, and making radiocarbon chronology difficult. What is certain is that the building phase continued over a number of centuries and the construction of long-chambered cairns had ceased by about 3200 BC. It is further suggested that the cairns were territorial and/or community centres, remaining in use throughout much of the third millennium until individual burial began to replace the communal tomb. Many had associated ploughed field systems which were only finally closed and abandoned with the opening of the Uplands about 1600 BC and the rejection of ostentatious burial and ritual. The cairn has the usual east-west alignment and to the south are associated free-standing stones and heaps of stones representative of field clearance.

But does any of this tell us what the people who lived here, and built this highly symbolic structure, really believed concerning matters of birth, life and death? Knowledge of these things would enhance understanding of this impressive edifice described in 1880 as "Druidical remains". In his marvellously entertaining read *The Modern Antiquarian*, Julian Cope offers insight and clues to the shape and form of Tinkinswood. The society was based around the Great Mother or Goddess often with lunar and/or solar associations and these longbarrows were about the birth and rebirth of souls with the stone chambers, usually at the east end, acting as a womb in which dissected bodies were placed and returned to the Great Mother. Imagine looking from above at the ground plan and you have a recumbent pregnant mother with open and truncated legs and a clearly defined vaginal entrance in between. Academics tend not to be as explicit in their descriptions as the amateur enthusiast Mr Cope, but his vision of this "outrageous paradise" rings true. A visit to this imposing cairn is awe inspiring in both the physical and spiritual sense.

Whitton

Near to what is now Whitton Lodge and the appropriately named field Whitton Mawr in the extreme south-west of the parish just south of the Roman road, there is archaeological evidence of early Iron Age roundhouses being succeeded by the rectangular structures of a Roman villa. This is a common sequence of events. It is thought that some 90 per cent of the Romano-British population lived a rural life and the villa was its most significant structure. In Wales villas were mostly a rarity except in the agricultural south-east with its fertile soil. A villa was in effect a farm, but one of some style, and comprised a range of structures besides the main house and barn. It may be assumed also that some of the nearby field systems are of Roman origin, and that the workforce came from a local settlement which could

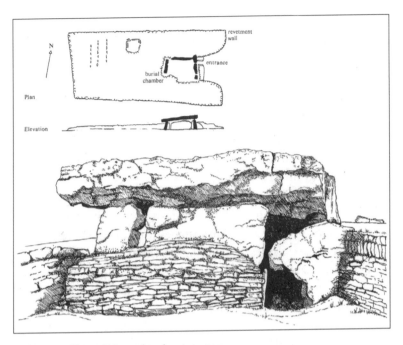

Tinkinswood Long Cairn – chamber entrance

St Lythan's Long Cairn

have been St Nicholas or Bonvilston, if they existed at that time. Little more can be said with certainty of Roman occupation in the rest of the parish, but there must have been a presence as the Caerleon to Carmarthen road passed right through what is now the village.

The Dark Ages

The period which followed the collapse of the Roman Empire, and known to history as dark because it was perceived as a time when civilisation, knowledge and culture receded is, in the case of St Nicholas, obscure. The intrusions of Saxons and Vikings who came to the Vale have left suggestions of their presence in one or two place names but no more – theirs was much more an oral culture than that of the Romans, and they built with wood. It is however likely that the nucleus of the village existed with the Roman road again being a vital artery.

Y Gaer, Cottrell Castle Mound and Coed y Cwm

These three sites straddle the A48 which, at different times, was the Roman road, the medieval Port Way and eighteenth-century coach road, and have long been the source of speculation about their origins. They have all been described as castles but with different assignations, respectively Iron Age, Norman and unknown.

When first researched in the 1970s, received wisdom held that Y Gaer was indeed an early British Iron Age hillfort to which the Romans had added an outer rectangular vallum to the south of approximately three acres, having a steep scarp to the west and the ·south. The vallum or earth defensive rampart is now thought to be a natural feature. In 1762 about a mile north of this vallum, a coin of Antoninus Pius, Roman Emperor between AD 138 and 161, was discovered along with an earthenware jar. A description of the site is instructive. It is a useful vantage point, as the Ordnance Survey realised, being the highest land for miles around situated on the summit of a ridge. The strategic significance was not lost on the original inhabitants of the area, commanding as it does views of the Bristol Channel to the south, the hills to the north and the course of the River Ely to the west. To the north there is a sudden fall of the land towards Peterston, adding considerably to the defensive capabilities of the site. It was suggested that this early British and Roman arrangement was similar to that at the Liege castle in Llancarfan parish. Y Gaer has also been described as a Dark Ages camp.

Physical descriptions show Y Gaer as being a ringwork, 200 feet in diameter and ten feet high with a deep and forbidding ditch. It is considered to be the best preserved castle ringwork in the county, and is bigger than the stone castles at Newcastle, Coity and Ogmore. Cottrell is a flat-topped motte 109 feet across at base and nine feet above the surrounding countryside and set in a commanding position. Coed y Cwm is a ringwork 120 feet across and 18 feet high with a peripheral inner bank and largely intact ditch. All three remain well-preserved to this day and are impressive earthworks.

It seems however that these three castles are likely to be part of a network that ultimately gave the Normans control of Glamorgan and were possibly motte-and-bailey constructions with a wooden stockade around the top of the mound and possibly even a timber tower. If there were baileys, little evidence remains of their imprint on the landscape.

Glamorgan has many castles dating from the Middle Ages but it would be wrong to suppose that they all exhibited the grandeur and imposing physical presence of say Cardiff or Coity castles. The St Nicholas examples are much more modest but would still have served their purpose of suppressing the local populace and imposing the will of the lord of the manor. Welsh resistance to Norman rule was still common in the twelfth century, despite the lordship of Glamorgan being assumed by the king Henry II. It was the Clares who finally completed the conquest of Glamorgan in the thirteenth century, some time before Edward I began his campaign to subdue the rest of Wales.

At about the time of the Fitzhamon lordship of Glamorgan

(1093–1107) grants at St Nicholas and Bonvilston, among others, suggest that early military ringworks were constructed. By 1217, when Gilbert de Clare became Lord of Glamorgan, well over 60 early castles had been founded of which 28 were ringworks and 16 were mottes. The lowlands of the Vale of Glamorgan essentially comprise a plateau cut through with valleys and a few sheer hills, and the three sites in the parish reflect this, with only Y Gaer being an obvious castle location. Cottrell motte is in rolling parkland (now a golf course), and Coed y Cwm is at the top of a gently sloping incline. It has also been discovered that the location of mottes and castle ringworks is closely related to the glacial deposits from the last Ice Age. All mottes are to the north of the drift and use glacial formations and material in their construction, whereas most ringworks are to the south of the glacial extent – Y Gaer being an exception, on fairly level ground with thin soil. It is not possible to say how long these castles were in use but, significantly, none were replaced by newer, stronger stone-built structures. They might possibly have remained in unchanged use until well into the thirteenth or even fourteenth century.

So why did this comparatively small area have three early substantial castles? The answer lies in the ancient subdivision of the parish and the lordship of St Nicholas which was held by three knights at Cardiff Castle. It is assumed that the Corbets – probably the first Norman settlers in St Nicholas – built and held as tenants-in-chief the most prestigious site at Y Gaer. Sub-tenancies or sub-fees were created at nearby Cottrell motte linked to Trehill and the Cottrell family (although not recorded until 1320), and at Coed y Cwm where the Mitdehorguill family held lands by the mid twelfth century. The extent of the boundaries of the lordship of St Nicholas is not clear, but certainly they reached beyond the parish limits. Roger Corbet paid eight marks for a sub-fee in 1202 to King John who was at that time Lord of Glamorgan. By 1262, William Corbet was responsible for and held all three fees of the lordship of St Nicholas. In 1280, William sued his tenant Adam de Someri concerning his wardship and marriage, the latter being heir to the Mitdehorguill lands of Coed y Cwm. These were troubled times, with St Nicholas being burned by the Welsh in 1226 and destroyed by Hywel ap Maredudd of Meisgyn in 1229. The tenancy eventually passed to the Flemings of St Georges and then the Malefants. It seems quite likely that these castles saw some military action, with the Normans and their successors meeting opposition from the indigenous population towards these unpopular invaders. The Welsh language was suppressed with Norman and English place names becoming common in the Vale and some villages and parishes assuming the name of their Norman lord, for example Bonvilston and Laleston. The typical Vale village, centred on a manor or castle with an adjacent church, is more typical of English settlement patterns than those of Wales. After the first thrust of the Norman incursions, it seems that the Welsh language made a comeback, with place and field names reverting to their original denominations. It is known that bards visited the homes of Welsh-speaking gentry, the sixteenth-century Meurigs of Cottrell being among them, even though the Tudor monarchs had banned Welsh as an official language under the Act of Union of 1536. In the 1570s, Rice Merrick of Cottrell remarked that the "castle of the Corbetts... [has] long since razed that no memory thereof remaineth, otherwise than a great field thereof called the castle hill".

The Middle Ages to the nineteenth century

St Nicholas was not an ecclesiastical parish with a lord of the manor and coextensive boundaries. It was divided into three – a division that was still noticeable in the twentieth century when the major land and property owners lived at Duffryn, Cottrell and Coedarhydyglyn. In 1578, the three knights' fees were devolved to Henry Earl of Pembroke (comprising the village, Pwll y Min, Homri and Doghill), Miles Button (Duffryn minus Doghill) and Rhys Meurig (Cottrell). The latter, also known as Rice Merrick, was the celebrated author of *Morganiae Archaiographia*, which he began writing in 1578 and left unfinished at his death. It is one of the earliest county histories of Britain, published just two years after William Lambarde's *A Perambulation of Kent*. Merrick, who was born *c.*1520, was the son of Meurig ap Hywel ap Philip, a freeholder and leaseholder of Bonvilston descended from Welsh families living in the Miskin lordship. After marrying the daughter of William ap John of Bonvilston, in 1546 Meurig bought the manor of Trehill or Cottrell in the parish of St Nicholas. This was a family with aspirations, and he built a new house at Cottrell sometime in the 1550s or 1560s. Adding to his father's acquisitions, Merrick obtained the manor of Bonvilston in 1574, land in the two manors then amounting in total to about 2,000 acres. Originally of yeoman class, the family had come far and sometime in the 1550s Merrick married Mary Fleming, which made him related to the Mansel family.

Merrick was a man of many talents functioning variously as a lawyer, clerk of the peace, genealogist and antiquary. He also enjoyed the patronage of William and then Henry Herbert, the Earls of Pembroke. In fact Merrick's eldest son Morgan married Martha, a member of the Herbert family.

Having observed some of the changes brought about among the rich and the powerful after the arrival of the Normans, it is instructive to consider the mass of the population and how they were affected. It is reasonable to assume that the social upheavals occuring in England were mirrored in this most anglicised of Welsh counties. By the middle of the fifteenth century labour, service and villeinage to the lord of the manor would largely have died out. In its place there would have been families of hired labourers and tenant farmers. The latter were then copyholders on the manor rolls, paying an annual rent to the lord and having no freedom of tenure unlike the freeholder. Later in the seventeenth century the decline of the small farmer and the village dwelling yeoman began, so that by the late eighteenth and early nineteenth centuries, villages consisted mainly of labourers and tradesmen. The Enclosure Acts had led to a redivision of open village fields, ploughland and common land, replacing scattered strips and common pasture with a series of compact and consolidated holdings. This allowed for more efficient farming, enabling the large landowners and tenant farmers, with some considerable acreage at their disposal, to flourish. Where the open fields of the three manors of St Nicholas parish were is not at all clear. In St Nicholas it is likely that most of the parish was already enclosed by the time of the Act, and that some of the scattered farms and mills are, at the very latest, of sixteenth-century origin and may have been farm sites for much longer. Enclosure, particularly in the midlands of Wales and England, caused the small farmer and peasant to lose his right of access to common and waste land, and thereby his fuel and pasture rights. This took away some of his self-sufficiency and had two side effects. Firstly, cash was needed for survival and so he had to sell his labour. Secondly, village stores appeared to provide those articles and foodstuffs no longer readily available. The effects in St Nicholas would have been less marked due to its much earlier non-parliamentary enclosure. Also, St Lythans Down common, a considerable expanse stretching to Wenvoe in the eighteenth century, touches a part of the eastern edge of the parish to this day, and would have afforded commoners' rights to some of St Nicholas' inhabitants. In his *Topographical Dictionary* of 1833, Samuel Lewis noted that the arable and pasture land was enclosed and cultivated "with the exception of only a small portion." At this time cattle and sheep fairs were held annually in the village on 19 May, 21 August and 17 December, and the St Nicholas Day fair took place on 6 December. There was also a fair at Worleton (Dyffryn) on 10 August which was discontinued owing to floods and transferred to the higher ground of St Nicholas. Those fairs were lively affairs. In the fifteenth century, the local coroner sought allowances, claiming 3s. 4d., but only being granted one shilling for keeping guard at different fairs – the object being to prevent robberies. A school for the "gratuitous instruction of poor children upon the National system" was supported by the rector and Mrs Grey, wife of the Hon. William Booth Grey of Duffryn House. Lewis described the church as an "ancient and venerable structure" in contrast to the "neat edifice" mentioned in Slater's *Commercial Directory* of 1880. In response to the Bishop of Llandaff's ecclesiastical questionnaire of 1946, it was noted that perambulations of the parish bounds were held within living memory but had been discontinued. The fact that St Nicholas never had been and never would be a destination for penitents and pilgrims was confirmed by the rector's affirmation that the parish contained no sacred pools or healing wells and witnessed no processions to deposit rings and pins. Furthermore, no water was taken away for special baptisms or procedures involving bathing of the eyes. Reassuringly, for the parishioners, no wells were used to inflict curses and none had a special guardian in either human or animal form. In a special rite still conducted in the twenty-first century, after being married in church, bridal couples would find the exit from the churchyard barred by a stout rope, which would only be removed on the production of small amounts of cash thrown by the groom for the children (and the occasional shameless adult) to scramble and fight over.

In the second half of the nineteenth century, increased mechanisation on farms depleted the workforce, causing hardships for village shop and inn keepers and bankrupting many village industries already hit by more centralised and efficient industrial production. In St Nicholas this was partly countered by influxes of mainly English settlers who, by their various endeavours, created new jobs. Occupations are sometimes difficult to describe, as a parishioner might need several employment outlets in order to survive. The mechanisation problem is encapsulated by William Wright of The Laurels/ Pikel House who, with Evan Yorath of Molton, had patented a hayloader enabling farmers to reduce the required number of hired labourers, while at the same time employing extra workmen to manufacture this and other pieces of agricultural equipment.

The Spenser Survey (1320), Exchequer Receipts Malefant (1541) and Earl of Pembroke's Survey (1570)

Parish surveys tended to be conducted to mark a change in ownership of a lordship. The tenants made a payment or mise to the lord in recognition of his beneficence in respect of franchises and liberties and the suspension of all penalties, amercements and forfeitures. An amercement was a fine at the mercy of the lord.

The Spenser Survey was a reassessment for Hugh le Despenser, Lord of Glamorgan, in order to make the most of his rights over ploughlands in the county. A ploughland in Glamorgan was measured at 80 statute acres of 4,840 square yards to the acre. Interestingly, the coastal areas of Glamorgan were well established as arable land, but St Nicholas, with poor-quality glacial gravels and clays, had less than a quarter of its land under the plough. The Malefant and Pembroke manuscripts relate to one of the three subdivisions of the manor and, being close in date, have many similarities, both containing lists of the freeholders and copyholders on the estate, and detailing manorial customs affecting the tenants and listing the payments to be made to the lord. There are descriptions of the lands and houses and a number of places appear in both including Peterston Mill, Pwll y Min, Homri woodland, Whitton and lands rented by the Buttons before they bought the Worleton manor and built Duffryn House.

Morganiae Archaiographia – Rice Merrick (*c.*1520–87)

"I dwell within two bowshots of the Portway" observed Merrick in his celebrated history and topography of Glamorgan, that dwelling being Cottrell House. Taking its name from Roger Cottrell, who owned about 200 acres in 1320, this was where Merrick wrote his manuscript, mostly in 1578, incorporating the Spenser survey, and offering valuable and fascinating observations of the people, buildings and landscape. Covering material from the Dark Ages onwards, he writes fondly of his native county. Running from Cardiff to the western towns, the highway or Portway, divided the Vale of Glamorgan into "two almost equal parts, and for the most part runneth straight upon a dry vein." He notes that the Vale "was always renowned as well for the fertility of the soil, and abundance of all things serving to the necessity or pleasure of man, as also for the temperature and wholesomeness of the air." The countryside had once been open and not enclosed and old men could remember stories of the time when cattle "for want of shade" had run all the way from the Portway to Barry, a distance of four miles. He paints a picture of abundance with rivers full of fish, pleasant meadows, fruitful pastures and fertile soil "replenished with great store of cold sweet springs."

More controversially, Merrick underlines a perceived and distinctive characteristic of the people marked by the previously mentioned "common travelling highway" – the Portway. Despite the fertility of the soil to the south of this line of demarcation, the so-called low-country produced people of a "boisterous, crabbed nature." These cross-tempered and churlish types were in stark contrast to the more tractable and pleasant folk who lived north of the road, whose breeding made them taller, mighty, active and valiant. The poor southerners had to content themselves with breeding "the greater and mightier beasts." Merrick talks of a magistrate, with considerable experience of both the north and south of the Vale, who concluded that to keep good order, low-country men should be ruled by severity and fear, and northerners with "fair words and good countenance." As St Nicholas parish is neatly bisected by the Portway, are we to conclude that there were two distinct types of physique and personality making up the people of the community? This contrasts significantly with Professor G J Williams, a founder member of Plaid Cymru, who wrote that Vale people were famous for their cheerfulness, welcome and generosity in this happy and neighbourly land.

Civil War

On Sunday, 7 May 1648, the most extraordinary event probably ever witnessed in St Nicholas unfolded before the bewildered inhabitants. The Royalist army assembled here prior to the battle of St Fagans. It was an army which, in sheer numbers, must have exceeded by far the Roman troops who conquered and colonised the area, an army greater in size than that which accompanied Henry IV when he camped at Ginkshill (King's Hill) before the battle of Stalling Down against Owain Glyndŵr.

Events preceeding the Royalist muster had seen Colonel Horton and his Parliamentary force leave Brecon to do battle with the Royalists under Colonel Rowland Laugharne who were advancing by way of Swansea and Neath to Cardiff. Laugharne's men consisted of disaffected and unpaid Roundheads, who intended to march on London to present their grievances. However, in the Vale of Glamorgan, they were joined by local Royalists, including Sir Edmund Traherne, Sir John Stradling, Captain William Button and Miles Button. This Royalist army was a hastily assembled mixture of Roundheads and Cavaliers. Facing them was a smaller force of Parliamentarians, which included the New Model Army Regiments of Okey's Dragoons and Horton's Horse.

By Thursday, 4 May, Horton had crossed the Taff at Llandaff and set up camp near St Fagans, in so doing frustrating the enemy who had also planned to dig in at that village. This meant that Laugharne and his troops were held up in St Nicholas and so, the next day, he withdrew his men and spread them among the Vale villages of Penmark, Llancarfan and Fonmon.

Then, on the aforementioned Sunday, the Royalists again took up their positions on the high ground north of St Nicholas 'neare Cotterell Miles Button's house on the hill.' A visit to this ridge overlooking the course of the River Ely clearly confirms why this was considered an advantageous assembly position. The Button family were staunch Royalists, an association which cost them dearly and resulted in the mortgage and ultimate loss of much of their property in the years after the war. It is estimated that this force was nearly 8,000 strong "above half armed, the rest Club men" using pitchforks, clubs and billhooks. They also lacked cavalry, may have been short of muskets and were suffering from desertion, with many leaving to join the Parliamentarians. This latter army was, by comparison, about 5,000 strong but with superior cavalry and better arms and discipline.

On Monday, 8 May, early in the morning, the Welsh advanced from the St Nicholas ridge and crossed the River Ely using two wooden bridges, one at Peterston-super-Ely and the other near a disused water mill at St George-super-Ely, and then headed towards St Fagans.

The battle lasted until about mid-morning, with the Parliamentarians gradually overcoming the Royalists who retreated in some disorder. There were some executions, but an estimated 3,000 prisoners were taken including about a hundred gentlemen and officers. The defeated made for the safety of Royalist strongholds in the Vale, pursued by Horton's men as far as ten miles and paying close attention to the ridge from Coed-Riglan to St Nicholas and on to Cottrell. It is not known how many died in the battle and subsequent skirmishes, but in the parish of St Fagans it was said there were 67 widows. Presumably, losses were similar in St Nicholas as it must be assumed that the Button family would have enlisted most of their servants and tenants. The Royalist leaders were singled out for punishment and eleven officers were tried by the council of war, with seven condemned to death (of whom four were shot immediately and one hanged). Captain William Button was one of those condemned to death but Miles Button was exiled for two years and fined about £5,500, a sum far in excess of his annual income. The Cottrell estate suffered badly, as did the whole local economy ravaged by the war and deprived of its manpower.

Communications

Travel within the parish in the nineteenth century was by means of footpaths and more significantly, the lanes or roads as they were then termed – Well Lane, Brook Lane, Duffryn Lane and Mill Lane, all of which lead to the turnpike road (A48); the first three also went directly into the village itself. It is likely that they are all of great antiquity and that they possibly linked ancient farmsteads. Although there are no documents which prove their early existence, it is probable that the Roman road network forms the basis of the nineteenth-century system. The Roman occupation of Whitton and other areas would have necessitated side roads from the main military route. Some of these lanes are, in part, well below ground level, a product of wear and tear over centuries – and others could even be Holloways, dug out as estate boundaries such as Mill Lane between the Cottrell and Duffryn estates. It is impossible to put a date to the origins of these routes. They could be Saxon, Norman, medieval or later, or indeed combinations of all of these.

Some of these lanes, such as Well Lane, take quite a direct route from A to B using the natural lie and fall of the land to good effect. However Mill Lane meanders with some abrupt right-angled bends for no immediately obvious reason. After initially running true and straight from the A48, it takes an indirect route before passing to the west of Y Gaer. Its width is variable too, up to 30 feet in places, and it changes from a steeply banked holloway to a ground level track. This suggests changes of route and rebuilding over a long period of time. The straight portion – although there is no evidence to prove this – is more typical of lanes produced by eighteenth and nineteenth century enclosure commissioners. The adjoining field system to the east of the lane immediately north of Pwll Sarn and including the school field, or Cae Pentre, closely conforms to the enclosure practice of squarish fields flanked with quickset hedges. A little fieldwork reveals a change in the route of this lane. By ignoring the first right-angled bend and carrying straight on into Cottrell estate and golf course on what is now a footpath, the ancient lane is clearly discernible. It can be traced as a slightly depressed holloway, running up to the ridge before dropping down towards Peterston on a much more acceptable incline than that taken by the current lane which is more precipitous. Following the old route, it is still clearly below the level of the adjacent ground, but with oak trees now standing at what would have been the original hedge line. At the foot of the hill, it then joins the side exit from Cottrell house now running parallel to the old lane, which can be seen slightly to the north as yet another holloway. Both of these lanes, ancient and modern, then rejoin Mill Lane on its watery way down to Peterston – this being an area of springs, with water frequently issuing forth from the underlying limestone. The current path of the lane clearly marks the eastern edge of Cottrell, as delineated on a map dating from the sale of the estate in 1942. In common with most estates, Cottrell has at some time been landscaped, to be more aesthetically pleasing, according to the new fashion of the Lancelot Capability Brown school of romantic vistas, which replaced the formal inward-looking gardens previously favoured. Nature was now lauded and these Georgian improvements dating from the middle of the eighteenth century and onwards created the artificial, yet so-called natural parkland, that we know of today. Landowners, as likely as not Emilia Gwinnett in Cottrell's case, were not above moving people, houses and lanes to create a pleasing panorama – could this be the reason for the change of route of Mill Lane?

On the map it can be seen that St Nicholas has now lost the northernmost part of the parish to Peterston, this including a number of important farms. It seems logical that the parish boundaries were redrawn to exclude the land, houses and farms north of Homri. The steep fall of the land presents a formidable geographical barrier, making transport and communication difficult and arduous. This area seems naturally to belong to Peterston, not St Nicholas. However, it was an indispensable part of the parish in the nineteenth century and had been so for many centuries. Its importance was as follows: it contained the two large farms of Lan y Lay and Pwll y Min; the vitally important mill at Peterston, which in the nineteenth century was gradually superseding the older Moor Mill which was closer to St Nicholas village; the occupants of these enterprises figured prominently in vestry and parish affairs; they employed between them a large number of labourers and servants; and finally Croes y Parc chapel seemed to attract more than a few St Nicholas parishioners in both life and death, as the gravestones graphically show.

Communications within the parish further emphasise the importance of this northern extremity. Today our sense of orientation is chiefly based on the main road, the A48, bisecting the village and passing east to west much as the Roman road did. This road governs our actions and the way we live – it is our conduit to work and to the city. In his county history, Rice Merrick records that before the conquest of Glamorgan, the Portway ran from Llandaff to St Fagans, Peterston, Pendoylan and eventually to Cowbridge. After the Norman invasion, it ran instead from Cardiff on a more southerly route, presumably through St Nicholas. Two centuries ago this was the turnpike road, unpopular with local residents who had to pay tolls like everyone else. Yet, most nineteenth-century travellers hardly needed to use it, because nearly all of the tracks connecting farms to each other and to the village run north to south. In the early twentieth century, children were expected to walk from the village to the mill to collect bags of flour. If, as conjectured, most communication took place on this basis then Mill, Duffryn, Brook and Well roads, as they were also designated, take on a new significance showing why they were so carefully maintained. Indeed Mill Lane, notwithstanding its steep inclines and twists and turns, was probably the busiest of all roads, being the shortest horse and cart route to two quarries, Peterston bridge, village and railway station as well as the way to two mills, four farms and a chapel.

Farming

In October 1818 the area of the parish was recorded as 1,521¾ acres in the Highways book. On the Tithe map of 1838, the estimate of 1,800 acres was subdivided as follows:

Arable – 726 acres

Meadow and pasture – 999 acres

Woodland – 75 acres

Cash payments to be made in lieu of tithes included:

1½d. on Hayland north of the turnpike road: 160 acres in total

£3 8s. 0d. p.a. paid for the Demesne lands of Duffryn, in lieu of small tithes

£1 0s. 0d. p.a. paid for the Demesne lands of Cottrell, in lieu of small tithes

56 acres of Glebeland belonging to the Rector.

In 1851 parish acreage was 2,104 and by 1881 it had increased to 2,172. The parish boundary, as shown on the Tithe map, is almost identical to that on the twentieth-century Ordnance maps suggesting that nineteenth-century estimates were too conservative. Over the years there is no discernible pattern to changing farm size, with increasing or decreasing acreage seemingly reflecting the different fortunes of the individual tenants rather than any meaningful sociological shifts.

Comparative farm acreages spanning 100 years:

	1838	1861	1881	1893	1937
Pwll y Min	218	133	133	133	122
Doghill	211	200	224	172	
Manor House	151	16	16	4	
Caia (incl. Broadway)	128	87			
Broadway (inl. Caia)	340	280	194	160	
Lan y Lay	109	99	109	78	34
Tinkinswood	82	110	120	146	179
Brook	75	83	80	80	
Vians Hill	64	85	160	126	

Homri	61	100	114	103	134
Moor Mill	38	20			
Gwreiddyn	35	95	73	42	

An interesting insight into farming practices of the mid-Victorian period is gained from a lease dated 2 February 1863 granted to Thomas Evans of Pwll y Min for 14 years. The landlord, John Bruce Price of Duffryn, exercised a strong hold over most farming activities. The farm comprised 135 acres and Mr Pryce reserved all lands, woods, buildings, minerals, sands and limestones for the use of the said farm. He retained all rights of entry with cart and horses; the rights to fell timber or such as required, to obtain minerals, make roads and use all game, rabbits etc., to hunt, shoot and fish; and to have access for repairs. Mr Evans, the tenant, was not allowed to sell more than one ton of hay, straw, turnips or other crops without first gaining consent. The lease further states 'that the land be subject to a four year rotation of crops with Corn following Turnips or Mangle Wurzles or fallow' and with 'not more than two fourths sown with corn.' The other fourth 'should have been the preceding year under clover, beans or vetches.' Therefore the rotation ran:

Year 1	Turnips, Mangles or Fallow
Year 2	Wheat, Barley
Year 3	Clover, Beans or Vetches
Year 4	Wheat, Oats or Beans

Thomas Evans, the tenant, was further bound:

to keep all the premises in good repair,

to replant quicksets in banks,

to cart stones, bricks, slates as required to make repairs to buildings,

to cut and flatten molehills and destroy all moles,

to cut thistles and nettles.

Also:

> manure and compost must be replaced on the land,
>
> any straw or hay unused must be retained for the use of the owner or any of his tenants,
>
> lime to be put on the land not more than one in six or eight years – not more than 25 crannocks per acre if done at six years or 36 crannocks per acre if done at eight years.

It is made clear that 'all must be in proper order during the last year of the lease and that seed and grain for the following year's crops must be gathered and belong to the owner for the following tenancy.' Such then were the duties of a tenant farmer – best practice was to be observed and with good reason.

John Bruce Pryce of Duffryn and his predecessor the Honourable W Booth Grey were both presidents of the Glamorganshire Agricultural Society and this august body had, for many years, been active in encouraging good farming procedures. At a meeting held at the Bear Inn, Cowbridge in 1773, the society had first introduced the four-course system mentioned above and for implementing this '… on farms of 10 acres and upwards a premium of 20 shillings per acre will be given, but the total amount shall not exceed £100.' Further to this '… a premium of 10/– per acre…' was offered '… for draining and cleaning the greatest quantity of black, peaty or boggy land not less than three or more than ten acres.' Good husbandry would then have been a prerequisite for Mr Pryce's tenants. The Misses Bassett, whose family owned Lan y Lay farm, frequently won the approval of the society for their contributions to farming, including the introduction of Cheviot sheep in the hilly areas and an improved plough. The society had long been interested in new and improved machinery, more of which is noted in the Wright family history outlined in Chapter 9.

Glyn-Cory

To mak' a happy fireside clime,
To weans and wife –
That's the true pathos and sublime
Of human life.

Burns

At the beginning of the twentieth century a scheme to develop the northern areas of the parish was proposed by the Cory family of Kingsland. It was bold, and for Wales revolutionary in concept, and if completed would have changed the environment of Peterston and St Nicholas, ultimately transforming them into suburbs of Cardiff.

Known as Glyn-Cory, the 'Garden Village of south Wales', and based loosely on the idea of the garden city or suburb, it was planned to build on a 300-acre site 'of beautifully undulating and well-timbered land' an estate of 1,400 houses with a population of 5–6,000 people. The land belonged to Mr John Cory, coal mine owner and philanthropist, and the plan was the brainchild of Mr Reginald Cory, director of First Garden City Limited. In a glossy brochure, liberally peppered with quotations from John Ruskin and William Morris, respectively those worthy champions of the Pre-Raphaelites and the Arts and Crafts movement, the thinking behind this praiseworthy, yet sometimes patronising ventu, is put forward. It claims to be based on the doctrine that 'in love of home, love of country takes its rise' and it was to be the answer to a 'dishomed nation.'

Mr Cory recognised 'the desirability of providing an example of town planning, on a rural area' which was 'unspoiled by the encroachment of ordinary suburban development with its cramped and monotonous rows of dwellings.' Glyn-Cory would provide for 'healthy, adequate and artistic housing' with 'preservation of existing natural features' and 'ample recreation space' and all this 'at rents comparable to those paid under existing crowded conditions.' The aforementioned houses would occupy about 160 acres of the site, with modern drainage and a gravitational water supply from a 250,000-gallon reservoir just south-east of Homri farm. The latter was constructed and can be found concealed in a clump of trees today.

Having regard for the fact that 'dependent, weak-willed, vicious, vulgar people leaven the composition of the State, whereas virtuous and refined citizens are the foundation of a nation's greatness', then this refinement and polish would arise from good housing. Mr Cory felt that not everyone could be helped; for example, the very poor and slums were insurmountable problems, but the lower middle-class (artisan, clerk or warehouseman) would appreciate a more refined environment. The health of this class was seen as a national asset to be fostered and, furthermore, these people could be relied upon to pay an economic rent.

It is worth pausing briefly to consider the motives of the Cory family in this regard. They were known for their strong Liberal nonconformity and for their opposition to the evils perpetrated in the name of alcohol abuse. Teetotalism had first surfaced in south Wales as far back as 1836 with the formation of the Cardiff Total Abstinence Society and John Cory, as a Wesleyan Methodist, was a fervent supporter. The final third of the nineteenth century had seen several revivals of teetotalism in the area, marked by prayer meetings and the Cory brothers had sponsored evangelical forays into the south Wales coalfield. In 1853 the United Kingdom Alliance was incepted in Manchester by a group of nonconformists led by the Quaker and cotton manufacturer, Nathaniel Card. In a premonition of prohibition in early twentieth-century America, the alliance promoted 'the total and immediate legislative suppression of the liquor traffic.' This was because both education and the provision of so-called counter-attractions to the public house had failed. John Cory subscribed to the alliance fund to the tune of £50,000 a year, a vast sum befitting his role as vice-president and indicative of his considerable personal fortune. It was part of the same thinking that, later on, caused Miss Cory to close the only public house in St Nicholas, the Three Tuns, and replace it with a coffee tavern for the use of the young men of the village. Fortunately what they thought about the matter is not on record and subsequent generations have been left to rue her autocratic decision and instead take the road westwards to the Red Lion in Bonvilston or eastwards to the Traherne Arms on the Tumble hill. All subsequent attempts to reopen the Three Tuns as a public house have been met with strong opposition, leaving the village without one of its most important amenities.

The Glyn-Cory estate was an attempt to replace haphazard and speculative urban growth with scientific development. If a public authority had taken on such a task the burden on ratepayers would have been too much, but the encouragement of public utility societies on private estates avoided this problem.

The advantages of a garden village included:

the planning of the site in advance,
the limitation of the number of houses per acre,
the preservation of open spaces,
the control over the character of the buildings.

Unlike the industrial village of Bournville in the Midlands and the self-contained community at Letchworth, Glyn-Cory was to be both accessible and detached. The chosen site between 90 and 350 feet above sea level had a 'dry and healthy atmosphere... free from smoke or fogs.' Sixty acres of land were reserved for allotments and a further eighty for a golf course just south-east of Homri farm. A report on the proposed links had been prepared by the eminent golfer Mr Willie Park, presumably on the assumption that social-climbing artisans might take up the sport. Willie Snr had won the British Open four times in his career, including the inaugural match of 1860 when he was first in a field of just eight players. However it was Willie Jr (1864–1925), also winner of the Open in 1887 and 1889, who was the consultant – this being one of 170 courses that he designed in his lifetime. One of the tees he constructed is still visible as a raised platform in the fields to the east of Homri farm. Not only would the lower classes have been busy playing golf but they might have gone boating or trout fishing had the proposal to deepen and widen the River Ely been adopted. There was also provision for houses of prayer, social institutes, a library, schools, a lecture hall, village hall, gymnasium and a reading room but, of course, no licensed premises.

The railway station at Peterston would have provided quick transport into Cardiff at 3¾ d. per day third class, or £9 19s. 6d. per annum for a first-class season ticket.

Access to the estate was provided by a new bridge over the River Ely (built before 1908 and now demolished) leading to the Main Avenue which was 100 feet wide. From this would fan three main semi-circular crescents, the Wyndham Park of today being evidence of the incomplete plan. In 1909, the first four houses were erected and there were plans for different sizes of house ranging in price from £150 to £1,000 or more 'so arranged that the smaller houses will not depreciate the value of the larger ones.' One obvious plus point was that rents would start at 5/– per week, this being about half the rate charged in Cardiff.

Security of tenure was by leasehold, as freehold was best avoided because it gave absolute freedom for individuals to erect objectionable buildings, for example a 'fried fish shop' on one side of a good residence and a public house on the other. Time and again great play is made of just how healthy it would be to live on this estate with its up-to-date sewerage system. In addition, Mr Cadbury of Bournville recommended gardening as "physically, morally and spiritually" uplifting and Mrs Barnett from Hampstead Garden Suburb claimed that the "larger gardens of the rich… keep the air pure." The quirky and out-of-touch notions held by the rich about the working classes are further emphasised with the claim that the cottage gardens would add that 'cosy, generous element which ever follows the spade when affectionately and cunningly wielded as a man's recreation.' Echoes occur here of Millet's noble peasants toiling in the fields, except his vision was not tainted with unrealistic sentimentality. The jostling of rich and poor, cottage and manor house are seen as 'distinctive attractions' in a village. The Corys were not unusual of course in their attitudes towards their fellow countrymen and women in what was a society divided into social classes. With new money from industry, and being part of the recently emerged Victorian upper middle-class which often embarked on philanthropic ventures commensurate with its new-found status, they lacked a certainty about their role and position in society, unlike the assured aristocracy and landed gentry. The idea of a hierarchy was universally accepted with little evidence of confrontation between the classes. This whole scheme was in the mould of previous ventures begun long ago by Arkwright and Strutt when designing suitable housing for their millworker employees. It found ultimate expression in the garden suburb which was an obvious reaction to the insanitary and totally unhealthy conditions experienced by the working classes in the nineteenth century. That millions of workers should have turned to excessive consumption of alcohol as a means of finding temporary relief from their miserable conditions, is not particularly surprising. Nor should we be surprised that the nouveau riche were moved through religious belief to help those less fortunate than themselves. It helped to justify their status in society. The estate brochure gives plans and elevations of two classes of house: the more luxurious four-bedroomed type with external half-timbering and three chimney stacks, and the plainer version with a multi-purpose chimney, three bedrooms, no upstairs toilet and other economy factors. Either way, there is

Pair of semi-detached houses erected at Glyn-Cory

no doubting the excellence of the design by Speir & Beavan of Cardiff. At a time when the outside toilet, in the back yard or at the bottom of the garden, was the norm, this was luxury.

It is common knowledge that the grandiose plans never fully materialised, and only a handful of houses were completed. However, it was designed from the outset to be carried out either on a limited scale or as a larger town.

Age structure of the parish

Between 1801 and 1931 the population of the parish fluctuated considerably from 351 persons in 1833 and 425 people in 1841 to 318 inhabitants in 1891. In 1851 the number of parishioners over the age of 70 was a mere 14 out of 414, nine of these being women. Interestingly, more than half the people were under the

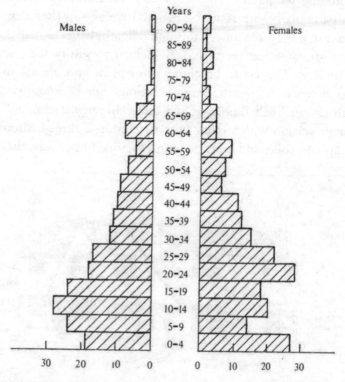

Age structure of the parish: 1851

age of 20. The predictable demographic pyramid caused by so many young children per family does not taper as quickly as might be expected. This is probably due to an influx of labourers, house and farm servants in the 15–30 age bracket. A chart based on the 1881 census shows a similar distribution, but with 17 people out of 349 over 70 years, twelve of them women. There is however a significant drop in the number of people between 25 and 39 years of age (89 in 1851 as against only 49 in 1881). Despite jobs being available on the farms and estates, it is likely that this age group had sought employment elsewhere.

County of birth

The 1841 census only revealed by a simple yes or no whether a person was born locally in the county or elsewhere. From 1851 onwards precise details are available as to an individual's birthplace.

In 1861 just over 280 people from a total of more than 350 were born in Glamorganshire and 130 of these were born in St Nicholas itself. The other counties of birth were: Somerset (10), Gloucestershire (7), Pembrokeshire (7), Devon (6), Carmarthenshire (5), Wiltshire (5), Monmouthshire (4) and Suffolk (4) plus seven people from Ireland.

Ten years later 310 people out of 419 were born in Glamorganshire, with exactly half of these in St Nicholas. Of the remainder, discounting half-a-dozen illegible names, eight people were born in Ireland and two each in Germany and Switzerland. From the counties of England and Wales residents originated from Somerset (31), Devon (13), Wiltshire (8), Middlesex (6), Hereford (6), Pembrokeshire and Monmouthshire (5 each) and Carmarthenshire (4).

In 1881, the high proportion of locally-born people was maintained. There were also seven people from Ireland, four from Scotland (due to the Mackintosh intrusion at Cottrell) and one each from India, Germany and Switzerland. Influxes from elsewhere in Britain originated in Somerset (19), Wiltshire (12), Pembrokeshire (6), Hereford (5) and Devon (4).

Burials and Baptisms in 5 year groupings

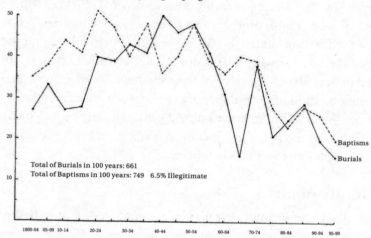

Total of Burials in 100 years: 661
Total of Baptisms in 100 years: 749   6.5% Illegitimate

Seasonality

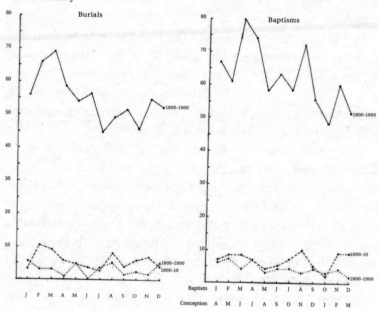

42

Piegraphs of Occupational Structures in St Nicholas Parish

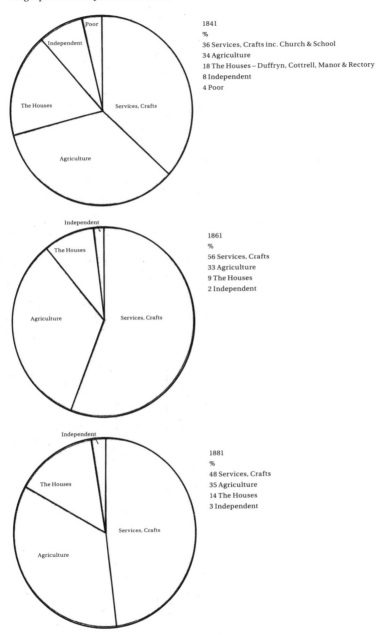

1841

%

36 Services, Crafts inc. Church & School

34 Agriculture

18 The Houses – Duffryn, Cottrell, Manor & Rectory

8 Independent

4 Poor

1861

%

56 Services, Crafts

33 Agriculture

9 The Houses

2 Independent

1881

%

48 Services, Crafts

35 Agriculture

14 The Houses

3 Independent

Occupations 1841–81

An analysis of occupations in the parish during this period reveals that:

- the whim of an enumerator in defining a job could produce a sharp rise or fall in numbers. This is graphically illustrated in 1881 when one Evan Evans drew a distinction between labourers (20), agricultural labourers (8), and male domestic servants (10) as had previously happened in 1851. In other years labourers had all been grouped together,
- the drop in the number of female servants was caused by a more accurate job description such as ladies' maid, differentiating the latter from general domestics,
- there were no scholars entered at all in 1841, although the village had a schoolmaster,
- paupers appeared only on the first two census returns; after this they were removed from the parish and sent to the workhouse in Cardiff,
- in 1861 there were sixteen carters in the parish – yet only one other appears, and that in 1871. What were they carting and where?
- no publican is mentioned in 1871 but this apparent oversight was due to Elizabeth Banner of the Three Tuns being away at the time of the census,
- the title female servant (1) includes domestic, house and general servant,
- female servant (2) is solely agricultural,
- male servant is domestic or house,
- engine drivers were agricultural and not railway,
- the journeyman blacksmith or carpenter having served his apprenticeship was qualified to work for daily wages,
- agr implmnt maker is Agricultural Implement Maker, specifically Benjamin Wright and his employees. The number of blacksmiths and carpenters in the village increased as a result of his manufactory,
- an annuitant was in receipt of a yearly allowance or income.

Occupation	1841	1851	1861	1871	1881
Pauper	8	7			
Scholar		49	44	96	69
Schoolmaster	1	2		1	1
Schoolmistress		1	2		
Female Servant (1)	41	32	27 (+1 ret'd)	15	13
Female Servant (2)			3		
Charwoman				3 (+2 ret'd)	2
Cook			1	3	3
Dairy Maid		2	6	2	1
Dressmaker		3	5	3	4
Governess			1	3	1
Housekeeper		2	3	1	5
House Maid		4	1	5	4
Kitchen Maid		2		1	1
Lady's Maid		4	1		
Laundress			2	5 (+1 ret'd)	3
Lodgekeeper				1	1
Nurse Maid			4	6	4
Scullery Maid		2		1	
Agricultural Lab'r	43	48	33	42 (+1 ret'd)	8
Male Servant	8	5	2	3	10
Labourer		12			20
Butler		1		2	1
Coachman		2	1	3	3
Engine Driver, Agr			2	1	
Errand Boy		4			
Footman		2		1	2
Gamekeeper	1	1		1	
Gardener		6	4	3	6
Groom		1	1	3	3
Shepherd			2	1 ret'd	
Farmer	12	11	15 (+2 ret'd)	18 (+1 ret'd)	14

Occupation					
Farm Bailiff		1	2	1	
Blacksmith	1	4	2	3	4
Blacksmith, Jrnyman	3	2			
Blacksmith, Apprtce	1	1		2	
Carpenter	5	6	4	6	2
Carpenter, Jrnyman	2				
Carpenter, Apprtce	2				
Agr Implmnt Maker		1	7	1	
Shoemaker	5	6	5	3	5
Shoemaker, Apprtce	1			1	
Glazier	1	1			
Mason	6	1	1	5	
Miller	2	2	1	4	3
Saddler		1	2	1	2
Tailor	3	2	3	3	1
Tailor, Apprtce	1	1			
Thatcher	1	1			
Butcher	1	2	3	3	5
Grocer		1		1	1
Shopkeeper	3	1			
Innkeeper/Publican	2	1	2		1
Carter			16	1	
Haulier				1	1
Sawyer		1	2	2	1
Woodman/cutter				1	3
Policeman		1	1	1	2
Annuitant				2	3
Clerk, Coal Merchant					2
Independent	7				
Landholder/owner			1	1	1
Merchant, Timber	1	1			
Preacher	1			1	
Rector			1	1	

The following occupations occur only once in the five census returns: Admiralty Surveyor, Baptist Minister, Brewer, Calvinist Methodist Minister, Commercial Clerk, Cordwainer, Cowman, Flannel Dealer, Gentleman, House Property, Journeyman Painter, Journeyman Shoemaker, Laundry Maid, Lodging House Keeper Retired, Magistrate, Major General, Master Painter/Glazier, Member of Parliament, Millwright, Newspaper Reporter, Ostler, Painter, Parlour Maid, Piper, Platelayer, Ploughboy, Post Office Master, Pupil Teacher, Railway Clerk, Railway Labourer, Schoolroom Maid, Seamstress, Shipbroker's Clerk, Stable Boy, Surgeon, Tax Clerk, Tiler/Plasterer, Washerwoman and Wheelwright.

The Tithe Map – 1838

For centuries one tenth (tithe) of a person's annual production, for example crops, livestock or wool, was paid to the local church. Also known as Great Tithes, mainly arable produce was paid to the rector, and Small Tithes went to the vicar. Tithes could also be bought and sold so that non-ecclesiastical people could in theory own tithes. In reality some tithes had already been replaced by cash payments before the introduction of the Tithe Commutation Act of 1836 which marked the end of payment in kind, replacing it with the tithe rent-charge. Three tithe commissioners were charged with determining how much commutation had already occurred and also with establishing every tithe district which in the case of St Nicholas, as with so many others, was in fact the parish.

An apportionment, that is a map and written schedule, was made of the parish, recording for posterity under plot numbers, the landowners and occupiers, and a description of every piece of land with its acreage but with no tithe rent-charge recorded. Not surprisingly most of the land is still grouped in just a few major holdings mainly reflecting the ancient manorial subdivisions.

A selection of plot numbers nearest to the village, mainly houses and associated land plus one farm, is listed below:

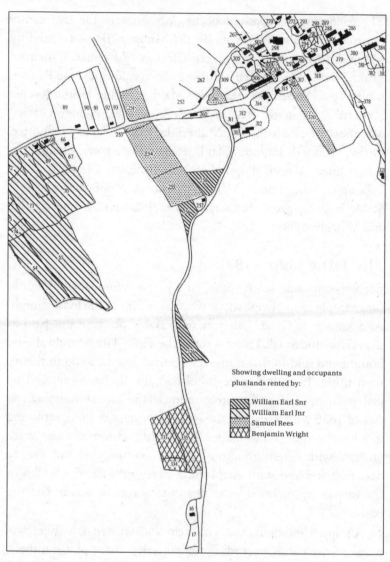

Saint Nicholas, the village – 1838

Showing dwelling and occupants
plus lands rented by:

William Earl Snr
William Earl Jnr
Samuel Rees
Benjamin Wright

No.	Name of Occupier	Description	A	R	P
256	William Earl Snr	Erw Madwls Cum	1		21
258	ditto	Erw	2	3	1
303	ditto	House, Garden		3	4
326	ditto	Close	1	1	6
54, 55	William Earl Jnr	(see Chapter 7)			
68–76		ditto			
251	Samuel Rees	Cae Trehill	2	2	3
253	ditto	Garden	1		
254	ditto	Pedwar Erw Trehill	2	1	28
255	ditto	Mwddwlls Cwm	2	2	3
261	ditto	Garden			32
302	ditto	Inn, Garden The Wivern			35
316	ditto	Stable, Garden			14
320	ditto	Erw Harry		1	16
294	Benjamin Wright	House, Garden		1	
333	ditto	Cwrt y wheod	1	2	37
334	ditto	ditto		1	36
335	ditto	ditto	2		21
16, 17	Thomas Minnett	Brook Farm, Homestead	75	2	7
66, 67	Mary John	House, Garden		1	10
89, 90	Richard Whapham	House, Cottage & Field	3	2	32
91	Thomas Jones		1	3	8
92	John Thomas			3	19
93	ditto			3	21
252	William Rees	Caia Trehill			
270	ditto	Garden			
295	ditto	House, Garden		1	10
257	William Thomas	House, Garden			
260	Mary Webb	House, Garden			28
262	James Pratt Brooks	Cae Tre Cefn y Scybwr			
297	ditto	House, Garden			28
309	ditto	Meadow		2	8

267	William John	House, Garden	1 32
271	Anne Morgan, John John	Cottages, Gardens	1 6
272	Phillip David	House, Garden	1 9
286	William Williams	Tuns Public House & Garden	2 18
380	ditto	Yard	
288	Evan Evans	House, Garden	15
289	Catherine Richards	House, Garden	16
290	Evan Williams	House, Garden	20
291	James Edwards	House, Garden	20
293	Jn Evans & Wm Williams	Barn Yards	
296	Evan Howard	House, Garden	12
317	ditto	Garden	19
299	Richard Lewis	House	10
300	ditto	Garden	
301	Anthony Lewis	House, Garden`	8
304	Richard Ellis	House, Garden	35
305	John Evans	House, Garden, Orchard	1 24
306	Elizabeth Gibbon	House, Garden	24
308	Edward Jones	House, Garden	24
310	Joan David	House, Garden, Orchard	
298	John Evans	Church Yard	
311	ditto	Barn & Yard	1 30
312	ditto	Parsonage House etc.	3 32
507	ditto	Barn Yard	
314	David Hopkins	Smiths Shop, House, Garden	
315	William Edmonds	House, Garden	26
318	William Jonas Watson	Great House	
379	ditto	Hayguard	
506	ditto	Buildings, Yard	
321	John Howard	Quarry House, Gardens	3 32
378	William Thomas	House, Garden, Pound	1
381	William Rees	House, Garden	16
382	Thomas Griffiths	House, Garden	16

| 383 | Edward Cule | House, Garden | 24 |
| 384 | William Kent | House, Garden | 36 |

Some of these characters will reappear in subsequent chapters.

The Parish Magazine

"A Sabbath well spent makes a week of content."

Over the course of a number of issues of this parish compilation magazine which are extant for the year 1912, the anonymous writers (presumably different ones for each parish) showed themselves to be not only concerned with parochial matters but with social and political concerns on a national scale.

A series of popular concerts were held in the Village Hall during the winter, the second on a wet night in January 1912 and the third on 17 February. The programmes included piano works by Chopin, solo and choral singing and pieces for solo violin as well as recitations and an impromptu speech. The secretary for these occasions was Mr R M Thomas of Homri and the adjudicator Mr D G Lewis of Cardiff. The Good Friday services at the church featured a performance of Sir John Stainer's setting of *The Story of the Cross* with Miss Doris Cole, the schoolmaster's daughter, singing the 'Appeal from the Cross' as a solo. The church had been beautifully decorated for Easter with greenhouse plants from Cottrell and Duffryn. The services on Easter Sunday were well attended with forty-eight communicants at the two celebrations of Holy Communion accounting for sixteen per cent of the whole population of the parish, even though two of the largest houses were empty at the time. Weekly meetings were also inaugurated in the Village Hall by the St Nicholas and District Men's Society – the aim being, by means of bright and attractive get-togethers, to provide something for the menfolk that was entertaining, instructive and generally helpful in a higher sense. In practical terms this meant musical items, recitations, lectures and debates all courtesy of Miss Cory who made no charge for the venue or transportation of performers and speakers. A sample of what was on offer included an address on the writer Charles Kingsley, a lantern lecture and a debate on 'Country and Town Life.' This is another example, along with the opening of the Coffee Tavern and the closure of the village pub, of religiously-motivated and wealthy parishioners attempting to steer men away from the perils of excessive alcohol consumption. Two points here are worthy of note. First, Charles Kingsley had connections with the area, staying at Sully House, Swanbridge in the 1840s. He took holy orders but was slightly suspect due to his radical and questioning views on religion, his Chartist affiliations and his membership of the Christian Socialist movement. Second, in 1904 and 1905 south Wales had been engulfed by an uprising of evangelical passion led by Evan Roberts, a miner, blacksmith and theological student from Loughor near Swansea. He single-handedly prompted the Welsh revival, ably backed by his own choir of young women, who filled churches and chapels alike. Roberts claimed to be led by the Holy Spirit in his preaching, stating that, "I never prepare the words I shall speak... I leave all that to Him." His meetings seem to have involved a kind of mass hysteria lasting for up to eight or nine hours in some cases and involving prayer, readings, spontaneous singing and confessions, sometimes with congregations numbering thousands. The positive side saw a significant reduction in alcoholism and the introduction of voluntary taxes paid by miners to build libraries and recreation halls as alternatives to pubs. The number of arrests by the police dropped and sobriety, industry, repaid debts and healed relationships became commonplace. Critics however pointed out that Welsh revivalism was nothing more than "a manifestation of Celtic instability." No doubt Miss Cory had observed these events with interest in her quest to improve and help the men of the parish.

On a more solemn note it was recorded that, "On Sunday, April 21st, there were special pulpit references made, and hymns sung, in connection with the terrible wreck of the steamship *Titanic*, 1,600 lives being lost on the previous Sunday night. The 'Dead March in Saul' was played at the close of the evening service."

It should come as no surprise to learn that the weather was a major discussion point in the September and October 1912 issues. August had been a bad month but St Nicholas being fortunately "set on a hill", had fared far better than many low-lying places avoiding the worst excesses of rain and flood. In neighbouring Bonvilston many parishioners questioned whether there should be a Harvest Thanksgiving service at all on account of the exceptionally bad harvest. It was recognised that the endurance and patience of farmers had been severely tried and losses were heavy. The magazine commented that although the price of foodstuffs would be sure to rise in the winter, at least there would be no famine because the country's needs would be more than supplied by "the vast wheat fields of Canada and Russia." It states further that, "The failure of the wheat-crop has not been universal. There will not be the abundance of other years perhaps, but there will be a sufficiency." Moreover, worshippers were cautioned to show their gratitude "for this and other inestimable mercies, temporal and spiritual, to the Author and Giver of all good" and to consult Habukkuk iv. 17–18, "Although... the fields shall yield no meat. Yet I will rejoice in the Lord, I will joy in the God of my salvation." The St Nicholas Harvest service held on the evening of 24 September was, despite everything, a big success. The "people did not seem to share in the prevailing doubt as to the fitness of these services this year, as the church was more crowded than usual." There had been a "delightful" change in the weather which had had its good effect enabling the farmers "to get in a portion of their crops in good order." Mr G Williams of Broadway Farm was congratulated on a successful conclusion to his harvest operations, with sixty extra acres under hay, drawing comparisons with the Canadian north-west. The whole tone of the writer is upbeat commenting on the new lamps which made the decorations more effective and the new ropes which had been fixed to the church bells with the promise of "many a merry peal" during the coming winter. A little more fancifully the singing by the congregation of the grand old hymn 'All people that on earth do dwell' was such a delight that "even the flowers, with their incense" seemed to say "For why? the Lord our God is good." Almighty God had remembered them when they had been in trouble and had sent the current glorious weather.

Divine intervention apart, the church was much exercised with other equally weighty matters. A threatened national coal strike which had been encouraged by paid agitators would have caused widespread misery and ruin to hundreds of thousands, but an attack on the Welsh Church by Parliament was also the work of political agitators. Any movement to injure the cause of religion was, by definition, not a religious one. So what had moved the Church to such annoyance with the Government? The proposed Bill for the disestablishment of the Church in Wales had been placed before Parliament and was a "glaring injustice." Tithes, instead of being paid to the clergy, would be paid to County Councils which would use them for secular or worldly purposes and, in the majority of cases, the parish would be left with little or nothing to carry on its work. Putting it bluntly, the Church felt it needed the money whereas the State did not. The converse thinking held that the privileges of the established Church were unjust, forcing British subjects to financially support it regardless of creed or belief. The Church should be dependent on its own adherents only. The Church in Wales however was unrelenting and anyone "with any sense of justice and fairplay" would spread the truth on the subject and defeat such a calamity. The Archbishop of Canterbury, no less, had presided over a meeting in Cardiff against the proposed disestablishment and, as had already been pointed out, "There is no Act of Parliament to be repealed which establishes the Church... for the Church established itself long before Parliament was invented." Gathering support from a leading Glamorgan Liberal and Nonconformist, who said that too little money was applied to religious work, this considerable owner of land paid his tithes to the Church and would be happy to pay two or three times that amount as long as it were used for religious undertakings. Contempt was reserved for those who sought "to take money from religious purposes and objects." The twin reasons for England (!) being "the greatest Empire the world has ever seen" were "the sacrifice of our forefathers and the religion under which they were brought up, giving them a backbone, a stamina and a spirit that nothing else can give." After strong pressure, the Church was allowed to keep six shillings and eight pence out of every pound, but this was still strenuously opposed as it was not a question of how much, but a matter of principle. The Church had held property by right and title for many centuries and continued to use it for the religious purposes for which it was originally given. It followed therefore that Parliament had "no moral right whatever, to divert it to secular purposes. To do so, whatever specious and fallacious and long-drawn-out arguments politicians [used] to bolster up their views, inspired by sectarian jealousy, malice, and spite [was] sheer robbery and sacrilege." It behoved "all fair minded men, whether Conservatives or Liberals, Churchmen or Non-conformists, to resist to the utmost, such monstrous injustice." Strong words indeed showing that, then as now, the Church was prepared to speak out against perceived wrong-doing by politicians. The disentanglement of church and state finally took place in 1920 with the previous bills of 1886, 1892, 1894, 1909 and 1912 all being defeated. This long and troubled debate had been given force in 1853 by the Liberation Society (the Society for Liberating the Church from the State), which had prompted the Tithe War of 1887 when resentment of having to pay tithes spilled over and, in 1891, had seen the transfer of tithe responsibility from tenant to landlord. A royal commission had inquired in 1910 into the provision of religion in Wales. In 1912 a Bill was presented to Parliament to remove established status from the Anglican Church in Wales plus two-thirds of its endowments, and this received assent in 1914, although the war forced its postponement for another six years.

Reminiscences

During Christmas 1939, Alexander Marriott Moore, who was born in the village on 4 August 1857 and was a master saddler and the village postmaster, penned some recollections of the parish from his retirement home in Stroud, just one year before his death.

He clearly remembered the transformation of Cottrell from country house to mansion and the rebuilding of the ruinous Duffryn to its present magnificence as well as the upgrading of many of the parish farmhouses.

Around the time of his birth the school and attached house were built and he recalls the teachers Miss Knowles and her successor Mr Bilby. The census tells that the latter was from London but Mr Moore asserts his Norfolk origins. He lived with the Moore family at the Post Office and Alexander's mother found him a "perpetual source of anxiety" because he "had slipped down the social scale by drink" and was also an indifferent teacher. At a time when "education was endured, not encouraged" he was however "perfectly harmless and well liked." Miss Knowles, as was only fitting for the village teacher, played the harmonium in church whereas Mr Bilby gave the key note for the choir and congregation. Reflecting its status at the centre of parish life, the church afforded other reminiscences which included the arrival of the Duffryn House party. "First the footman would arrive with a large bag containing prayer and hymn books", followed by the old squire and the ladies. Quite unremarkable compared to the arrival of Mr Lewis Bruce of the Manor House who, because he had lost the use of his legs, had to be lifted from his horse at the lych gate and carried into church. The Cottrell contingent were regular attendees and sat behind the door.

Transport services were sparse with the populace relying on the good nature of the farmers and traders for lifts into Cardiff. On Saturdays there was a two-horse bus which came from Llantwit Major and William James of St Athan had a light wagon with seated accommodation – both of these conveyances proceeding into Cardiff. Walking into the city was not uncommon and Mr Moore remembers one old lady, Sarah Ellis, who walked into Cardiff every Saturday to purchase her weekly groceries yet still arrived home in time to cook dinner for her family. This was Sarah Morgan (1821–89), born in Wenvoe, who married James Ellis, a shoemaker, in 1844 and produced eight children.

The village was well noted for the high proportion of old people, with Kitty Earl and John and Anne Morgan being over eighty-five years, and Mr Howard nearly ninety, closely followed by Barbara and John Rees and William Earl and spouse. Also remembered are Tommy Minnett, gardener at Duffryn House, who is described as an old man, and his father who lived to be a hundred. Old John Jenkins, the village tailor, was "young and sprightly" at just over eighty and Edward and Betty Jones of Tŷ-To-Gwellt were old enough to be mentioned. Fortunately "only one or two were bedridden out of the lot and [the rest] were able to walk to the door when the poor law officer [Mr Eagleton] called on Thursdays with a little help from the Parish Funds."

Shortage of water for domestic use during the summer months was always a concern as it had to be fetched and carried from the bottom of Well Lane by a procession of women and children carriers. Indeed, in very dry years, a longer journey to Homri was required with a punishing uphill return leg. In a true sense of community spirit the water was divided equally amongst the toilers, none of whom had the advantage of wheeled casks. Unfortunately this harmony was marred by one Tom Morgan who went down to the well at midnight with casks and emptied it. Mr Moore particularly admired "Mary the Muddlescombe" (see Chapter 4) the wife of John Jenkins who "would lift a big milking pail full of water, place it on her head and walk all the way home without resting or spilling any water." How times have changed.

CHAPTER 2

Houses and Farms of the Parish

PWLL Y MIN FARM

Derivation: possibly Pwll-lymin – the kids' or fawns' pool.

Certainly inhabited since the sixteenth century, the farm site lies just to the south of the River Ely and once had its own water wheel. Despite the discrepancies in the spelling of Pwll y Min in the Malefant and Pembroke surveys below, a comparison of buildings and land clearly indicates that it is the same place.

1541 – Malefant

Free… Gitto holding 1 messuage [dwelling house and outbuildings] and curtilage [enclosed land attached to a dwelling house] 30 acres land and meadow in pulfuyne and returned per annum… 11s.

Morgan ap Morgan holding free 2 messuages and 3 curtilages called pollvin and returned per annum… 10d.

1570 – Earl of Pembroke's Survey

Freeholders:

William William holding 3 messuages and 3 acres of court adjacent to 15 acres of land plus George Cole… returned 3s. 10d… and [other] messuages of 30 acres of land lying in the place called Pullfyne… returned 6s. 4d. and so in total… 10s. 2d.

Thomas Edwardes jn law left by Jacob Mathew namely 2

messuages 3 acres of curtilage lying in Pull myne and returned annually... 10d.

Copyholder (copia dat – copyholding usually dated on three lives):

Nichus Howell Ricus Nichas his son... and Kather[in] wife [of] Nichi... by copy dated the last [day of] November in the... reign of Edward VI first settlement of £20 one messuage and holding called Pull moyne containing 26 acres of free land arable meadow pasture and cattle and returned... 9s. 2d. 2 capons.

1670 – 15 August, The Will & Inventory of William Wrinch of St Georges

A particular of what moneys are due unto mee from others

Itts ffrom Mrs Lettice Morgan of Pwllmin... £2 0s. 0d.

In the will of one Henry John dated 1672 Mr George Morgan of Pwll y min owes him £1 2 shillings.

1730 – 6 May, The Will of Jane Morgan of Poollymyn Widow

By a deed of settlement dated 19 Nov 1720, made on the marriage of her daughter Elizabeth with Edward Deere Esq., Jane has the power and authority to bequeath £80, charged on messuages, lands, tenements and hereditaments in St Nicholas, to Henry Morgan the youngest son of her stepson Morgan Morgan. This money is to be raised from the rents and profits of these premises but only after the death of Elizabeth. Henry will also receive £100 twelve months after Jane's decease. Elizabeth, the sole executrix, will have all her mother's "Goods, Chattles and personal Estate." Probate was granted in April 1731.

1733 – 13 October, The Will of Elizabeth Deere of Pwllymin Widow

Although in good health and possibly spurred on by the recent death of her mother, Elizabeth settled her affairs six years before her death. To her brother Evan Morgan and two nephews Henry Morgan son of Evan and Morgan Morgan of Monachty she bequeaths one guinea apiece to buy mourning rings and to her cousin Mary Jones £10 and all her wearing apparel. Elizabeth had recently purchased a lease for three lives from Martin Button Esq... "upon that house Garden and Barn called Llan y Llay vach ... with all the Lands thereto belonging" and this she gives to her loving nephew Henry Morgan, son of her brother Morgan Morgan deceased, and sole executor when the will was finally granted probate on 19 September 1739.

1810

Burial of Harry Harries of Pwllmyn.

1820

John and Hesther Evans (see Chapter 5).

Poor Book (see Chapter 6)

Details of a quarterly rate paid by a tenant to the Vestry towards the support of the poor of the parish. On the left is the tenant's name, followed by the owner of the property, its name, rateable value and the amount of rate paid according to the levy in the pound. The glebeland belonged to the church as did any monies accruing from its rental.

1824

John Evans	Hon W B Grey	Pwll y min	£79 15 0	£2 19 10
John Evans	Rev. T Davies	House & Glebe	£54 12 6	£2 1 0

1838–4 – Rate Book

John Evans J B Pryce Esq. House & Land, Pwll y Min Farm 178 acres 2 roods 17 perches

John Evans Rev. R T Tyler Glebe Land, St Nicholas 50a

1838 – Tithe Map

No 150	John Evans	The Green	1a 1r 27p
No 151	John Evans	Homestead	1a 2r 15p
	Total land rented		218a 1r 36p

1829–30, 1832–3, 1836–7

John Evans   Overseer of Poor

1820–9, 1830–1, 1833–4

John Evans   Surveyor of Highways

1841

Burial of John Evans of Pwll y Minn Aged fifty-nine. John Junior, to distinguish him from his father John Senior of the School House, made his will on 14 February and died two days later. As a wealthy farmer he was able to leave his sons Evan and William £450 each plus £500 to his son Thomas. All the remainder of his real and personal estate he left to his son John and wife Esther and the total value of his estate was valued at under £3,000.

1841 – Census

Esther Evans	57	Farmer
John Evans	20	
Evan Evans	18	
William Evans	16	
Thomas Evans	14	
James Howard	16	
Edward Cule	14	Ag Lab
Catherine Jones	23	Servant
Jane Williams	16	Servant

1850 – Lease dated 26 January

Lease between J B Pryce and J W Bruce of Duffryn (the owners) and John Evans of Pwll y Min Farm detailing the erection of two Messuages or Dwelling houses occupied by John Evans or his undertenants. These are delineated in an accompanying map. The term of the lease is for the life of the said John Evans, however he must not erect a "Chapel for the purpose of Public Worship" or use the new buildings as "a Licensed Public House, Inn or Tavern", nor sell beer, ale, porter or cider.

Within a year John had left for the Three Tuns, taking Evan with him. William moved temporarily to the parish of Llancarfan, leaving the youngest son Thomas to farm here.

1863 – Lease

Lease between J B Pryce and Thomas Evans for fourteen years on Pwll y Min farm. Extent of land 135 acres seven perches.

1871 – Census

Thomas Evans	Head	M 44	Farmer 136 Acres,	
			3 labs, 1 boy	St Nicholas
Anne Evans	Wife	M 44	Llanharry	
Henry Evans	Son	U 10	Scholar	St Nicholas
Thomas Evans	Son	U 8	Scholar	St Nicholas
Mary A Evans	Dau	U 2	St Nicholas	
John Williams	Visitor	U 50	Tailor	St Nicholas
John Murphy	Ser	U 60	Gen Servant	Ireland
Philip Hopkin	Ser	U 17	Farm Servant	St Nicholas
Dedimia(?) Korrell	Ser	U 19	Gen Servant	Penmark
Catherine Rees	Ser	U 10	Gen Servant	Cardiff

1881 – Census

John Davies	Head Wdr 34	Farmer 133 Acres, 1 man, 1 boy		St Hillary
Mary Jane Davies	Dau	U 10	Scholar	Pentyrch
David J Davies	Son	U 8	Scholar	Swansea
Thomas Davies	Son	U 7	Scholar	St Brides
Elizabeth Davies	Dau	U 4	Scholar	St Brides
Edmund Davies	Son	U 2		St Nicholas
Barbara Williams	Hkr	M 34	Housekeeper Domestic	Llantwit Vardre
Lydia Thomas	Ser	U 19	Domestic Servant	Tonyrevil
John Sheppard	Ser	U 34	Farm Servant Indoor	Somerset
John Luvlock	Ser	U 14	Farm Servant Indoor	Welsh St D'nats

Ser – Servant Wdr – Widower Hkr - Housekeeper

1891–5

Occupier: Robert Davies Owner: John Cory.

Robert who was in his fifties came from Ystradyfodug and spoke both Welsh and English.

1901

Occupied by John Bowen from Pembrokeshire and four farm servants plus Lizzie Barlow, a domestic from Birmingham.

1919

E G Williams

For many years Pwll y Min Farm held the glebeland instead of the church and this entitled the occupier to a reduction or refund of the parish rates.

The Evans family

The problem of distinguishing between three gentlemen of the parish called John Evans is a difficult one. Mr Evans Snr lived at what is now called the School House between 1838 and 1841 and was a member of the Vestry. He does not appear on the census of 1841. His son of Pwll y Min was also in the Vestry but had died by the same year. Their signatures were almost identical and only occasionally did they use the Jnr or Snr suffix. After 1841 John Jnr's son John, aged twenty, took over the parish duties along with his younger brother Thomas. The following are just a few of the many Rate Book entries concerning these men.

Poor Book	*£ s d*
1824	
Allowd Jn Evans in consideration that he holds the Tythe Lands	3s. 7½d.
Allowd J Evans Balance in poor rate J Bassett Esq. would not pay	4s. 4½d.
1826	
Pd John Evans Board & Lodging for Ann Cule & her Son for 4 Days	4s. 0d.
Mr John Evans Paid William Rees for Journey to Myrthir on	
Parish business	7s. 0d.

1829

Paid John Evans for Hay for Thos Fords Asses   £1 5s. 0d.

Paid John Evans for keeping Jane Deer's child the Third Quarter   £1 3s. 9d.

Highways Book   £ s d

1814

paid John Evans for raising 40 perch of Gutter at 2½ d. per perch   8s. 4d.

1819

John Evans Jun 2 days cart & horses   14s. 0d.

1833

John Evans Jnr 2 days Cart & 2 Horses Haulling Earth   12s. 0d.

1838

Paid John Evans for 8 yds stones 4d. 2/8; for 1 Load & hauling 1/–   3s. 8d.

1848

Paid Thomas Evans for 2 Horses & Cart 1 day on Duffryn road   6s. 0d.

1851

Thomas Evans for 4 Yd of stones and hauling the same to Lan-y-Lay   4s. 0d.

Thomas Evans for hauling Earth from Mill Road   6s. 0d.

Paid Thos Evans, Majistrates Clerk as p Bill   15s. 6d.

1852

for John Evans Hauling Stones, 1 day Cart 1 Horse & Man   4s. 0d.

1854

John Evans for Draing [sic] Pipes   2s. 6d.

1859

Thomas Evans for hauling & spreading

45½ yds of Stones at ½ p yard for Mill Road   £2 13s. 2d.

1860

Thomas Evans for hauling 52 yds of Stones

to Croes y Park at 1/– p yard   £2 12s. 6d.

LAN Y LAY FARM

Derivation: Glan Elai – bank of the River Ely.

1812 Land Tax Returns

The farm was owned by John Bassett Esq. and occupied by William Williams.

1814

Occupied by David Edmunds.

1814–24 – Records of The Glamorganshire Agricultural Society

Although the Bassett seat lay outside the parish, throughout this period the Misses Bassett of Lanelay, presumably related to the owner, received a number of awards for their agricultural prowess. They were first awarded the society's honorary medal in 1814 for ten acres of swedish turnips and were congratulated in 1819 for their introduction of Cheviot sheep into the hilly districts. In 1820 they received a premium for rearing 217 lambs from 220 ewes and their ploughman, David Morgan, had two guineas, a reward probably not unrelated to the superior plough that the ladies had introduced. Further premiums followed for more turnips and "hilly sheep."

1819

7 September Baptism of three children of Captain Robert & Elizabeth Chapman:

> Robert, born at Dublin, 9 October 1812,
>
> Arthur, born at Ashes, Buckinghamshire, 9 October 1815,
>
> Mary Anne, born at Cottam near Bristol 22 September 1817,
>
> A third son Leicester had been baptised on 1 January 1819.

1820

The Hon. W B Grey now owned the farm which was occupied by John Thomas who also rented Kingsland.

1827

Baptism of Evan son of William and Mary Thomas of Little Lanelay Farmer.

1827–8, 1830–1, 1834–5

John Thomas Overseer of Poor

1830, 1833, 1841–2

John Thomas Surveyor of Highways

1838   Rate Book

John Thomas	House & Land, Lanelay & Kingsland	63a 2r 7p

1838   Tithe Map

John Thomas	109a 1r 20p

All through the nineteenth century, probably until the 1890s, Kingsland, housing one or two labourers' families, was rented out as part of Lan y Lay and was not a farm in its own right.

Lan y Lay itself comprised three dwellings:

The Homestead	2r 6p	Great Lanlay
House & Garden	1a 16p	Great Lanylay
Cottage & Garden	1r 4p	Little Lanylay or Llanlaifach

1841 Census

Great Lanlay		
John Thomas	60	Farmer
Elizabeth Thomas	55	
Ann Thomas	29	
William Thomas	19	
Thomas Thomas	19	
John Thomas	17	

Were William and Thomas twins? It seems likely, as within eight years William himself was the father of twins.

The house at Great Lanylay was occupied by an assortment of servants, labourers, visitors and a ninety-four-year old pauper.

The cottage housed a farm labourer Evan Miles (55), his wife Mary (50), and their three children William (10), Jane (7) and Elizabeth (5).

By 1851, John Thomas was a seventy-three-year-old widower, but he kept four servants to help him run the house and farm. Ages on the 1841 Census were sometimes estimated and this would account for John gaining thirteen years over a decade.

1852–3

William Thomas Surveyor of Highways.

1856–7, 1861–2, 1868–9

William Thomas Overseer of Poor.

1861   Census

Little Lanley

William Thomas	Head	M 29	Farm Labourer	Bridgend
Frances Thomas	Wife	M 23		
Mary Thomas	Dau	U 4 mos		St Nicholas
James Pascor	Brdr	Wdr 45	Railway Labourer	Cambridgeshire

mos – months, Brdr – Boarder

Lanley

William Thomas	Head	M 39	Farmer of 99 Acres, 1 man	
				St Nicholas
Catherine Thomas	Wife	M 36		Flemingston
Evan Thomas	Son	U 12	Twins Scholar	Peterston
David Thomas	Son	U 12	Scholar	Peterston
Elizabeth Thomas	Dau	U 10		Peterston
William Thomas	Son	U 4		St Nicholas
Catherine Thomas	Dau	U 2		St Nicholas
John Thomas	Brdr	Wdr 83	Retired Farmer	Welsh St D'nats
Ann Howard	Ser	U 17	House servant	St Nicholas
James Radcliff	Ser	U 20	Carter	Pendoylan
David Reynick	Ser	U 20	Carter	Brody, Pembs

William died c.1869 leaving the widowed Catherine with seven children to support and a farm to run. This she managed to do, with the help of her widowed mother Elizabeth Hopkins and her twin sons, certainly until 1891. By 1893 the farm acreage had dropped to seventy-three acres, one rood, thirty-eight perches. In 1901 daughter Elizabeth was running the farm with one labourer. David Thomas died in 1912 as a result of falling when boarding a tram-car in Cardiff.

Lanlay Fach was rented by railway platelayers, namely George Lawson and family in 1891 and William Leyshon in 1901 with his wife Alice and children William, Lewis, Blodwen and John.

1895

Evan Thomas.

1919

Elizabeth Thomas.

1926

Selwyn Morgan.

Poor Book	£ s d
1828	
Paid John Thomas a Journey to Cowbridge after J David	2s. 6d.
Paid John Thomas 2 journies to Wenvoe on p Business	4s. 0d.
Highways Book	£ s d
1819	
To a Rate unpaid for Lanlay	15s. 0d.
1833	
Myself [J Thomas] 2 day Haulling Stones for the Culvart	12s. 0d.
1835	
John Thomas for Cart & 2 Horses Hauling Earth by Lanlay	6s. 0d.
John Thomas Lanlay Cart Clearing Road from Croes y Park to Bridge 1 day	6s. 0d.
1844	
John Thomas 2 days Hauling Earth by the Meeting House	12s. 0d.

1848

Paid John Thomas for breaking 30 yards of Stones on Doghill & Witton Road	£1 2s. 6d.

1850

William Thomas for 8 Yards of Stones & Breaking Do at 1/3	10s. 0d.

1853

W Thomas for hauling stones on Witton Road 2 days at 6/–	12s. 0d.

KINGSLAND

The present house bearing this name bears no similarity to the original dwelling. Originally it seems to have been a pair of cottages or one cottage housing two families.

1814

Baptism of Richard, son of William, a labourer, and Anne Rees.

1823

Burial of Thomas John aged eighty-three.

1831

Burial of Elizabeth Rees aged ten weeks.

1838

Baptism of Thomas son of David, a labourer, and Jennett Morgan.

1838 – Tithe Map

John Thomas	Kinsland House, Garden	2r 16p

1841

Occupied by two labourers' families – George (21) and Ann (25) John and their daughter Ann (4 months) plus Thomas (25) and Elizabeth (25) John and their children Thomas (5), Elizabeth (3) and William (1).

1851

Occupied by:

Thomas Hopkins a thirty-two-year-old butcher from Welsh St Donats, his wife Sarah (26) and son William (14 months).

Thomas Davies a thirty-five-year-old labourer from Pendoylan, his wife Maria (38) and a daughter Jane (2 months).

1861

Occupied by:

Robert Thomas, widower, a fifty-two-year-old labourer from Ystrad Devodog and his daughter Elizabeth (13).

William Radcliff a thirty-three-year-old mason, his wife Ann (35) and their children William (4) and Thomas (1) plus Evan Morgan (30) a millwright and son of Thomas Morgan of Moor Mill.

1871

The Radcliff family was still in occupation but with two more children, John (9) and Mary (7).

1881

No entry on the census return suggesting that rebuilding was under way.

1887

Baptism of Charles George Francis, son of Charles Edward and Matilda Mary Waring. Mr Waring was an architect and a member of the parish Vestry. Obviously a different class of people to the previous occupants.

1891–5

| Charles E Waring | Land, Kingsland | 20a |

Mr Waring is entered as a surveyor on the 1891 Census and maintained a household of two servants and a school governess from Cambridgeshire for his three children.

1919

John Cory   15a 3r 4p

1926

Charles Cory.

MOOR AND PETERSTON MILLS

The origin of these water mills is obscure but likely to be very ancient. It is thought that mills originated during the eighth century with a preponderance in eastern Britain. Corn mills often have Saxon beginnings and the Domesday Book records that Somerset had 371 mills and Devon 98 but Cornwall had only six.

Although on different sites it is convenient to treat the mills together as, during the nineteenth century at least, they were both rented by one person and not as separate units. St Nicholas, due to its high position and lack of streams, had no water mill, which meant a journey for villagers and farmers either to one of these establishments or down the lane to Duffryn Mill.

Peterston Mill, with the River Ely as its power source, still stands. It was here that the corn millers practiced their trade well into the twentieth century.

Moor Mill had ceased to function by 1919, at the very latest, reverting to a house and today scarcely a trace remains. The water supply came from the powerful springs which flow down from the woods on Cottrell estate.

1541 – Malefant

Thomas Morgans ap Morgan Morgans son… holding by copy… corn mill… called peterston Mills… and returned per annum… 66s. 8d.

1570 – Earl of Pembroke's Survey

Mill Lands

Hugo Richards Custodian of the Lords Castle... Kayrdyff holding... one corn mill called Peterston Myll... and returned annually... 66s. 8d.

1806

Burial of William Evan of More Mill.

1819–20, 1846–7

Thomas Morgan Surveyor of Highways.

1824

Poor Book

Thos Morgan	The Right Hon. E Clarendon	£30 16s. 6d.	£1 2s. 10¼d.

1828–9, 1831–2

Thomas Morgan Overseer of Poor.

1838–43

Rate Book

Thomas Morgan Captain Tyler	2 Mills & Land	38a 2r 31p

1838

Tithe Map

Moor Mill Thomas Morgan No 124	Mill House	2r 30p
No 125		4a 2r 32p
No 126		20a 2r 28p

In total Thomas rented thirty-six acres, one perch paying £2. Plus:

Peterston Mill Thomas Morgan No 494	House Garden	2r 6p
No 495 Mill Green Pasture		2r 10p
No 496 The Green Pasture		3r 28p
Total – two acres four perches paying 10s. 0d.		

1841

Occupied by: Thomas Morgan (50), his wife Mary (45) and their children Maria (25), Thomas (21), John (20), Jane (16), William

(15), Ann (14), David (12), Evan (10) and Morgan (8) plus mother-in-law Mary Thomas (85) and William Kopeland (15), an apprentice miller.

1851

Thomas and his family lived at Moor Mill. At the Lower Mill lived:

David Davies	Head	M 43	Miller	Pendoylan
Mary Davies	Wife	M 39	Wife	Welsh St D'nats
William Williams	Ser	U 12	Millers Servant	Llantrisant
David Davies	Ser	U 11	Servant	Ystradowen

The Morgans were Nonconformists and some of the family were buried at Croes y Parc chapel including:

Thomas Morgan	2 Jan 1852	Aged 62 years
Mary Morgan	25 June 1855	Aged 63 years
Their infant daughter Johannah and their son-in-law.		
William Radcliffe	30 June 1895	Aged 67 years
Ann Radcliffe his wife	19 May 1901	Aged 75 years

After the death of his parents, David Morgan took over the tenancy and lived at Moor Mill with his wife Sarah and children Thomas, Elizabeth and Charles. In 1856 he was Overseer of the Poor. By 1865 there was a new miller, James Ball, a member of the Royal Agricultural Society of England who, unlike his predecessor, lived at Peterston Mill. In 1871 James was fifty-seven years old. He had come to St Nicholas from Norton Bavant in Wiltshire with his wife Frances (57), his brother William (43) and two friends Henry (28) and Sidney Watts (26). With him too had come an older brother George (59) who had settled in Pendoylan to farm 110 acres at Hefnllys. George's daughter, Georgina (11), lived at the mill with her uncle and other people continued to arrive from Wiltshire to help with the work.

By 1891 Henry and Sidney Watts had taken over the Peterston Mills which were rebuilt in brick alongside the original stone structure, but Moor Mill was now probably no more than a house.

In 1901 Sidney Watts is recorded as living at Cae Bout and still working as a miller. Also in the household were his widowed sister-in-law Mary, twenty-one years his junior and styled 'housekeeper', and her three young children.

1919

| Wm Howell | The Mackintosh | Mill Peterston | 1a 2r 23p |
| James Evans | Miss Cory | Old Mill House | 3a 1r 21p |

Highways Book		£ s d
1816		
Evan of Mill for Cleaning a Water Course		2s. 0d.
1819		
paid Evan of the Mill for opening a Gutter for two year		2s. 0d.
1820		
Thos Morgan cart 2 horses Duffryn		7s. 0d.
1844		
To Thomas Morgan for rising 22 perches of Hazards on Logod road at 1d.		1s. 10d.
1849		
Paid Thomas Morgan for Hauling one Day at 6/– p day		6s. 0d.

GWREIDDYN

Variously spelt: Gwruddin, Gwryddin, Grithyn, Garythyn, Grythen, Groiddin, Groithin, Grwyddin, Gwreiddin, Grwythin, Grythin. A literal translation of this word from the Welsh is 'root'. Situated on a damp north-facing slope numerous springs have their source here and flow down to the River Ely.

It is difficult to put a date to the original farmhouse but it is not on the 1838 Tithe Map despite existing in the Rate Book of the same year. Whether this indicates the date of construction of the house or merely the inaccuracy of the map is not clear. What is certain is that the farmland known as Gwreiddyn existed in 1812, whether the house was there or not.

1812–14 – Land Tax Returns

Tenant Mary John.

1816

Marriage of Henry John and Ann Miles both of St Nicholas.

1824 – Poor Book

Sir Charles Tyler rented from The Right Honourable E Clarendon paying £1 6s. 7¼d. based on an annual rateable value of £35 10s. 6d. Sir Charles lived at Cottrell.

1838 – Rate Book

Henry John was the tenant renting house and land of thirty-five acres, three roods, twenty-three perches from Captain Tyler. The John family continued to live here until the 1850s. In 1851 the widowed Ann (58) farmed fifty acres of land and kept three servants and a lodger.

By 1861 there were new tenants: David (34) and Elizabeth (33) Llewelyn and their children Jane (7), Edward (5), William (3) and Thomas (1). They also baptised more offspring, David in 1862, Windsor Morgan in 1863 and Elizabeth Louisa Ann two years later. The farmland had increased to ninety-five acres.

| 1863–4 | David Llewelyn | Overseer of Poor |
| 1864–7 | David Llewelyn | Collector of Rates   Salary £8 per annum |

1871

Another new tenant who was to stay here until 1895.

David Hopkins	Head	M 41	Farmer of 50 Acres	Welsh St Donats
Hannah Hopkins	Wife	M 57		St George
Ann Hopkins	Dau	U 19	Farmers daughter	Peterston
Thomas Minnett	Fn Law	Wdr 95	Formerly farmer	Llandaff

In 1838 Thomas lived at Brook Farm. His daughter Hannah was sixteen years older than her husband but they had at least two daughters as Eliza was baptised in 1873 at the age of twenty.

1873

David Hopkins was now farming sixty-one acres, two roods, fourteen perches. In 1881 he had increased his acreage to seventy-three but this fell by 1893 to forty-two acres one rood four perches. He was assisted by his brother William in 1891.

1901

With the demise of David, Eliza and her husband, Evan Evans took over the farm along with the now widowed Hannah. Evan (1850–1927) and Elizabeth (1853–1935) Evans lived here until 1926 and both are buried at nearby Croes y Parc Chapel.

Also living here and occupying two rooms were William, described as a coachman or groom, and Mary Palmer.

Highways Book	£ s d
1818	
Henry John 2½ days Cart etc.	17s. 6d.
1844	
To Henry John for 10 Cartloads of Stones and Hauling to Lanlay	12s. 6d.
1849	
Paid Ann John for Cart & 2 Horses Hauling Stones 1 day	6s. 0d.

HOMRI

Also known as Hornby(e) and probably a farmstead with very early origins. The Old Norse personal name Horni plus the Danish ending –by, meaning farm, give Horni's Farm which can be dated to the late ninth century. Many Scandanavian or Danish settlements were built on Anglo-Saxon sites. In the 18th century the farm is recorded as Great and Little Hombury.

1541 – Malefant

The same [Milo Mathew] holding one woodland called Horneby... 8d.

1570 – Earl of Pembroke's Survey

Miles Button Knight secretly heirs and children... one woodland called Home bye containing fifteen acres and returned... 8d... the tenants are doubtful on this one.

It is unclear what this entry means. In Rice Merrick's *Morganiae Archaiographia* three woods are mentioned – Y Cotrel, Y Kynehed and Hornby – suggesting that they are owned by the three Lords of the Manor of St Nicholas but they had been sold to "men of Bristol."

1719 – 27 May, The Will of John Thomas Rector of St Nicholas

The rector, who wanted "to be decently interred in ye Chancell of my Church", held the lease of Homebury Vawr for the life of one Henry Chiny. He had granted this lease to his granddaughter Lettice Miles for four years after which it was to go to another granddaughter Elenor Miles for four years and then on to his grandsons William and Morgan Miles for a further four years. At the end of this term it was to revert to his daughter Elinor Miles for the rest of the lease as long as Mr Chiny was still alive. John left his study of books to his grandson John Miles and the residue of his effects to grandson Morgan, who was still an infant. The rector's failing health is indicated by a very shaky signature. His inventory totalled £9 13s. and the probate was granted on 12 June 1720.

1772 – 29 May, The Will of Elinor Thomas, Widow

It would seem that Elinor is related to John the rector and could be the one mentioned in his will. She too has a leasehold estate comprising a messuage, tenement and farm called Great Hombury and purchased from the late Martin Button on two lives. She leaves the lease to her son John Jones on condition that he pays his brother Richard an annuity of £6 from the profits of the estate. To John's son William she bequeaths £20 which is to be invested for interest purposes until he is twenty-one. Should he die then the sum goes to his sister Elizabeth along with Elinor's wearing apparel, both linen and woollen. To Richard Jones, relationship unknown, she leaves Little Hombury and £52 which is chargeable on the estate of her late brother, the Rev.

Morgan Miles clerk. When making her will Elinor claims that she is in perfect health, an assertion borne out by the granting of probate nearly five years later on 17 March 1777.

1790–1821

John and Margaret Evans lived here with their children Mary, Evan, William (died) and William.

1795

Birth of William Evan.

1824–36

John and Ann Evans were the tenants with their children Evan, Ann, Thomas (died) and Thomas.

1824 – Poor Book

John Evans rented the farm from the Hon. W B Grey paying £2 11s. 2¼d. per quarter.

1837

Baptism of Rees, son of Rees Morris, Village Servant and Catherine Griffiths, Omri Servant.

1838 – Rate Book

David John rented the farm from J B Pryce Esq. with house and land comprising forty-eight acres, two roods, sixteen perches.

1838 – Tithe Map

Richard Thomas probably the son of Richard of Doghill Farm also lived at Homri – the accommodation at this time consisting of a homestead plus a small cottage and garden.

1839 – Rate Book

Rented by Richard with the same acreage as before plus an extra twelve acres of land. By 1841, David Thomas, probably the brother of Richard, rented the house and land comprising seventy-four acres, five perches and stayed until c.1866. His first wife, Phoebe, bore him three children Gwenllian, Morgan and

Mary. His second wife Jane, who died in 1852 aged forty-three, also had three children Mary, Julia and Jane.

1844–5, 1849–50, 1855–6, 1860–1

David Thomas Surveyor of Highways.

1850–1, 1854–5

David Thomas Churchwarden.

1853–4, 1859–60, 1863–4

David Thomas Overseer of Poor.

1861–2

David Thomas Collector of Rates.

When David Thomas left the farm he moved to No. 4 Mail Road in the village where his son-in-law's younger brother, Robert, ran Broadway Farm.

1871 – Census

David Thomas	Head	Wdr 68	Annuitant	Ystrad Yfoddu
Morgan Thomas	Son	U 32	Taxes Clerk	Llantrisant
Mary Morrish	Dau	M 23	Farmers Wife	St Nicholas
John M Morrish	Sn Law	M 48	Farmer	Somerset
Walter Morrish	Gr'son	7 mos		St Nicholas

1866–84

Thomas Harbottle and family, assisted by his brother Henry, were the new tenants. They were the sons of George and Emelia Harbottle of Tinkinswood Farm. Thomas was twice married, his first wife Jane bore him three children Edith Mary, George Kempster and Henry Percy. Mrs Harbottle was buried on 28 October 1872 aged thirty-seven years. Thomas's new wife was called Catherine and they too had three children Morgan Thomas, Douglas and Ernest Alexander. By the 1880s the farm had expanded to 114 acres or 103 acres three roods ten perches according to which source is quoted. Thomas Harbottle gave parish service as Churchwarden (1869–70, 1877–8), Guardian

(1881–2) and Overseer (1888–9) before leaving the farm. The eldest son George Kempster married Mary Catherine Moore daughter of William and Elizabeth of the Post Office in St Nicholas. This was in 1914 when they were both forty-six years of age and they lived at Cartref.

1890

Baptism of Edward Reginald, son of Reginald William and Ellen Jackson, Commercial Traveller.

1891–1926

Richard Thomas, probably the nephew of David Thomas, was the tenant renting from Charles Waring and Miss Cory. He was Overseer from 1892 for two years. He and his wife Lydia produced ten children.

Churchwardens' Account	£ s d
1851	
David Thomas for Hauling stones, sand & mortar	6s. 0d.
Highways Book	
1833	
John Evans Homry 1 day Haulling Cart & 2 Horses	6s. 0d.
1850	
David Thomas for Cartload of Stones and Hauling the same to a Culvert by Peterstone Bridge	1s. 6d.
1860	
David Thomas for 12 Yds of Stones at 4d.	
1861	
Pd David Thomas for hauling 27 yds stones to Pwllymin Road @ 1/1 per yard	£1 9s. 3d.

TAIFFYNON or WELL COTTAGES

A pair of cottages, now demolished, close to St Nicholas' Well in Well Lane (Heol y Ffynon) and built *c*.1850. They were used as housing for labourers.

1851–3

John and Mary David occupied one cottage with their children Julia and Elizabeth. He was a stone mason. David (28) and Hannah (38) Hopkin lived next door with their stepdaughter Ruth Thomas (15).

1853–61

The new residents were David and Elizabeth Jones and children Thomas, Rachel, Ann, William, David, Elizabeth and John. David, a widower by 1861, was a farm labourer.

1858

Charles, another labourer, and Mary Pocock and children John and Agnes.

1861

The occupants were William (43) and Sarah (41) Griffith and five children Daniel, a farm labourer like his father, Mary a dressmaker, Lewelyn, Amelia and William.

1867–71

John and Mary Anne (née Jenning) Chidgey with their children James and Thomas. The parents were from Heathfield, Somerset.

1871–81

Robert and Mary Vickery, another West Country family, lived here with their children Jane, Emma and Harry. Robert was an agricultural labourer.

1875

Henry, a carter, and Mary Boll were resident with their son Albert Henry.

1876

William, a labourer, and Harriet Mary Bartlett lived in one of the cottages with their daughter Edith.

1891–1901

William Walters, a thatcher, lived with his family in one cottage and George Young, an agricultural labourer, occupied the other but the latter was empty by 1901.

1919

John Ward and Walter Walters lived here. Mr Walters, William's son, who died in 1947 aged seventy-six, at one time worked at Homri lime quarry and his parents William and Ann lived in the parish as early as 1881.

COTTRELL HOUSE

The old house has been demolished and the surrounding area developed as the centre of a thriving golf course. The origins of Cottrell House and estate have already been discussed and written about here and elsewhere. To this day the estate still retains an isolated identity within the parish.

1320

Roger Cottrell.

1546–58

Meurig ap Howell.

1558–87

Rice Merrick.

1587–1624

Morgan Merrick inherited from his father and increased the estate to 870 acres, by buying land and property in Bonvilston and Llantrisant. Merrick was variously a Coroner, Justice of the Peace and Sheriff.

1624–c.1640

The estate passed to Barbara Merrick from her grandfather, Morgan, as her father Rice had already died.

c.1640–?

Miles Button of Worlton (Duffryn) married Barbara and became the new owner of Cottrell. His support of the Royalist cause in the Civil War proved costly – a fine of over £5,000 set against his annual income of £400.

1669 – 2 December, The Will of Ales Griffith alias Williams, Widow

This is the earliest of a number of wills made by occupants of Cottrell and deposited at the National Library of Wales in Aberystwyth. Ales leaves money towards the repairing of Llandaff Cathedral and for the poor of Llanblethian and St Hilary parishes. She bequeaths £20 each to the children of her "well beloved" sons-in-law, Thomas Mathew Esquire and Thomas Button Esquire and everything else to her daughter Gwenllian Williams, her executrix. The will, made on 2 December 1669, is signed by mark and her inventory values her assets at £202. The inventory was compiled on 7 January 1669 which is not a dating error as the New Year began on 25 March until 1752.

1670 – Will of Thomas Button Esquire

Thomas's considerable wealth is disbursed and bequeathed through his wife Gwenllian, daughter of Sir Thomas Lewis of Penmark. The Esquire of Cottrell had lately bought lands, messuages and tenements from Anthony Thomas of Brigam and these he leaves to his wife of twenty-one years to generate £1,000 for "hers and my children not already provided for whereby the same may bee set forth for their best advantage." Already the mother of a daughter, we learn that his wife is pregnant and if she gives birth to another girl she will have a share of the thousand pounds but if the child is a boy he will not benefit presumably because eventually he would inherit the Cottrell estate. Thomas appoints overseers to carry out his wishes – namely his father Miles, his grandfather William Thomas of Aberthin, his "good brother" Thomas Mathew, his loving brother Thomas Bassett of Llanvithin and his cousin Miles Button of Miskin. Gwenllian is his executrix entrusted with disposing his bequests and legacies. A detailed inventory gives a good account of the possessions of a 17th-century squire. He had one hundred sheep "of all sorts" valued at £35, twenty cows and a bull at £55, eight oxen £30, five steers £12, eight young beasts £12, ten yearlings £6 13s. 4d. and "One Nagge belonging to his owne Saddle" £6 plus horses, pigs, poultry, wheat and corn within and without doors. There were also carts, wains, implements, household stuff, furniture in the hall and parlour, thirteen feather beds and bedding including thirty pairs of sheets, tablecloths, napkins, brass, pewter, implements for the brewhouse, buttery and kitchen, more furniture, plate and wearing apparel. The total value came to £300. The fine that his father had incurred through his Royalist affiliations during the Civil War seems to have been overcome.

1682 – Will of Edward Lewis Esquire

Edward was the second husband of Gwenllian, widow of Thomas Button. His estate was worth slightly more than that of Thomas Button at £342 16s. 4d. but he owed almost as much at £329 18s. His assets comprised twenty-nine cows, four young calves, thirty-seven oxen, three bulls, three steers, twenty-eight beasts, fourteen calves, forty-eight wethers, five rams, one hundred and sixteen ewes, ninety lambs, nine horses, eighteen acres of wheat, three mows and two ricks of hay, fifteen acres of barley, fifteen-and-a-half acres of oats, pigs, poultry, linen, pewter and brass. He was also owed £110 in the form of three bonds in the name of Lady Ann Lewis.

1710 – 22 December, The Will of Thomas Button Esquire

Thomas wished to be buried "in a plain and decent manner" in the parish church of St Nicholas and left all his manors, messuages, lands, tenements and hereditaments to his son of the same name. He left £2,000 to his daughter Barbara which was part of the sum due to him "from Thomas Mansell Esq. Late of Britton Fferry by mortgage." Of the remainder of the mortgage of £500, the majority, that is £450, went "unto my dear mother I having borrowed Soe much of her." The mortgage remainder of £50 went to his son Miles, plus two tenements of lands recently bought from William and Evan Treharne in Llantrisant and Peterston-super-Ely estimated at fifty-eight acres and called Lloyn Gibbon and Langesvach and another tenement in Eglwys Ifan. Should Thomas and Miles die without issue, then all assets revert to Barbara and if she has no issue then the estate passes to Thomas's brother Robert. His mother, Gwenllian Lewis, is to exercise legal control, that is, guardianship, over the children until they reach twenty-one. Should she die, then brother Robert will care for the children and, in the event of his demise, then the very eminent Sir Thomas Mansell, Sir John Aubrey, John Laugharne Esquire, Charles Button Esquire and Oliver St John Esquire would jointly fill the parental role. The will was witnessed by Eliza Basset, Joan Howell, Jenkin Mangell and Will Turbervill and probate was granted to his mother Gwenllian and not Thomas, his son, the chief executor.

1713 – The Will of Gwenllian Lewis, Widow

The will was drawn up on 24 November 1711 with instructions that she be buried with her husband (was this Edward Lewis or Thomas Button?) within St Nicholas church. To her grandson, Thomas Button Esquire, she left £30 for mourning and the furniture of her chamber and her daughter, Susana Savors, likewise received £20 plus her sermon book. Daughter-in-law Emilia Button had £10 for mourning but granddaughter Barbara Button, spinster, already the recipient of £2,000 through her father's will, had the £450 which her father owed Gwenllian at his decease. This money came from profits generated by property held in the county of Brecon. Granddaughter Emilia Button gained £20 for mourning and Gwenllian's sister, Elizabeth Bassett, widow and niece, Margaret Mathew, both received a mourning ring and gloves. Furthermore, Emilia was to have best advantage of the profits from letting customary-held land and tenements in Llanblethian until she was sixteen years old, plus the rents and issues from similarly held land in Llanmaes,

Llantrisant, Llanwonno, Pentyrch and Llantwit Vardre, as well as the fishing of the Taff and the river of Cowbridge "in as large and ample manner" as confirmed in an indenture of lease. To her maidservants, Kate George and Margaret Rosser, she gave respectively £10 for mourning and a legacy and fifteen shillings. Her manservant, Christopher William, received thirty shillings. The executor of the will was Miles Button and the overseers were Charles Button Esquire of Columbar (Worlton/Doghill), Oliver St John Esquire and Edward Jenkins, Gentleman of Llandough.

1718 – July, A Bond in the name of Thomas Button

The deceased Thomas's goods, chattels and credits are granted to his brother Miles.

1718–30

Miles Button.

1728 – 21 August, The Will of Jenkin Mangell, Yeoman

Although resident at Cottrell, there is nothing in his will to connect him to the Button family, so it is likely that he was one of their employees. His executor and main beneficiary was his nephew and farmer William David of Ewenny. William's sisters Catherine, Mary, Elizabeth and Eleanor received £10 "to be paid them and every of them at three Months End after my decease."

1729 – 10 October, The Will of Evan John, Yeoman

It would seem that Evan, presumably a bachelor, worked for the Cottrell estate and his bequests make an interesting comparison with those of his employers, the Buttons. To his niece Mary, daughter of Rees John of Llantrisant, he left twenty shillings. To the whole family of Cottrell, his cousin Catherine John, her sister Margaret and to Florence, wife of John Bevan his cousin, he left a pair of gloves each. Illtyd Thomas, a fellow servant, received a razor, a cravat and a looking glass. Likewise William Rosser gained a mirror, William John a flannel shirt, leather britches and socks and Griffith Thomas a shirt and razor. Robert William, a tailor, received a coat and a white flannel waistcoat. Evan's body was to be interred in his father's grave in Llantrisant and the five pounds for his funeral expenses were at the disposal of his cousins, the aforementioned John Bevan of Llantwit Minor and Lewellyn Howell of Llantrisant, yeoman. He bequeathed forty shillings yearly to his sister Mary, his executrix, till all his money was gone and probate was granted on 22 May 1730.

1730 –7 April, A Bond in the name of Miles Button

Barbara Button (1695–1755) inherited the estate from Miles under the terms of her father's will. The bond is signed by Barbara and by Susanna Savors who is Gwenllian Lewis's daughter. She never married and bequeathed the estate to her cousin Emilia.

1747 – 4 February, The Will of Edward Lewis, Yeoman

Presumably another single employee of the Cottrell estate, Edward bequeathed his nieces Elinor and Mary Richard, offspring of his sister Anne, twenty shillings each. To his nephews Evan and Lewis Richard and nieces Anne and Cecil Richard, more progeny from the same source, one shilling each. The rest of the estate went to his brothers and executors William Lewis and Lewis Howell, with probate being granted in November 1748.

1748 – 8 October, The Will of Susana Savors, Widow

Susana, daughter of Gwenllian Lewis (d.1713), had made her will eighteen years earlier on 20 April 1730 around the time of Miles Button's death. She left her niece Emilia Button £150 and her cousin Margaret Matthews a silver coddle cup. To cousin Anne Watkins, widow, she gave ten pounds to buy a mourning suit and to nephew John, Anne's son, £50. Niece Gwenfrid Watkins, Anne's daughter, was the recipient of £50 also. Miss Mary Ratcliffe received a silver salver, Chrisogon Lewis, wife of Thomas Lewis of Garnlloyd, three guineas and maidservant Elizabeth Jones ten pounds. To the poor of the parish of Llanblethian she gave six pounds to be distributed within a week of her decease and likewise five pounds to the poor of St Nicholas "to be given them in Bread att the months end next ensueing my decease." Forty pounds was allocated for her funeral expenses in marked contrast to Evan John's five pounds in 1729. Other bequests included two guineas to Robert Bradford of Llanblethian and two hundred pounds to her niece and executrix Barbara Button.

1754 – 20 December, *The Will of Barbara Button, Spinster*

Cousin, executrix, and at that time spinster, Emilia Button was the main beneficiary of the will inheriting the Cottrell estate. Barbara's aunt, also Emilia, received £100 plus her grandfather Price's picture set in gold. To her cousin Anne Gwinnet, wife of Samuel Gwinnet, clerk, she gave £20 to buy mourning and to Samuel Gwinne, son of Samuel Gwinnet, the large sum of £200. Her godson Button Gwinnet, son of Samuel the clerk, gained £100, whereas John Price and Emilia Gwinnet, more offspring of Samuel, only managed £50 each although there was a separate annuity of £30 for Anne. To Joseph Radcliff Esquire and cousin Mary his wife, Barbara bequeathed £50 apiece to buy each of them mourning and also to Mary a ring with her father's hair set with diamonds. Cousin Mary, daughter of Joseph and wife to a surgeon, received £20 once again to buy mourning apparel. Her cousin, Ann Radcliff, daughter of Joseph and wife of Benjamin Radcliff Gentleman, received £100 but godson Miles Allen and cousin Margaret Allen, children of cousin John Allen Esquire, late of Crosselly, Pembroke only £50 each. A clerk, John Basset of Bonvilston, inherited a small, silver coffee pot and Thomas Morgan, Gentleman of Kilvynidd in the parish of Eglwsilan £30. Mindful of the lower orders, five pounds was left to Elizabeth Jones, maid to her late aunt Susana Savors, whilst Mary Morgan, spinster, Barbara's own maid, received a generous £100 plus all her clothes "if she lives in my service at the time of my decease." Another maid, Cecil Russel, was left £10 and Jennet Rees half that amount. In 1785 this same Cecil, widow of Trehill, seemingly having climbed the social ladder, left the leasehold of the Mansion House, garden and orchard held under Samuel Gwinnett clerk, to her two nieces Margaret and Jane Williams.

Like her aunt Susana, she left money to the poor, this time £10 in Bonvilston for those without parish support to be distributed within one month. A further £10 was expended on the poor of St Nicholas. Further generosity came in the form of one year's wages for all the rest of her servants and an annuity for life to her cousin Anne Gwinnet of £30, money arising from the letting of tenements at Downs farm in St Andrews and Cogan. Probate was granted on 24 March 1755.

1755

The new heiress of Cottrell, Emilia Button (1785) married the Rev. Samuel Gwinnett (d.1792) of St Mary Hall, Oxford, she being twenty-four years older than the new squire.

1792–1807

Already the owner of the Penlline estate, Emilia Gwinnett inherited from her brother Samuel.

1807–24

Thomas, Earl of Clarendon and executor of Emilia's will, had temporary custody of Cottrell pending the maturity of George Tyler. It seems that George, an unlikely beneficiary, profited indirectly from Samuel Gwinnett's unrequited love for George's mother, Margaret Leach, who had married instead Sir Charles Tyler.

In 1813 Walter and Anne Meynard Esq. residing here baptised a son, Walter.

1824–62

Sir George Tyler lived at Cottrell as both tenant (1817–35) and owner.

In 1824, Robert Christopher Mansel of St Peters, Carmarthen married Emila Tyler of St Nicholas.

1824 – Poor Book

Sir Charles Tyler was renting the estate valued at £147 8s. and paying the poor rate of £5 10s. 8¼d.

1826

John Augustus Sullivan of St Marks married Jane Tyler of St Nicholas.

1827

Highways paid Sir Charles Tyler for 23 Cart of Stones at 3d. pr load 5s. 9d.

Baptism of Georgina, the daughter of Robert Christopher, a Lieutenant Colonel in the Army, and Emilia Mansell.

1828

Burial of Mark Sargent aged 38 years.

1835

Burial of Dame Margaret Tyler aged 76 years.

Burial of Admiral Sir Charles Tyler GCB aged 75 years.

1838 – Rate Book

Rev. Roper Trevor Tyler renting from Captain Tyler the house and garden of three acres and demesne land of 100 acres.

1839

Baptism of Alice Grey, the daughter of Roper Trevor, Clerk MA, and Isabel Tyler. In the 1880s the Reverend Tyler was Rector of Llantrithyd living at Tyfry.

1841–3, 1846–7, 1849–50, 1851–2

Sir George Tyler, Churchwarden.

1841 – Census

The Cottrell household comprised twenty-nine people including thirteen servants:

George (45) and Harriet (45) Tyler and their children Harriet Georgina (20), Anne Marie (18), Charles Frederick (15), Caroline (11), Edward (10), John (9), Louisa (8) and St Vincent (6). George Tyler was governor of the island of St Vincent in the Windward Islands from 1833–40.

The Pullman family of Louisa (40), Jane (35), Roper (14), Emelia (9), Frederick (6) and James (4).

Among the servants was Marie Baklin, a lady's maid from France.

1845

Burial of Alfred Tyler aged 18.

1851 – Census

On this occasion the Tyler family numbered just six but had ten servants most of whom were maids born in Glamorgan.

1850s

Baptisms of Augusta Maria and Frederick Hobart, children of Lieutenant Frederick and Katherine Tyler.

1861

The Tylers were absent at the time of the Census and there was only a skeleton staff at the house.

1862

Burial of Admiral George Tyler RN, aged 70.

1863

Baptism of Frederick Howe son of Major George and Louisa Browne.

1863–4

Colonel Tyler, Churchwarden.

1869

Burial of St Vincent Tyler aged thirty-four also resident at Wisteston Court, Herefordshire.

1870

Burial of Thomas Jones, aged 65. Servant.

1871 – Census

The head of the household was Harriet M Tyler, now a widow of seventy-six and born in London and she was assisted by her unmarried daughter Anna M (49) born in Buckinghamshire. Four grandchildren, all scholars, come next: Harriet D A Richards (13) of St Nicholas, Godfrey (11) and Basil (8) Mundy respectively born in South Sea, Hants and London and fourteen-year-old Wyndham Luin, also of London. The Mundy's father Major General Pierpont H Mundy (55) of Hallam, Derbyshire completed the family line-up.

The staff are listed in descending order and were all unmarried, except for the widowed housekeeper and nurse, a not unusual situation for those given to a life in servitude. They were: Eleri Evyne (29) a governess from Switzerland, from the same country a housekeeper Maria Jones (63) – the surname suggesting that she had married a local man; Annie M Coldwell (37) a lady's maid from Fulham, Sophia Kirtland (33) a cook from Oxford, also from that place, a nurse Sarah Stopes (53), two housemaids: Mary A Eddols (27) of Penmark and Katheryn Found (21) from Coity. Three local girls follow – the nursery maid Eliza Hopkins (17), kitchen maid Annie Hopkin (19) and scullery maid Amelia Griffiths (16). The male staff were Puis Henn (47) the butler from Baden in Germany, Richard Holly (32) the coachman from Bacton in Herefordshire, George Richards (19) a groom from Cardiff, and last of all Edwin Lewis (17) the footman from Penmark. A cast assembled from far and wide and quite a cross section of society no doubt.

Harriet Tyler died two years later and the estate passed to her granddaughter, the young Harriet Diane Arabella Mary Richards. On 14 April 1880 she married Alfred Donald Mackintosh Esquire of Moy Hall in Scotland. Their first child, Violet Charlotte, was baptised on 14 April 1881, but she lived to be only two years and two months. Their household consisted of fifteen servants, including Hugh Fraser the piper and Mr Henn again who was, by now, a nationalised British subject.

By 1891 there were seventeen servants to care for the house and estate, Alfred and Harriet and their five-year-old son Angus. Marie (note the change of the last letter) Jones was still present but now hailed from France and the rest of the staff came from all over the country. More exotically, there was a visiting major-general on half-pay born in Florence, Harriet St Leger a family lady's maid and Gladys Hewitt, an instructress on carving.

1895

The Mackintosh   Parish Churchwarden

1906

Coming of Age of

Angus Alexander Mackintosh

Chief of the Clan Chattan

6 August 1906

This booklet produced to commemorate the twenty-first birthday of Alfred Mackintosh's son clearly shows the grandeur of the occasion. Vast celebrations took place at Moy Hall the ancestral home of the Mackintosh. Presentations of silver dessert dishes were made by the servants from both houses – Moy and Cottrell. After the thanks given by the new Laird, the old Mackintosh announced that a pipe of port (a cask of about 105 gallons) laid down at his son's birth would be handed round. The following is a first-hand account of the setting.

"A spacious ballroom, measuring one hundred feet in length and forty feet wide, was erected in the Italian Garden adjoining the Mansion House, the balcony forming an ideal entrance. The steps were covered with crimson cloth and the balcony was transformed into a beautiful reception room, with French casements. The room was upholstered with ottomans and easy chairs, and there was an exquisite display of flowers. The guests entered the ballroom through a massive Gothic arch, resting on white and gold pillars. The interior of the ballroom presented a dazzling view. The scheme of decoration and furnishing was remarkable for its beauty of design and the splendour of its effect. The sides of the room were lined in white silk wallpaper and stretching beneath the entire roof was white wavy drapery. Suspended from the roof were eight massive 30 light brass chandeliers, while the sides of the room were panelled with oval gilt mirrors and brass pendants. At each corner of the ballroom were groups of palms and the mirrors and ornamentals were completely wreathed in flowers. Floral decorations were also displayed hanging from the roof and on the white walls trailers of smilax had a very fine effect. At one end of the room was a raised platform for the band, finished off with four Gothic arches resting on gold and white pillars fitted with open lattice work. The flooring consisted of polished oak parquetry, with an excellent spring for dancing. Access to the buffet was obtained through another white and gold arch situated opposite the main entrance... The buffet was beautifully lined in green and white wavy drapery and was finished with easy chairs and gilt edged couches. The sides were panelled with mirrors framed in white and gold, and lights shone from two magnificent brass chandeliers. A long buffet table ran the entire length of the room, on which was displayed massive silver candelabra and old Sheffield plate. Lovely flowers gave the finishing touch to the beautiful arrangement of the table. The spacious room led out from the ballroom through two handsome Gothic arches draped with very fine old gold French curtains. The walls of this room were completely lined in green and panelled with gold mirrors ten feet high. There were ormolu wall pendants corresponding to these in the ballroom. The room was lit with three magnificent crystal chandeliers. The arrangements for seating the guests consisted of round tables, each set for eight. One huge Brussels carpet covered the floor and the chairs were solid dining room chairs in red leather."

A not surprisingly ostentatious display for a family which had made its money in fur trading in the New World and derived a considerable income from property developments in Roath, Cardiff. This sumptuous occasion clearly illustrates the wealth and opulence enjoyed by the landowning gentry during the nineteenth and early twentieth centuries. Such families, when the old estate system was flourishing, employed a large number of people who, in exchange for long working hours, were given a roof over their heads and a modest income. This was the British class system in full working order and was seen by many as preferable to factory or mine employment. Evidence gleaned from old documents often reflects a feeling of gratitude and even affection towards those who provided employment and favours for their services. No wonder, as the extravagance of the ballroom was made available to the Scottish tenants and servants on the following evening. A true act of benevolence and no doubt much appreciated.

Cottrell, as everywhere, experienced severe changes in lifestyle during the years of World War I, the most noticeable of which was the reduction in male servants. Most pre-war table service was undertaken by the butler and his understaff. During the war additional parlour maids were employed to replace the butler, and women and girls occupied other positions formerly filled by men. This was how the now famous Gardens of Heligan were 'lost', as all the men left the land when drafted into the army.

At Cottrell the parkland was not lost and a semblance of normality was retained. Though social life was necessarily less active than before, the Mackintoshes continued to follow the seasonal pattern of former years. Cottrell was favoured for the hunting season and this meant that the family was in residence at Christmas. Some older inhabitants of the village still remember the Christmas party and the large tree provided at Cottrell for the children.

The beginning of summer demanded a move to London for the racing at Ascot and associated social events. The Mackintoshes owned a house at 8 Hill Street, Mayfair and it was here that they stayed and entertained their society friends.

Autumn necessitated yet another move, this time to the ancestral home at Moy Hall north of the border. It was here that they spent their time shooting grouse and, in pre-war years, entertaining on a grand scale with royalty included in their guest lists. The hall with its many richly filled rooms and parkland full of deer must have made a deep impression on the servants who travelled with the family from house to house.

All three establishments were kept in order during the absence of the family. Major cleaning and redecorating was done for convenience sake while the family was not at home. The travelling staff consisted of a head parlour maid, assistant parlour maid and the piper whose services were required every day to pipe in the evening meal. Mrs Gwendoline Prosser, who was travelling parlour maid during the war years and lived well into her nineties, remembered her service under the Mackintoshes with great affection. Mrs Mackintosh was always very solicitous of the well-being of her servants and watched over their health and recreation. Permanent staff at Cottrell included the cook, four kitchen maids, one scullery maid, a housekeeper (Mrs McCulvery), a hall boy (Bernard Littley), the head housemaid (Mary Flynn), second housemaid and three parlour maids. Interesting comparisons can be made with the household in 1871. All had particular and specific work to do and were expected to keep to it. The scullery maid cleaned the everyday cutlery while the parlour maids cleaned the silver and entrée dishes. Parlour maids served at table and the housemaids made the beds. Before the war, male servants had been entitled to what was known as 'boys' beer' and so the women received the equivalent in money.

Of interest in view of the strong family hunting connections was the keeping of a tame fox tied up in the yard outside the house.

1929 – 8 May, Complaint of Dangerous Driving of Motor Cyclists

P S Hamilton reported receiving "a complaint from Col The Mackintosh of Mackintosh, Cottrell, respecting The Dangerous Driving of Five Motor Cyclists [his capitals] who were competing in the Reliability Run, on Croes y Parc Kingsland lane about 7 p.m. that evening".

The Mackintosh stated "that accompanied by Mrs Mackintosh and several other persons also Mr C K Cory and Mrs Cory, Kingsland they were walking on the above stated lane when the Five Cyclists… came down from the direction of St Nicholas… round the corner… at a very fast speed without sounding their Horn or giving any other warning of their approach and the whole of the party, who were walking on the Lane, had to get up on the Bank out of the way".

COTTRELL LODGE

Thatched with an unusual semi-circular end and once used to house estate workers, Cottrell Lodge now provides an attractive aspect to the entrance to Cottrell Park.

1820s

David and Catherine Dawkin lived here with their children David and Thomas. He was a gardener.

1835

Burial of Elizabeth Large aged 53.

1838

Listed number 80 on the Tithe Map with an extent of 38 perches.

1841

Occupied by David and Mary Jenkins, their son David and Mr Jenkins's mother Mary a 75-year-old pauper. He was a labourer.

1851

John (50) and Margaret (45) Patrick lived here. He was a farm bailiff.

1854

Gardener John Keel lived here with his wife Anne. They lost a son aged three months.

1861

New arrivals from Wiltshire were Edward Taylor (65), a farm labourer, and his wife Anne (55).

1868–73

John and Eliza Hill were resident with their children John H, Mary E, William, Ellen who died in 1870 aged fifteen days, Eliza and Thomas. The family came from Herefordshire and John was a gamekeeper.

1869

The Collector of Rates was asked to assess the two cottages on the Cottrell estate, viz., the Lodge and the house on the opposite side of the road, the Laundry, occupied by a Mr Nicholls, at £3 each.

1879 – Rate Book

Mary Jones rented the cottage and garden of one rood, 30 perches.

1881 – Census

| Ann Jones | Head M 43 | Lodge Keeper not Servant | Pontypridd |
| Clara Bond | Niece U 18 | Scholar | Canton |

1891 –

Daniel Rees a farm bailiff lived here.

1893 – Rate Book

David Rees was the new tenant.

1914

John Colston and Lily Phillips lived here and their son John Colston. J C Snr was a warehouseman.

1915

A cowman Stephen Lord was now in occupation along with his wife Annie and their son William Arthur.

THE OLD LAUNDRY

Situated on the opposite side of the road to Cottrell Lodge and demolished some time after 1929.

1838

The Tithe Map shows Grant Morgan renting plot number 82, Laundry House and Garden with an area of one rood, 20 perches making it roughly the same in extent as Cottrell Lodge.

1891–1901

The resident self-employed laundress was Margaret Flynn from Ireland and her two daughters Julia and Mary.

1920s

Occupied in succession by John Edwards, a Mr Sweetland and Cecil Trigg a postman.

THE BREACH

The Tithe Map of 1838 indicates two, possibly three, houses. The occupant on the map is not the one listed in the Rate Book because the latter ran a small farm here, his name being used in official documents. The other occupants were farm labourers. The Breach was part of the Cottrell estate and had a steady flow of skilled and unskilled workers who laboured at the big house throughout the nineteenth century.

1813

William, a smith, and Hannah Owen with their son Thomas.

1815

William, a labourer, and Mary Jenkins and their children John who died aged one year, Mary and John.

1815

Phillip, a labourer, and Elizabeth Griffiths and son Phillip.

1816

Burial of Catherine Lewis, aged 26.

1816

A cooper Thomas Richards lived here with his wife Ann and sons Thomas and William.

1821

Thomas, a labourer, and Gwenllian Williams with sons John and William.

1821

Lewis, a smith, and Mary Barrett and son Moses.

1822

Thomas, a carpenter, and Laurannah Rowland with son Joseph.

1825

Burial of William Griffith aged 40.

1826

James, a shepherd, and Mary Hazel, plus daughter Susan.

1827

Labourer John and Catherine Howard and daughters Elvira and Harriett.

1828–41

A long tenancy by agricultural labourer Edward Milward or Miller and his wife Maria with children Anne, Jane, Maria, William, Harriett and Catherine.

1832

Labourer Edmund Miles, his wife Ann and their children Llewellyn and Eliza.

1833

The resident labourer was Morgan Grant with wife Joanna and children Robert, David and Harriett.

1833–41

George Harding, Farmer, Churchwarden, Overseer and Surveyor.

1838

Philip, a labourer, and Susan Griffith and son William.

The Tithe Map shows that Samuel Griffith rented one house of one rood, 24 perches, Edward Miller another of one rood and George Harding rented the 30 acres of Breach Farm from Captain Tyler.

1839

Burial of Llewellyn David aged four months.

1839

Labourer David Jenkin lived here with his wife Mary (nèe Morgan of St Hilary). They married in July 1838 and had children David, Ann, William and Mary.

1841

Agricultural labourer Samuel Griffiths lived with Elvira his wife and children Daniel, Charles, Edwin, Matilda and William.

1842

George Harding had left and the farmland reverted to the owner Sir George Tyler.

1843–52

Sometime labourer and gamekeeper John Thomas was resident with wife Anne and children Thomas, John, James (died), James, Edwin and William.

1848

Gamekeeper James Morgan and wife Mary, plus daughter Margaret.

1851

Samuel and Charlotte Humphrey had moved in with children John, William, Mary, Sarah and Ann. Mr Humphrey and his two sons were farm labourers.

1853

Labourer John Gill with wife Eliza and daughter of the same name.

1861

Thomas and Amy James lived here with their children John, Mary and Eliazer. He was a labourer and woodcutter.

1861

In the other house were James (died 1873, aged 81) and Agnes Hewitt (died 1886, aged 92) from Devon and their children Agnes, a servant, who died in 1870 aged 35, William who died in 1879 aged 52, Mary, a farm servant, and their grandson Isaac. James was a shepherd.

1871

John Nicholls, gardener and 56-year-old widower lived here. His wife Margaret (55) had recently died. Also in the house were his two sisters-in-law, Jane Stevens, laundress and 60-year-old widow and Elizabeth Williams (59), also a laundress and unmarried. Elizabeth had less than two years to live. Two years earlier Mr Nicholls had lived at the Laundry Cottage.

1874

John and Eliza Hill, formerly of Cottrell Lodge, in occupation with their six children.

1879

The Rate Book tells of three occupants all having a cottage and garden – the smallest that of Daniel Gibbon at 38 perches, Thomas James a more extensive one rood, 24 perches while Mary Hewitt had something in between at one rood. Mr Gibbon, a tailor, was from Bonvilston and his wife Eliza, five years his senior, came from Limsbury, Somerset. There were three children – Lilly, Amelia and Mary.

1891

The residents each occupying three rooms were Thomas James with wife Amy and William Morgan a retired farmer with a housekeeper, his niece and a lodger called Harry Burrows.

1893

The occupants were John Hutchings, Thomas Davies and William Hutchings.

1901

With one cottage uninhabited, the only occupants were Thomas (52) and Ann Griffiths along with his niece Alice John. Thomas was a farm bailiff from Wick.

1919

Edward William.

1929

John Edward Williams.

CAIA FARM

Variously spelt: Caua, Cauau, Cauia, Caeau, Caiae, Caya, Cairau.

1822

Burial of Anne David.

1824 – Poor Book

Llewelin Price renting from the Hon. W B Grey and paying 10s. 2d. on the rateable value of £13 11s. 0d.

Llewelyn was the son of Thomas Pryce, miller, and was baptised on 30 October 1785. He had three sisters: Mary, baptised on 23 December 1787, who died as an infant; Mary, baptised on

23 May 1790 and Anne who was baptised on 19 August 1792. It is not known at which mill he lived. On 26 December 1812 Llewelyn married local girl Rebecca Jones. There are two known children of this marriage, a son William, baptised in April 1824 and Anne born in March 1827. Llewelyn was a carpenter by trade and he and his wife lived first at Ty'n y caia (was this a cottage adjoining Caia farm?) and then Caia where he turned his hand to farming. He was also an Overseer (1826–7, 1833–4) and Surveyor (1835–7).

1826

Journey to Wenvoe for Lewellyn Price 2/6 Oath 1/– [in role of Overseer] 3s. 6d.

1833

Paid Lew Price for Returning Jury List and Lunatic Bill to Wenvoe 7s. 0d.

1836

[L Price]... Cart & Horses 5 day on Witton Mawr £1 10s. 0d.

1838

To L Price Cart 2 horses 1 day 6s. 0d.

The Rate Book and the Tithe Map both record that Llewelyn Price rented from J B Pryce Esq. both Broadway and Caia farms with a total acreage respectively of 128 acres, three roods, 13 perches or 137 acres four perches. For many years Broadway and Caia were run as a single unit, the latter being the homestead. At this time Broadway farmhouse had not been built and the site consisted only of labourers' cottages. Each had assumed a separate identity by the mid-1850s and from 1861 until the late 1870s, the Caia served as a labourers' household and Broadway was the home farm.

Llewelyn Price stayed at Caia farm until the 1850s on occasions employing as many as seven labourers.

1861

The census reveals that Robert Grant lived here as farm bailiff along with John and Ann Potter and their daughters Jane and Sarah. Mr Potter was a carter.

1871

Isaac and Mary John and their children William and Mary Ann plus a lodger Thomas John. Isaac and Thomas were agricultural labourers.

1872

John and Mary Morrish and children Walter, John and Jane lived with father-in-law David Thomas, a retired farmer from Homri. Mr Morrish was also a farmer and brother to Robert who ran Broadway.

1878–9

Robert James Meyrick, farmer, also Overseer and Surveyor.

1881

William, a labourer, and Joan Kent were in residence with their sons William and John. Also Christopher and Catherine Bassett and children Catherine, Florence and Lewis Thomas. Mr Bassett was a farmer and parish Churchwarden, Overseer and Guardian.

1891

David Thomas, farmer and Overseer, lived here with his wife Margaret and one-year-old son.

1901

Farmer David Evans, his wife Edith Maud and daughter Dorothy Olga Maud.

1912

Farmer Morgan David Morgan, his wife Annie May and children Annie May, David Randal, Ethel Margurite and Doris Muriel.

VIAN'S HILL FARM

1762–3

Survey of Wenvoe Estate Vianats [or possibly Vianars] Hill.

1820

In residence were Captain Robert and Elizabeth Chapman and their six children including Fanny Louisa and Herman. Formerly of Lan y Lay.

1824

The Poor Book shows that Mr MacGregor renting the farm from The Hon. W B Grey paid £1 12s. 7½d. to the Overseer of the Poor on a rateable value of £43 9s. 0d.

1826

Also living here was labourer James Edward and his wife Elizabeth with children Sarah and William.

1835

Thomas and Jane Minnett and daughter Amelia. He was the son of Thomas Minnett of Brook farm.

1838

The Rate Book indicates that William Richards rented the house and land of 85 acres and three perches from J B Pryce Esq. whereas the Tithe Map assesses the land at 64 acres.

1843

The new occupant was George Price Esq.

1848

A farm labourer lived here, namely Joseph Richards with wife Jane and children Jane and John.

1848–61

The farmer was John Harris, unmarried, and having 65 acres increasing to 85 acres. He was a Churchwarden, Surveyor and Overseer.

1850

John Harris for removing 8 yards of stones on Duffryn Road 8s. 0d.

There were usually a number of servants and farmworkers living on the premises at Vians Hill yet they were all women and included two widows.

1864–72

George (died 1872, aged 53) and Anne (died 1871, aged 41) Hooper. He was an agricultural labourer from Usk and his wife came from Bristol. They had four children – Thomas, George, Annie and Elizabeth, plus an adopted daughter Minnie Williams whose father was the captain of a merchant ship.

1866–71

George and Amelia Barkway and their children Richard, Stephen, George and James. Mr Barkway was a carpenter from Suffolk and had formerly worked for Benjamin Wright of The Laurels, St Nicholas making agricultural implements. His descendants lived in the eponymous Barkway's Cottage, on The Downs adjacent to Vian's Hill, a tiny one-up one-down building now demolished and one totally lacking in basic facilities even by nineteenth-century standards.

1871

Agricultural labourer Thomas Kent, his wife Sarah and children Mary Ann and William.

1874

Thomas Yates or Yeats, a haulier from Wiltshire, his wife Olivia and a proliferation of children – Ben, Edith Jane, Mary Elizabeth, Olive, William, Anne, Blanche, Beatrice and Emma Margaret. The family also lived on The Downs and in St Nicholas village.

1875

On Easter Sunday labourer George Stevens and his wife Catherine baptised their six children, Anne (13¾), Alfred (9), Ellen (6), Ernest (5), Sarah (3), and William Charles (7 months).

1881

The farm now comprised 160 acres and was run by Morgan Williams from Ogmore. His wife was Catherine and they had four children – Thomas, Morgan, Margaret and Samuel. They had an Irish servant girl Annie Lisburn and a lodger Thomas Phillips, a carpenter from Somerset.

1884–94

Now farmed by John Wesley Ford with his wife Jane who had died by 1891 and three sons the youngest bearing his father's names. From 1892–4 he was parish churchwarden.

1901

The new occupier was John Morgan, his wife Emma and family.

1919–29

David William Evans.

BROOK FARM

Now a complete ruin but with the walls of a barn still standing.

1809–14

John and Margaret John and their sons Thomas and Morgan.

1818–20

Morgan Grant was the farmer and also Surveyor of highways 1818–19.

1823–30

David Harry farmer and Overseer of the poor 1829–30.

1824

Mr Harry was a tenant of the Right Hon. E Clarendon paying a poor rate of £1 10s. 6d., the rateable value of the farm being £40

12s. 6d. Also a Mr M Morgans rented a part of the farm valued at £11 12s. 6d. and paying a poor rate of 8s. 9d.

1831–41

Thomas Minnett farmer, Overseer of poor 1831–2, 1835–6 and Surveyor of highways 1838–9. Mr Minnett's daughter Hannah married Richard Thomas in 1833 and his son Thomas married Jane Morgan of St Georges two years later. Thomas and Jane had a daughter Amelia and lived at Vians Hill before finally farming at Tre Ywbwb, St Lythans. They also had two sons Thomas and John.

1838

The Tithe Map and Rate Book both record Thomas Minnett renting the farm from Captain Tyler, with the house and land totalling 75 acres, two roods, seven perches. John Jones now had the smaller portion of 24 acres.

1841

At the time of the census Daniel Williams (25), an agricultural labourer lived here with his common-law wife Mary Cole (30) and their nine-month-old daughter Jane.

1851–1904

Throughout this period the John family, Thomas and Ann and their children Ann, Thomas and Jane were tenants farming 83 acres. Thomas and Jane never married and took over the farm when their parents died. Thomas John Senior or Junior (it is not known which), gave service to the parish as Surveyor, Overseer and Churchwarden on five occasions between 1850 and 1865. The children Thomas and Jane were Nonconformists and were buried at Croes y Parc Chapel.

1919

Evan and D Jones farming 74 acres, three roods.

Poor Book	*£ s d*
1832	
paid Thos Minnett for keeping Jane Deer	£1 1s. 3d.
Paid Thos Minnett for Returning the List to Wenvoe	10s. 0d.
Highways Book	
1811	
John John purchased the Highways book on 2 September.	
1822	
Morgan Morgans 1 day Cart & Horses	6s. 0d.
1829	
Dd Harry 1 day Haulling	6s. 0d.
1845	
To Thomas Minnett 3 days Hauling on Brook Road at 7/–	£1 1s. 0d.
To Thomas Minnett For 54 Cartloads of Stones at 3d. per load	13s. 6d.

WINCH PIT

A modern house on the site of an old cottage. In the nineteenth century it was usually rented as a smallholding with a few acres of land.

1820–69

Occupied by the Morgan family. In 1820, William Morgan, aged 79, was buried and more tragically in 1829, Martha Morgan aged eight died. The Tithe Map, number 369, and Rate Book of 1838 show William Morgan renting the house and land amounting to six acres, two roods and 39 perches from J B Pryce Esq. William lived with his wife Ann and their daughter of the same name. He was a farm labourer and cowman from St Georges and died in 1869 aged 84.

1871–81

The new occupants were Thomas and Ann Evans with their children Martha Jane, John and Ann. Thomas was a haulier but he rented land extending to eight acres, two roods, nine perches and was parish constable between 1864 and 1867 and also 1870 to 1879.

1891–1920

John Penny from Cadoxton lived here with wife Mary and seven children – George, William, Helena, David, Harriet, Harold and John. He was a bootmaker and sometime farmer.

TINKINSWOOD FARM

1815

Farmer Thomas Williams was the tenant along with his wife Mary and son Morgan.

1817

Richard and Elizabeth Rees and their daughter Mary now in occupation.

1824

Phillip Davies rented Tinkins Wood and Castell Carreg from the Hon. W B Grey paying a Poor Rate of £1 6s. 10½d. on a rateable value of £35 15s. Mr Davies was Overseer of poor in 1826–7 and again in 1830–1 when he was also Surveyor of the highways.

1838

George Harbottle was in residence renting from J B Pryce Esq. number 354 on the Tithe Map, the house and land estimated to be 82 acres, one rood, 24 perches. George came from Northumberland and farmed here until about 1856. He served the parish variously as Surveyor 1840–1 and 1847–8, Churchwarden 1843–6 and 1852–4 and Overseer 1852–3. His wife Emelia came from Berkshire and their children, Hannah, John, Mary, Elizabeth, Henry, Thomas and William, were all born in Aberdare, plus Sarah, Amelia, George and an unnamed baby who were all born locally. Henry and Thomas farmed at Homri in the 1860s and daughter Hannah, a maidservant, gave birth to an illegitimate son

111

John in 1856. George died in 1862 in Llandaff aged 64 and his wife died nine years later, aged 72.

1857–78

William and Catherine Evans and family, farming 112 acres (see Chapter 5).

1877

On the motion of Mr WT Wright and seconded by the Rev. W Bruce of Duffryn, a remuneration of £2 10s. 0d. was made to Mr W Evans Overseer "for his trouble in making the new valuation of the Parish. This valuation £2,806 6s. 0d. at 8d in the £ = £93 11s. ½d.". Subsequently the Evans family moved to Broadway.

1878

Phillip Harry, from Llantwit Major, farmed here until his death in 1888 at the age of 68. He was Overseer in 1878–9 and rented variously 120 acres and 144 acres. His wife Eliza was fifteen years his junior and came from Nine Wells in Pembrokeshire. There were six children of this union – Richard, William, Thomas, Phillip, Ann and Edith.

1891

The widow Eliza Harry from St David's, Pembrokeshire was the farmer assisted by her two sons.

1893–1901

John and Mary Dunn and family initially farming 146 acres. This reduced to 90 acres in the early twentieth century.

Poor Book	£ s d
1827	
Paid Phillip Davies 2 Journeys to Landough	5s. 0d.
Highways Book	
1818	
To paid Mr Rees Tinkingwood 2 days Cart & Horses	10s. 6d.

1826

Paid Phillip David for 9 Cart load of Stones at 3d. per Cart Load   2s. 3d.

1841

Paid George Harbottle for Cart & 2 Horses for 5 days at 6s. per day.
Hauling Stones to Brook Lane   £1 10s. 0d.

1848

John Harbottle 3 Horses & 2 Carts 1 day on Witton Road   10s. 0d.

1850

George Harbottle's Bill for repairing Culvert   6s. 0d.

1851

G Harbottle for improving the side of the Road by Tinkinswood   10s. 0d.

1853

Paid George Harbottle for hauling lime & slates   14s. 0d.

1859

Wm Evans for hauling stones on Witton road 2 days for 2 Carts &
3 Horses at 12/– p day   £1 4s. 0d.

DUFFRYN LODGE

1832–44

Occupied by gamekeeper George Sandland, his wife Ann and children Charles, Jane who died in 1844 aged nine, Elizabeth, who sadly died within two days of her sister, aged seven and George.

1851–81

Head of the household was the widowed Mary Miles formerly of Little Lanelay and Pendoylan. She was a gardener and lodgekeeper. For a short time her daughter Elizabeth kept house but probably left to get married. Mrs Miles' son Miles was a farm labourer and engine driver.

1891

Working as coachman and groom for the occupants of Duffryn House was Edward Curtis from Banbury in Oxfordshire. He was

113

much travelled, for his wife was from Bayswater, his eldest son was born in Yorkshire, three more in London and the youngest boy was a Cardiffian.

1901

Occupied by Charles Day the estate gamekeeper and his son.

Two new Duffryn Estate dwellings appear for the first time on a census return, namely Duffryn Gardens and Duffryn Yard. They were respectively occupied by Charles Lucton and his son who were gardeners, and George Mullett, the coachman and groom.

DUFFRYN HOUSE

From the seventh to the sixteenth century, the Manor of Duffryn, also called Worleton or Columbar, belonged to the Bishop of Llandaff. The manorship and property of Worleton then passed to the Button family, initially on a lease when they lived at Doghill Grange, and then by outright purchase. They moved to Duffryn House, which presumably they built, around 1571 at which time William, Earl of Pembroke was Chief Lord. The Buttons were Royalists and strong supporters of the church, and they also combined the manor by marriage with the Cottrell estate of the Meyricks. In the year 1688, the Buttons of Duffryn and Cottrell bought out the third knight's fee of the manor of St Nicholas still held by the Earl of Pembroke and became sole lords. This was the first time that the whole of the parish had been owned by one landlord or family. The support that the family gave to Charles I meant that the estate had to be heavily mortgaged and, in 1749, the foreclosure was enforced by Truman Harford, a Bristol merchant to whom the estate had been pledged in 1735.

Thomas Pryce of Court Carnau bought 415 acres of the demesne including Duffryn House and other lands for £13,758 2s. 0½d. and it was his daughter Frances Anne, by then married to William Booth Grey, who inherited Duffryn. John Bruce Pryce from 1837 and his heirs then held the estate until 1891.

The old Elizabethan pile was probably in decline in the

nineteenth century and may not have reached the standards of comfort and convenience required by the Bruce family. The census returns of 1861, 1871 and 1881 show that they did not live here permanently but preferred the manor house and rectory in St Nicholas village or estates elsewhere.

John Cory demolished the old house in 1891 and built the present structure.

1541 – Malefant

... holding free 8 acres of land called Hewe Butons lands and returned per annum... 16d.

1570 – Earl of Pembroke's Survey

This survey was conducted about the time the Buttons moved from Doghill to Duffryn and states:

> Miles Button Knight holding one messuage and 32 acres of land lying in Worletowne falling away to the west and so returned likewise... 10s. 7d.

and:

> Miles Button holding one house without a court three acres of land... recently belonging to Robert ap Rice in Worleton... returned 16d.

See also Doghill farm.

1662 – Will of Robert Button of Worlton

Married to Jane, his executrix, daughter of Sir Thomas Aubrey of Llantrithyd.

1692 – 24 October, The Will of Martin Button of Worlton

Son of Robert, Martin leaves everything, "Cattells, Corne, Household stuff, Plate, Mony, Bonds, & all other my Goods, & Chattells", to Mary his wife and probate was granted under the old calendar on 16 January 1692.

1693 – 5 October, The Will of Myles Button of Dyffryn

Myles, brother of Martin, bequeaths all his possessions to his true friend Charles Jevans, Gentleman. However ten years later, through a bond, Charles Button, his nephew and administrator, inherits the Worlton estate.

1713 – February, The Will of Charles Button Esquire of Columbar

In this extensive and detailed will Charles covers all aspects of his possessions, family care, inheritance and funeral arrangements. Charles desired to be buried "privately in the night tyme" in his father's and brother's grave "using only those short prayers ordered by the Established church at the grave for burying the dead and my request is that no escutcheon [coat-of-arms] nor any pompous thing be used in and ab[ou]t my funerall nor much Expense but lett it be done with decency." He wished his soul and spirit to be precious in the sight of almighty God, "washed in the blood of the immaculate lamb that was slain to take away the sins of the world" so that "whatsoever defilement it may have contracted in the midst of this miserable world thro' the lust of the flesh or the wiles of Satan" may be purged and done away with so that his soul is "pure and without spott" before God. This is a strong and personal expression of his spiritual needs.

More prosaically he leaves his daughters Mary and Jane £1,500 each and to his son Charles £1,300 plus messuages, tenements and premises in St Mellons. He asks that his "personall Estate of whatkindsoever" be converted into money "with all convenient speed" to pay the aforementioned sums. His children are also to receive £1,000 secured on an estate in Monmouthshire in his wife's name upon her death. Also the rents and profits from his properties in St Nicholas, St Georges, Ystradevoduck [sic] and elsewhere, amounting to £1,240, are for the children's legacy. Charles Van of Llanwern and Roger Jones of Buckland in Brecon were to manage the rents and profits from this, the purchased estate, as opposed to his ancient estate. Furthermore there are "the yearly rents issues and profitts of the severall Messuages Lands tenements and premises" at the Dogghill, Cortfarme and the Caia Bach in possession of the widow Catherine Bevans plus the Great House or Castle farm under David Richard and the Cae hill with David Anthony. More money came from Maud's tenement in possession of David Morgan, David Anthony and Christopher

Williams, the Kingsland rented or leased by George Giles and the widow Hawkin and Llanylay Vach taken by the widow Morgan of Pwlymin (see Pwll y Min, Jane Morgan's will, 1730) and Mr Jones, her brother-in-law. More money was forthcoming from tenements in the possession of William Thomas bailiff and Thomas Lewis malster, land with his Aunt Lewis of Cottrell and more property occupied by Rosser Richards, John Thomas als Griffith, Ann Thomas als Griffith spinster, Elizabeth Reignolds widow, John Morgan, joiner and John Williams, gentleman. Charles requests that some honest, discreet person be appointed bailiff and collector of these rents, issues and profits and that every midsummer this money be used to support three of his four children. His fourth child, eldest son and main benefactor, Martin, received two-thirds of the ancient estate and his wife Mary, executrix, the rest. If Charles were to inherit the estate due to Martin's demise, then his £1,300 would revert to his sisters. Several people who were to assist his wife in carrying out his wishes as expressed received plain, gold mourning rings valued at twenty shillings each.

As a caring father he wished his wife to be guardian of their four children as they were all under 21 years of age. He charges his children to be dutiful and respectful to their dear mother and wanted his sons "to be brought up in the Doctrine and Discipline of the Established Church" so that "they take upon them the respective callings and vocations herein after mentioned." Son Martin wished to be admitted to a college for two years before entering Lincoln's Inn to "take upon him the proffession of a Barrester." Younger son Charles was to enter college to study divinity and "such degrees as may fitt him for a Divine [clergyman] in the Established Church."

To Mary, his wife, he also bequeaths "all her Gold new or old, ye five pound peese of Gold the Gold medall given at the revolution & other medalls." There are also gold rings "plaine morning or those sett with stones", plus diamonds, a picture set in gold, gold buttons and earrings, silver coin, gold and silver held in trust for the children. His daughters will receive £120 each for a "little schooling or education", scant when compared to the largesse extended to the sons but representative of the age. To encourage his wife to stay at Columbar during the children's minority, she can have the malt in the storehouse and corn in the barn. Assuming she was of no great age, this might appear to be a combination of a bribe not to remarry and a desire not to unsettle his maturing family.

In a touching final request he asks his wife and son to be kind to the poor of St Nicholas and St Lythans. Probate was granted 26 October 1714.

1824

In the Poor Book William Booth Grey is listed as owner and occupier paying £3 9s. 10d. on a rateable value of £93 2s. 0d. He was churchwarden from 1824 to 1840 inclusive and his wife Frances Anne died in 1837 at the age of 57.

1838

John Bruce Pryce Esq. was now resident with Duffryn House and lands totalling 88 acres and 26 perches.

1841

The household comprised five children of the Bruce family and 12 servants.

1843–67

John Bruce Pryce was churchwarden for most of these years.

1845

Burial of Major-General Sir Burges Carmac, aged 71.

To repairing the road leading from St Nicholas Village to Duffryn the half paid by the [Highways] Trust for the use of Mr Pryce's stones £5 3s. 0d.

1846

Paid J B Pryce Esq. for lime for Dog Hill Road 2s. 0d.

1850

Henry and Annabella Bruce with their daughter Jessy Frances.

1851

J B Pryce, his wife and four children had fourteen servants including a butler, footman, groom, two gardeners and maids of all descriptions.

1861

The house was now occupied by only three people – the housekeeper May David (41) from Bridgend, a dairymaid Mary Morgan (24) from Lanvabon and the farm bailiff Jonathan Howells (41) from Llanblethian.

1871

Mr Howells still ran the farm but there was a new dairymaid plus a groom.

1872

Burial of Alicia Grant Bruce Pryce aged 81.
Burial of John Knight Bruce Pryce aged 88.

1873

Burial of Shadrack Cox aged 26. He was coachman to the Pryce family and was killed suddenly by a fall from his horse riding down to Duffryn late at night.

1874

Baptism of twins Alan George Cameron and Edward Maunsell, sons of Alan Cameron and Anna Mary Synnot Bruce Pryce.

1881

Occupied by an agricultural labourer from Middlesex and his family. They were Morgan Grant (51), his wife Gwenllian (52) from Ystrad Rhondda and children Gwen (24) a dressmaker, David (22) and Robert (20) both labourers, Elizabeth (13), Margaret (10) and granddaughter Ethel (1). They had previously lived in St Lythans.

1885

Newly resident was Henry Ellis Collins, a bank manager originally from Clifton in Bristol, his wife Mary and their children Mary, Kate, Gwendoline, Henry, William, John Duffryn Powell, James Denis Ellis and Isabel Frances. The household was completed by a French governess, an English cook, Welsh and German housemaids, and Victorine Baron, a nurse from Paris.

1889

Burial of Lewis Hobart Bruce of Llandogo Chepstow, aged 28.

1901

John Cory, a coal merchant originally from Bideford in Devon took up residence with his wife Anna and two unmarried children, Florence aged 43 and Reginald aged 29. At the time of the census there were three visitors: a solicitor's clerk, a corn merchant from Essex and unsurprisingly, given the family's religious inclinations, Edward Telford, an Evangelist preacher from Northumberland. They were attended by a staff comprising a butler, footman, cook, four housemaids and two scullery maids.

1909

Burial of Anna Maria Cory, aged 73.

1910

Burial of John Cory, aged 81.

The new house built by Mr Cory comprised 227 acres of grounds and gardens, parklands, two entrance lodges, estate yard, head gardener's cottage and woodlands. In the house there was a grand hall, billiard room, large and small drawing room, morning room, red library, white library, dining room, boudoir, breakfast room, secretary's room. First floor: end bedroom, bedroom no. 2, Italian bedroom, Tynsal room, four single bedrooms, two bathrooms and pantry. Second floor: seven single bedrooms, eight staff bedrooms, housemaid's sitting room, linen and blanket rooms.

DOGHILL FARM

The farm includes the site of a moated grange or fortified manor house and there is evidence of masonry foundations. From the twelfth century onwards it is known that Cistercian monks practised sheep-farming on ranch-like granges, particularly in the Yorkshire Dales and Wales. This medieval grange, belonging to the Bishops of Llandaff, was probably supplanted by the present farmhouse, which is reputed to be very old, after the Buttons left for Duffryn House. The name Doghill would seem to be a corruption of 'Mitdehorguill' the name of the family which had a sub-tenancy of the manor of St Nicholas.

1570 – Earl of Pembroke's Survey

Margareta wife of Miles Button Edus and William his sons... holding by copy dated 24 June... ninth year of Queen Elizabeth... one parcel of land and pasture called Dogghill containing seven acres and another parcel called namely Knolle containing 30 acres and a third parcel called Colyngstote containing five acres and returned annually... 20s.

1816

On 31 March, Thomas Furber, bachelor of Doghill married the widowed Hannah Branch in Michaelstone le Pit. Hannah (née Greatorex) of a family originally from Derby, had married Edward Pranch, elder son of Edward Pranch of Nantbrane and St Fagans. He was buried on 2 March 1813 leaving Hannah with seven children – Edward, Margaret, Elizabeth, Hannah, Mary, Thomas, and William. Hannah and Thomas Furber themselves had a son bearing his father's name. When the Furber family left Doghill, it is thought they went to Maes y Felin farm just up the road. The name Furber is found in the list of Welsh archers at Agincourt.

1824

The Poor Book shows that Mr Furber rented the farm from the Hon. W B Grey paying £5 9s. 2½d. on a rateable value of £145

12s. 0d. He was an Overseer of the poor in 1825–6 and again in 1827–8.

1826

Mr Furber Relieved William Thomas & Wife sundry times: 7s. 0d.

Ditto John Ford & Wife 5/– Ditto Ann Cule & Son 4/– 9s. 0d.

1829

Baptism of William, illegitimate son of William John and Mary Branch, both servants at Doghill.

1835

Baptism of Maria, daughter of William Williams, farmer of Doghill and Margaret Richards, servant.

1838

The Tithe Map, number 436, and Rate Book indicate that Richard Thomas and his son Job now rented Doghill from J B Pryce Esq. farming an estimated 224 acres, one rood, 15 perches. The following year they were assisted by William Thomas.

1841

Still in residence were Richard (82) and Gwenllian Thomas (70) and their three unmarried sons Richard (45), Robert (30) and Rees (28). (See Chapter 5.)

Richard Senior lived to be 95 or 96 years of age and after his death, his son of the same name, having finally married when he was over the age of 55, took over the farm. By 1871 Rees Thomas ran the farm. He too had waited until late in life to marry, being at least 40, but his wife Ann bore him six children. In 1891 Rees, by then a widower of 79, had the help of two sons, Robert aged 25 and Rees aged 24, plus his son-in-law John Dunn, also of Tinkinswood Farm, who lived here with his wife Mary and Rees Senior's three grandchildren.

The Thomases had the longest tenancy of any farming family

in the parish during the nineteenth and early twentieth centuries, the last occupant of that name being the above mentioned Robert, who ran the farm by 1901 and was certainly there in 1926.

The last two cattle of the now extinct Glamorganshire breed were kept here and were called Swan and Sweet.

1854 – January, The Will of Richard Thomas, farmer

Richard left money to his children as follows: Thomas £50, Rees £150, Robert £10, David, Gwenllian and Jane £1 each. All the remainder of his real and personal estate went to his son and executor Richard and the will was witnessed by William Bruce, rector and Morgan Howell, farmer of Baily Mawr, St Lythans. Richard Senior had died on 4 August 1855, probate being granted 7 November on an estate valued at under £450.

Taking into account that Doghill was one of the largest farms in the parish, it is instructive to compare Richard's farming assets with those of the 18th century Buttons at Cottrell. The inventory of live and dead stock was taken by his son Thomas and William Lougher. Downstairs accommodation in the farmhouse consisted of a kitchen, back kitchen, dairy and parlour, although puzzlingly the latter contained three beds. Possessions, which comprised only a very small part of the estate value, included the ubiquitous dresser, a cheese press and vats, 24 milk pans, churns and a buffet sideboard.

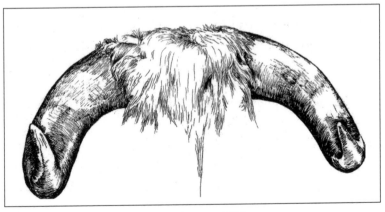

A pair of Glamorganshire cattle horns from Doghill farm

Livestock were listed as: twelve cows at £6 each, ten steers and heifers at £5 10s. each, eight two-yearlings at £4 each, eight yearlings at £2 10s. each, nine calves at 15s. each, three draught horses at £9 each, two fillies at £6 each, one pony £5, two colts at £2 10s. each, 29 sheep at £1 each, 21 lambs at 10s. each and one ram and four pigs at £1 10s. each. Implements of husbandry included a wagon, three carts, a plough, two pairs of drays, a halter, shaft and ploughing harnesses, a winnowing machine, a turnip scuffler (possibly some sort of hoeing device) and a turnip cutter. Of considerably more value were six small ricks of wheat valued at £48, four small mows of hay at £40 and three small ricks of oats at £12. The total value of Richard's estate was £433 12s. 6d.

Highways Book	£ s d
1851	
Paid Richard Thomas for 21¼yds of stones & hauling the same to Doghill Road at 1/– per yard	£1 1s. 3d.
1860	
Paid Richard Thomas for making culvert on Doghill Road	4s. 0d.

WHITTON LODGE

Adjacent to Whitton Mawr, a huge field at the south-west corner of the parish.

1541 – Malefant

John ap John ap Willm and Jhoana wife... and Johes son... holding by copy... one cottage... meadow... white downe... 14d.

Milo Mathew holding by copy... whyte donne... and returned per annum 12s 9d.

1570 – Earl of Pembroke's Survey

Jevanus ap John, Johnna his wife and John his son... holding by copy dated 23 May... 8d. one cottage one acre of meadow lying in Whyte Downe and returned... 14d. 2 capons.

Ricus... Jana wife... and John, son of Lodovici Madock, holding by copy dated 12 October seventh year Queen Elizabeth... one closure called Whyte & downe containing 15 acres and returned... 12s. 9d. and 2 capons 2 gallini.

One Ap Morgan and Hoell ap Morgan holding by copy dated 9 October... two acres in Morva Whittdon.

1824

The Poor Book shows that Thomas Hopkin rented Witton Mawr from the Hon. W B Grey paying £1 9s. 3d. on a rateable value of £52 6s. 6d. This would be for the land not the house.

1838

The Rate Book and Tithe Map indicate that David Smith rented a house and land from J B Pryce Esq. amounting to 56 acres, eleven perches and David Hopkins rented apportionment number 479, a house and garden of one rood, twelve perches. David and his wife Elizabeth were resident in 1841 with their children Joseph, Thomas, Sarah, Rowland, David, Elizabeth and Anne. Mr Hopkins was both a gamekeeper and agricultural labourer.

1841

William Smith.

1842

Lewis Lewis.

There is no record of Whitton Lodge on the 1851 census, and a decade later it was empty.

1871–91

Agricultural labourer and grocer Daniel Griffiths from Llandisilio or Narbeth, Pembrokeshire (depending on your source) lived here with his wife Mary and children Jane, David, Margaret, Hannah, Mary and Gertrude. Mrs Griffiths had an illegitimate daughter Catherine, only a year older than Jane, who was baptised in 1872 at the age of 15.

ST NICHOLAS A GLAMORGANSHIRE PARISH

1893

William and Jane Thomas and their daughter Alice Mary Rebecca. Mr Thomas was an army reservist.

1901

Mr Davies, a roadman, lived here with his wife and four children.

BLACKLAND FARM

Not actually in the parish yet having land in and connections with the area.

1879 – Rate Book

William Griffiths rented the house and land of 20 acres, 32 perches from Gwinnett Tyler.

1893

John Thomas rented from Fred Tyler.

REDLAND FARM

1812–20

John Jones farmed here until his death in 1818 at the age of 83. His wife was Mary and there are two known sons, Richard buried in 1783 aged 17 and John who died in 1836 aged 72.

1820

Burial of Cecil Lebert aged 49.

1824

The Poor Book reveals that John Jones Junior rented the farm paying 19s. 9d. on a rateable value of £26 6s. 6d.

1839

Evan Prosser rented 65 acres, one rood, 26 perches from Captain Tyler.

1854

A labourer John Moore, his wife Drusilla and son Charles lived here.

1855

Labourer Stephen Stokes with his wife Sophia and daughter Janet.

1871

Occupied by David Davies (29) born in Carmarthenshire, his wife Elizabeth and daughter Margaret. He was the Baptist Minister from Croes y Parc chapel.

1879

John Richards rented 76 acres, three roods, six perches from Gwinnett Tyler.

1881–93

Daniel Lougher rented the same from Fred Tyler.

1919

James James.

CHAPTER 3
The Village

THE DATE OF the shift of the population from the old and prehistoric sites and dwellings of the parish to the present village site can only be a matter of conjecture. As in most villages the rise of Christianity and the rule of the Normans played a significant part. The building of a stone church, often to replace a wooden original, and the organisation of the manor of St Nicholas may not have been contemporaneous, but they would have served as focal points encouraging settlement. We associate both, rightly or wrongly, with Norman rule. Another factor to consider is that churches were often built on sites which previously had some pagan or ritualistic significance pre-dating Christianity. The yew tree, as with all evergreens, was important to the Celts and these long-living trees are frequently found in churchyards, suggesting a Christian need to seek to consolidate itself within the context of ancient rituals. It is possible, then, that the church occupies what has been for many thousands of years a special place of worship, the early material evidence of which has long since disappeared.

St Nicholas has all the appearances of a street village with the houses mostly built on an east-west axis flanking the main road, the Roman military route of the Via Julia Maritima, constructed shortly after 75 AD. This constitutes at least a 3,000-year gap between the early settlers around Tinkinswood and those attracted by the passing and permanent trade generated by the Roman road, and another thousand years before Norman settlement took place.

Many of the older village dwellings are to the north of the main road in order to take advantage of a south-facing front elevation with direct access onto the road, and the possibility of a cool northern aspect for the construction of kitchen space and food storage facilities. These old houses have few, if any, windows in their northern walls. If the church is of Norman origin, then most of the houses built since appear to have turned their backs on it, thus confirming the importance of the main artery of communication with its commercial prospects of hostelry and trade. Mammon before God. Alternatively, this could suggest that the village pre-dates the church, which did attract a few related buildings in the form of a tithe barn, a poor house and an associated village green. There was also some early lateral development along Duffryn Lane, namely the Manor House, the Pound, Quarry house and the Winch Pit.

Over the centuries many villages have been deserted, abandoned, destroyed or moved as a result of evolution, changing social patterns, local and national politics, and disease and pestilence, but there is no evidence of this happening in St Nicholas. Infilling in the twentieth century linked the village to Trehill, which in the eighteenth and nineteenth centuries had consisted of no more than half-a-dozen houses with a suitably lofty soap-box site for itinerant Wesleyan, or other Nonconformist preachers.

With the exception of the church it would be unreasonable to expect any building to pre-date the sixteenth century although the houses could occupy reused sites of considerable antiquity. The old village houses are listed below:

- The Manor House – also known as Great House Farm and largely rebuilt
- The Three Tuns – probably sixteenth century with later additions
- Smiths Row – eastern half *c.*1620, western half *c.*1700
- Trehill Cottage – possibly eighteenth century
- Tŷ To Gwellt – seventeenth to eighteenth centuries, once thatched

- Manor Cottages – once thatched, rebuilt early twentieth century
- Blacksmith's House – old smithy now demolished
- The Post Office – formerly two houses
- The Rectory – now The Court
- Twyn Bach – house here pre-1838, possibly rebuilt
- School House – single-storey cottage, rebuilt
- 1 & 2 Smith's Row – partly demolished and rebuilt
- Church Row – formerly a barn
- Pryce's Arms – 1841
- The Laurels – 1846
- Pwll Sarn – 1846
- Broadway Farm House – 1850s, confusingly known as Great House Farm
- Police Station – 1858
- Trehill House – possibly the Meeting House for Trehill Chapel

Until the middle of the nineteenth century St Nicholas followed the pattern of all Vale villages in having white, cream or even yellow ochre-washed rubble stone houses with thatched roofs. The erection of the Pryce's Arms, the Laurels and Pwll Sarn would have marked quite a departure from a long Glamorgan tradition of using only the local materials of limestone and straw. They required the importation of slate, the occasional framing of windows and doors with brick, the building of thinner, more regular walls with larger sash windows, and the implementation of a more obvious symmetry of design. Vernacular architecture was dying and the progress that was the Industrial Revolution, with its mass-production and national communications by means of the railways and canals, meant that building materials could now be imported at not too prohibitive a cost. In the twentieth century the building of council houses enabled some of the locally-born young families to remain in the village, but from the 1950s onwards only expensive new housing was sanctioned, and this began the transition to the modern commuter village. Reference to the Tithe Map gives an accurate assessment of the number of buildings which in the last 150 years have been neglected, replaced, razed or fallen prey to property developers. The losses include:

- The Wivern – replaced by the Coffee tavern, now Westways
- Broadway Cottages – former labourers' cottages and shop
- Malt House
- Village Farm – replaced at the same time as The Wivern
- Old Barn – demolished prior to Ger y Llan development
- Poor House – demolished
- Trehill Farm – derelict and replaced
- The Beeches – former farm and carpenter's shop, demolished
- Quarry House – a ruin
- The Pound – replaced
- Mwddwls Cwm – a ruin

CHAPTER 4

Houses and Farms of the Village

TREHILL

THE METHODIST CHAPEL

Richard Jones, who died in 1783, was a farmer with Trehill connections and could afford to leave £350 to each of his two nephews Richard and John, sons of his deceased brother William. Possibly inspired by John Wesley's 1740 visit and, as a man of substance, he bequeaths the Society house, stable and half an acre of land "which said house has been for the use of preaching of the Gospel of Christ for this many years past which said house and stable and the said half an acre of land are in the parish of St Nicholas which are held by lease under Samuel Gwinnett Cl[er]k of Cotterel for and during the term of the life of John Morgan of Drope in the parish of St Georges which said house… I give and bequeath during the life of the said John Morgan for the use of preaching of the Gospel" plus five shillings a year for the maintenance and repairs thereof. There is a certain irony here in that land and property held under lease from the Rev. Samuel Gwinnett of the established church should eventually become the site of a purpose-built non-conformist chapel

In her will of 1840, Jane Rees, widow of Bonvilston, left £20 to Edward Jenkins of Fynonwen Peterston "in trust that he will apply the interest thereof for the benefit of the Methodist Society at Trehill... and should they... have occasion to erect or build a new chapel or meeting house for a society of the like persuasion then my will is... that the said sum of twenty pounds be given in aid of such building". Her funeral expenses are listed in detail: "Shroud 6s. 6d., Coffin £3, Laying out the corpse 2s. 6d., The grave 6s., Beer for the cause [the Methodist one presumably] 13s., Meat for the funeral 8s., Bread 5s., Cheese 4s., 3lbs of butter 3s. 3d., Candles 10½d., Tea & sugar 3s. 4d., Currants & raisins 1s. 8d. Total £5 14s. 1½d. Doctor's bill £1 1s."

THE BEECHES

The various building stages of this old cottage were clearly visible before demolition.

Occupied throughout most of the nineteenth century by William Earl Junior and family (see Chapter 7). He was a carpenter and farmer.

TREHILL FARM

The farm also included a labourer's cottage and the original building was a ruin before rebuilding took place.

The Whapham family farmed here for the first half of the nineteenth century. Richard Whapham (1770–1822) from Chaily in Sussex and his wife Elizabeth (1770–1833) lived here with their nine children, although only eight are known by name. Mary (dates unknown), married William Wenmouth (1796–1825) of Bonvilston in 1820. William (1798–1847) farmed Sheepcourt in Bonvilston with his wife Elizabeth (1796–1852). The exotically named Philadelphia (1800–43) also lived in Bonvilston. Third daughter Amelia (1805–36) married Henry Lloyd of Swansea. Richard (1809–51) assisted his father at Trehill, although he died in Welsh St Donats. Parish service was given by Richard as Surveyor (1834–5, 1836–7) and Churchwarden (1837–40). The three other children were Thomas, born in 1811, Jane (1814–37) and Harriett born in 1820.

William and Elizabeth of Sheepcourt had six children: Jane

Trehill Farmhouse, No 89 on the Tithe Map of 1838

born in 1820, Amelia (1823–40), Maria born in 1826, Richard (1828–48), Thomas born in 1830 who was a footman at Cottrell House and Charlotte born in 1831.

Richard Junior and Elizabeth had two children for sure: Thomas baptised in 1837 and Amelia born in July 1841, who died five weeks later.

Meanwhile, a different William Whapham, possibly Richard Senior's brother, had been active in siring an illegitimate son, William, by Mary. This child was baptised on 17 August 1802 but tragically, and all too typically for the times, was buried on 23 November just over three months later.

1824

Elizabeth Whapham took over the running of the farm on the death of her husband and paid a Poor Rate of £2 6s. 1d. on a rateable value of £74 14s. 6d. She served as Overseer of the poor between 1832 and 1833.

1838

Son Richard was now in complete charge, renting 99 acres and one perch from Captain Tyler and numbers 89 and 90 on the Tithe Map, a house, cottage and field totalling three acres, two roods, 32 perches.

1851

The new occupant was Thomas Williams (30) from Radyr farming 138 acres and employing five labourers. Mr Williams was Surveyor of highways (1853–4, 1855–6), Assistant Surveyor (1858–9) and Overseer of the poor (1858–9). With him on the farm were his wife Mary, children Edward, John, Hannah and Ann and five farm and house servants.

1861

Occupied by Evan Jones from Welsh St Donats farming 143 acres, reduced to 103 acres in 1879, and employing one boy and three men. Mr Jones was Overseer on three occasions. He lived here with his wife Adlina or Sinai and their ten children William, Mary, Thomas, Evan, Jane, John, David, Elizabeth, Louisa and Henry. The family remained at Trehill Farm for the rest of the century. Evan died suddenly in the autumn of 1912 at the age of 78 after a tenancy of 52 years.

TREHILL COTTAGE

Thatched, possibly eighteenth century. Very little is known about the dwelling or its occupants.

1838

The Tithe Map shows John Thomas renting two dwellings, numbers 92 and 93, of three roods, 19 perches and three roods, 21 perches respectively. On the 1841 census John was 91 years of age and a pauper, so too his wife Ann who was 83. Ann Hughes, a widow of 76, lived with them. John fell just short of his century finally being buried on 2 April 1847 aged 97 years.

1880s and 1890s

Thomas Ellis, a shoemaker, lived in the cottage with his wife Susan. One of their children drowned in the well (see Chapter 5).

THE PRYCE'S ARMS

For details of the building of this public house, see Chapter 8.

1881

Occupied by the widowed Hannah David and her two daughters.

1919–26

AW Harry lived here. Formerly of the Blacksmith's House and 4 Smith's Row.

1937

Mrs Jane Harry had 2.213 acres comprising a five-roomed cottage, outbuildings and land.

COTTAGE

1838

The Tithe Map shows a cottage, numbers 66 and 67, estimated at one rood, ten perches occupied by Mary John.

ST NICHOLAS VILLAGE

MWDDWLS CWM

Variously spelt: Mwdwlscwm, Muddlescwm, Mudlscwm, Muddwlcul, Moodlescwm, Muddlescombe. This translates as Valley of Tumps and refers to the many mounds, reputedly anthills with a grass covering (and an indicator that the land has not been ploughed), to be found in the fields between this ruined building and Coed y Cwm earthwork. The cottage is not recorded on the 1891 census.

1788–1841

William Thomas, who was 87 in 1841, lived here for many years. A mason by trade, he was married to Jennett and she died in 1842 at the age of 88. Their children were Jennett, baptised in 1788, Jane who died in 1789 aged two days, William who died in

1792 aged four months, William baptised 1795, and Anne born in 1799, died 1804.

1838

The house is listed number 257 on the Tithe Map.

1845–51

Occupied by Samuel Griffiths, a farm labourer formerly of Bonvilston and the Breach, his wife Elvira and children Edwin, Matilda, William, Samuel, Frederick, Edward, Henry and Elvira.

1853

The new tenants were Morgan, a labourer, and Mary John, and two daughters Martha and Susannah.

1861–81

Occupied throughout this time by the Jenkins family. John Jenkins and his son Richard were both sawyers and the former lived here with his second wife Mary from Llysfaen.

1919

Morgan Radcliff rented agricultural land of five acres, three roods, nine perches.

COTTAGE

Demolished.

On Boxing Day 1824 Robert Alexander Webb married Mary John. There are only two known children, Mary Anne (1827–32) and Samuel Alexander born in 1834 but the existence of a grandchild with the surname Innes indicates that there were more offspring. Unfortunately Mr Webb died between 1834 and 1838 leaving Mary destitute and living in this cottage, number 260 on the Tithe Map. Mary lived here with her mother Margaret and son Samuel who was an apprentice tailor. Both women were paupers. Indeed, Mrs John had been receiving weekly poor relief since 1824. On the death of her mother Mrs Webb took a lodger, a farm labourer from Pendoylan, to help make ends meet.

PWLL SARN

Literally translated as 'causeway pool' presumably due to its proximity to the main A48 highway, formerly the turnpike road.

1838

This area is number 252 on the Tithe Map. At this time it was just a field called Caia Trehill and apportioned to William Rees who lived in the village.

Register of Freehold Land 2 February 1887.

Lease dated 12 August 1848 by J B Pryce and J W Bruce to Thomas Watts the Younger from 1 May 1846 for 99 years of so much of the hereditaments numbered 252 on the Tithe map...

Presumably Mr Watts built the farmhouse in 1846. He had formerly lived at the rectory and a cottage on Broadway and was a butcher and farmer. Thomas was also Churchwarden, Overseer and Surveyor in addition to running the 120-acre farm. He was married twice. His first wife Sarah died in 1866 aged 49 having borne him three children Margaret (1840–6), Jane (1842–5) and Thomas. The second Mrs Watts, Mary Ann, died in 1879 aged 60, but Thomas himself lasted until 1896 and is buried at Croes y Parc chapel. Thomas Junior was living here in 1891 and 1901 with his wife Anne, six daughters and three sons.

1919–37

Occupied by Wilfred H Cometson formerly of the Laurels and farmer of 57 acres.

TWYN BACH

The small twyn or green in front of this house disappeared not too many years ago when the village roads were resurfaced.

1838

William John rented this parcel of land, number 267 on the Tithe Map, a house and garden of one rood, 32 perches. He was an agricultural labourer who died some time before 1861 and left a widow, Ann, who became a flannel dealer.

1871

Occupied by Edward Jenkins, carpenter and widower, and his son John. Edward was formerly the husband of Susan Earl of 5 Smith's Row.

1881

The tenants were Edward and Elizabeth Davies, their daughters Edith and Gwendoline and the wife's parents John and Jane Rees. In 1879 they had been granted a 39-year lease on this property. Mr Davies was a wheelwright and employed one man.

1893

John Piodrigize (?)

It is said that during the twentieth century one of the occupants of Twyn Bach used to set mantraps beneath the trees in the orchard to warn off apple scrumpers!

COTTAGES

Listed number 271 on the Tithe Map and now demolished.

1838

There were two occupants: Anne Morgan and John John, renting a total area of one rood, six perches.

1898

James and Lucy Ford and children Alice, Charles, Henry, Albert, Fred and Daisy lived here. Within three years Lucy, at this time 44 years old, was widowed.

HOUSE

Listed number 272 on the Tithe Map and now demolished.

1838

The house and garden consisted of one rood nine perches and Elizabeth and Phillip Davies lived here until their respective deaths in 1852 and 1858. Previously they had farmed at Tinkinswood.

HOUSE

Listed number 291 on the Tithe Map and now demolished.

1838

Occupied by James Edwards with an extent of 20 perches.

VILLAGE FARM

Formerly a thatched cottage with an adjacent tithe barn. The new house was built at the same time as the Coffee Tavern early in the twentieth century and the tithe barn was controversially demolished, before a conservation order was sought, in order to facilitate the building of the Ger y Llan development.

1838

Occupied by Benjamin Wright (see Chapter 9).

1891

Occupied by Anne Thomas, a widow. Her sons Peter and William farmed here, and ten years later Peter only with a wife and four young children.

1919–26

Morgan and Mary Elizabeth Radcliffe farmed 47 acres.

HOUSE

Listed number 295 on the Tithe Map and now demolished.

1838

House and garden of one rood, ten perches occupied by William Rees.

MANOR COTTAGES

Formerly three thatched adjoining cottages, renovated and slated possibly at the beginning of the twentieth century and finally becoming two cottages when the porch was added in 1912.

1824

Evan Williams occupied one of the cottages.

1838

The Tithe Map shows that number 288 at 15 perches was occupied by Evan Evans, number 289 at 16 perches by Catherine Richards, and number 290 at 20 perches by Evan Williams.

Evan Evans had married Anne Williams of the parish in 1823 but he died in 1839.

Evan Williams (1766–1847) was a village carpenter who rented seven acres of land. He and his wife Catherine (*c.*1763–1846) had at least four children. They were Amelia, who died in 1798, Amy born in 1800, Evan born in 1803 and Hannah (*c.*1799–1842). The latter married William Llewellyn of St Brides Major on 26 April 1823 and by that October they had baptised their first child William. He was followed by Thomas, baptised in 1825, Mary (1827–43), Catherine baptised in 1829, Hannah who died in 1832 aged eleven months, Jane baptised in 1833, Elinor baptised in 1836, Edwin (1838–40) and Hannah baptised in 1841. At different times William and Hannah lived at Manor Cottages and The Old Post, Bonvilston, as the husband's employment changed from being a gentleman's servant, presumably in the Manor House, to a victualler. This dwelling was used from very early days as a post office:

1824 Paid Evan Williams Post Office delivering a London letter 1d.

also:

1830 Paid Evan William for a coffin for John Foord 18s. 0d.

In his will Evan made generous provision to his daughter Ann Watts £5, granddaughter Margaret Watts £10, three granddaughters Ellen, Jane and Hannah Llewellyn, £5 each, and grandchildren Catherine and Thomas Llewellyn, £4 each. With £27 in the bank, three tons of hay in the field worth £8 5s., £8-worth of sheep plus cattle in calf, Evan was quite comfortable. The total value of his estate was £79 7s. 6d. set against debts of £9 16s. 6d. which included doctor's bills and funeral expenses.

From her house in 1838 Catherine Richards (c.1771–1844) ran a grocer's shop. Her niece, Catherine John (c.1810–94) of Llanblethian, lived with her but worked at Duffryn House as a servant. Here Miss John met Edward Branch (1798–1877) the stable boy and later coachman to the Hon. W B Grey and Mr J B Pryce. Edward, orphaned at the age of 14 on the death of his father, and Catherine married in 1845 and occupied all three cottages, as on her own the new Mrs Branch ran her late aunt's shop and the Post Office, and they lived in the remaining portion. Catherine Branch also rented 16 acres of land with cows, pigs and poultry to manage while Edward put in 40 years of service at Duffryn.

The couple had three sons. Thomas became a saddler or harness-maker known for his craftsmanship and, as a sideline, he bred chickens in one of the rented fields. He was secretary of the local Oddfellows Society and to the parish council. He had a difficult relationship with the rector, for reasons unknown, and attended church only once a year at Easter, sitting near the door for a quick escape at the end of the service! He never married and voluntarily entered the workhouse in Cardiff when he retired to receive the food and clothes he felt were his due, after a life of labour. He died at the age of 76 and is buried in Llandaff.

The second son, Edward, died of rheumatic fever on 10 May 1863 aged 14 years.

In contrast the youngest boy William (1851–1947) lived to be 96. Educated in London in mathematics and building construction, he qualified as a clerk of works. Before this he had been apprenticed to his uncles Abraham and Isaac John who were carpenters and woodcarvers in Cardiff. He married Annie Griffiths and they had eight children. On his return to St Nicholas he supervised the erection of the Coffee Tavern (Westways).

1937

Number 1 amounting to 30 perches was let to Mr L D Francis of Broadway for £5 per annum.

Number 2 assessed at 26 perches was let to Eli Bradley for 5s. a week.

THE THREE TUNS

This was one of the village taverns until it was closed through the religious zeal of the Cory family. It has been suggested that the house originated in the sixteenth century and was subsequently extended, with later additions to both east and west. The front elevation clearly reveals the piecemeal organic development traditionally associated with vernacular architecture. The now-continuous ridge line was once much lower over the western portion. In 1913 the walls had the customary white limewash. It was used for magistrates' meetings in the reign of Elizabeth I.

Most of the residents, in addition to innkeeping, ran a small farm or butcher's business.

1813–19

James, a victualler and butcher, and Margaret Rees lived here with their three children James, Thomas and Margaret.

1821–41

Occupied by William (*c*.1783–1863) and Catherine Williams (*c*.1783–1861) and their children William, Eliza (*c*.1811–42), Henry, John (who was baptised in 1821 and became a tailor) and Catherine (who was baptised in 1823). William was a publican, farmer of 27 acres and undertook parish duties as Overseer of the poor. His oldest son of the same name was a glazier, often working at the church. He appears to have been popular with local servant girls called Jane.

6 January 1833: Baptism of Kate, daughter of William Williams, glazier and Jane Williams, servant.

7 September 1834: Baptism of William, son of William Williams, glazier and Jane Davies, servant.

1851

By this time the new tenants were John and Ann Evans, their daughter Mary Esther, John's brother Evan and two servant girls. John came from Pwll y Min farm, leaving behind his widowed mother who herself was a publican's daughter. At the Three Tuns John combined the roles of publican and farmer. By 1856 they had all left and moved across the road to the newly-built Broadway Farm House.

1856

The Banner family (see Chapter 7).

1860s–1930s

The Earl family (see Chapter 7).

1937

Extending to three roods and with a rental of £23 per annum, the accommodation comprised three living rooms, kitchen, larder, store room, five bedrooms, a coach house (formerly an old barn and now converted to a house), and a thatched cowshed to tie five.

CHURCH ROW

In 1838 the Tithe Map shows that the building here in Church Row was a long barn. Whether the present cottages are a direct result of its conversion or whether they were built anew is unclear.

1871

The first known occupants.

No. 1 William and Sarah Griffiths formerly of Well Cottages. He was an agricultural labourer and they had two sons, Llewellyn, a groom and William, still at school.

No. 2 John and Mary Thomas lived here with their six children Ann (10), William (9), John (6), Elizabeth (4), Richard (2), and Samuel (2 months). John was a labourer and Mary was a charwoman.

No. 3 William and Margaret Cule in occupation with their children Edward (13), Ann (10), Margaret (8), Susannah (5), and Thomas (4). William and his eldest son were both farm workers and the extent of the cottage was one rood, nine perches.

There is no evidence of a fourth cottage at this time. By 1881 the Thomas family had left to be replaced by George and Elizabeth Langdon and their children Ann (3) and Harriett (2). George was a shoemaker from Somerset and they later moved to Smith's Row. The Griffiths family now had a lodger, William Cole, a certificate schoolmaster from Lincolnshire.

1891

No. 1 Now occupied by John Edward, a coachman and groom, and his wife who was a laundress.

No. 2 Alexander Moore, a saddler from the Post Office, lived here with his wife and family.

No. 3 Another laundress, Mary Griffiths, lived here with her two grandsons.

Interestingly a dwelling called The Laundry is listed next to No. 3 on the census return and was occupied by a widow, Ann Evans. Could this be No. 4?

In the twentieth century No. 4 Church Row was at one time let to the occupants of the Manor House for the use of their workers.

COTTAGE

Numbers 299 and 300 on the Tithe Map and now demolished.

A house and garden of ten perches occupied by Richard Lewis in 1838.

COTTAGE

Number 310 on the Tithe Map and now demolished.

House and garden of eight perches occupied by Anthony Lewis and family (see Chapter 6).

TÝ-TO-GWELLT

Although now slated, 'Tŷ-to-Gwellt' translates as 'house with thatched roof'.

From 1838 right through to the early 1880s this cottage and garden of 24 perches extent was occupied by one childless couple with the occasional lodger. Edward Jones (c.1807–82) from Wenvoe had married Elizabeth Price (c.1797–1884) and they probably moved in shortly after their wedding in 1834 so that Edward could practise his trade, that of carpenter, in the workshop which was then part of the premises. Despite such a long residence in the village, little is known about Mr and Mrs Jones, except:

> 29 February 1856 Edwd Jones as p bill for repairing Belfry etc. 4s. 0d.

Their lodgers were William Morris, a preacher (in 1841) and a decade later, Edward's poverty-stricken mother, Mary.

SCHOOL HOUSE

Beneath the Victorian exterior has been uncovered the original gable end of a one-storey, presumably thatched, cottage. This would account for the variations in wall thickness which is apparent in different parts of the building. It is not known exactly when the house took on its present form but probably c.1856 when the new National School, which is an extension of the house, was opened. It is thought that the original cottage was the often-quoted 'village laundry' and that the school changed sites and moved here after the demolition of the parish Poor House, which served the dual purpose of education and shelter for paupers (see Chapter 6).

Throughout the first half of the twentieth century the various headmasters of the school lived here but this was not always the case. In the 1830s and 1840s, J P Brooks and other subsequent teachers lived in one half of the present Post Office while in the 1880s a farmer lived in the School House.

In 1838 John Evans Snr lived here, renting nine acres and 25 perches including a house, garden and orchard numbered 305 on the Tithe Map. His son of the same name farmed at Pwll y Min. John Snr undertook work for the parish and on the roads, and served as churchwarden from 1824 to 1840, after which he disappeared from records.

It is known that James and Martha Ann Walker, both teachers, and their seven children lived in the village school house between 1851 and 1857 but whether this or some other building is the one referred to cannot be ascertained.

In 1861 the village school was staffed by two sisters, Martha T Knowles, aged 25, and her assistant, Mary, nine years her junior. They were born in Lancashire and Worcestershire respectively and had succeeded George Arnold who taught here in 1859. It is not known where any of them lived.

In 1871 the schoolmaster, following a precedent, lodged at the Post Office. He was James Bilby, a 58-year-old widower from London. Ten years later the census states quite clearly that School House was occupied by Peter and Ann Thomas and family. He was a farmer of 46 acres employing two boys, and Ann was a half-sister of Catherine Branch of Manor Cottages. It is also known that the Thomases lived at Village Farm in the 1890s.

By 1874 the new master was William Cole whose wife, Sarah Jane, née Moore of the Post Office, bore him at least four children. They lived in the School House certainly by 1891, although William was living on his own in Church Row at the time of the 1881 census. There was also a schoolmistress at this time named Mary Vickery. Mr Cole stayed a long time in the village and was highly thought of, for at a parish meeting on 23 March 1874 it is recorded that: "The meeting desires to give expression to their feeling of confidence in and entire satisfaction with the present Master Mr W Cole, whose energy and perseverance has contributed so largely to the present successful position of the school."

In 1895 Mr Cole could accommodate 103 children in the school, yet the average attendance for the year was a mere 59, reflecting the demands of a farming community where unpaid child labour was frequently needed in the fields.

Mr Cole was Sidesman in the church for most years between 1889 and 1905. The Coles lived in the School House until his retirement in 1913, when they moved to Cartref near the Three Tuns which had been built for Sarah Jane's father. She lived there until her death in 1947.

In 1919, David Timothy Jenkins was the schoolmaster and known for introducing the Welsh language into all the lessons in the school. He taught the children the history of their village, the social life, the work and occupations of their parents and the names of the farms and the fields. He had a great awareness of the history of the Vale and its people, and was awarded an OBE in recognition of his services to education.

THE LAURELS

Also known as Pikel House. For the early history of this house, see Chapter 9.

1937

Mr William Hobby lived here under a service tenancy at will and free of rent. The extent of house and garden was three roods, 39 perches and comprised two sitting rooms, an office, a kitchen and back kitchen, larder, five bedrooms, a two-stall stable, trap house, two pigs' cots, a spinney and paddock.

1 & 2 SMITH'S ROW

See Chapter 9.

1838

Number 310 on the Tithe Map: a house, garden and orchard occupied by Joan David. On 16 August 1780 Joan Lewis (c.1760–1845) married William David (c.1759–1826) a carpenter from St Georges. There were five known children: Thomas, baptised in 1785; Jennett, who lived only a few days; Richard, baptised in 1789; Susanna, baptised in 1795 and Margaret, baptised in 1799.

Partial demolition of the building took place when Benjamin Wright lived next door at The Laurels and used the building as a showroom for his agricultural machinery.

When it was converted and reoccupied by 1899, one of the tenants was Robert Whitefoot, another carpenter.

1937

| No. 1 Mr D G Cule | Extent 9 perches | Rent 4/– per week |
| No. 2 Mr J J Penny | Extent 10 perches | Rent 7/6 per week |

3, 4 & 5 SMITH'S ROW

See Chapter 9 for explanatory drawings of the development of Smith's Row as a housing unit.

See Chapter 7 regarding the Earl Family.

See Chapter 5 for the Ellis family tree.

NUMBER 3

1838–41

Occupied by Elizabeth Gibbon a farmer and shopkeeper. See Chapter 8.

1895–1926

George Henry and Elizabeth (Granny) Langdon lived here. He was a boot maker by trade and church bell ringer by vocation.

1937

The house extended to 15 perches and was rented by Mr W Samuel for a weekly tenancy of six shillings.

NUMBER 4

1838

Occupied by Richard and Ann Ellis and family. He was an agricultural labourer and farmer of 11 acres.

Late nineteenth century

The village blacksmith Abraham Harry lived here with his wife Jane and family. They moved to the Pryce's Arms *c*.1908.

1919–26

In residence was Harry Lee, a farm worker at Caia.

1937

Mr Thomas Picton let the house of 15 perches extent to representatives of the late M D Morgan of Caia for a quarterly rent of £1 5s.

NUMBER 5

1838–50

Occupied by William and Elizabeth Earl and family. At some time the house was divided in two, the circular stone staircase being boarded up and replaced by two straight wooden flights, and accommodated the Coles and Tanner families. Early in the twentieth century the tenancy was held by Edward and Minnie Cule who had single occupancy.

1937

The pre-war tenancy was two shillings a week for a house and garden of 15 perches.

THE WIVERN/ TRAVELLERS' REST/ COFFEE TAVERN/ WESTWAYS

The names refer to two different buildings on the same site. The Wivern was the first building here, a thatched public house until the late 1830s, when it became a dwelling house. It was possibly known as the Travellers' Rest as well. After demolition it was replaced at the start of the twentieth century by the Coffee Tavern or Duffryn Tea Rooms, a new and novel village amenity, now known as Westways.

1824

Occupied by Roger and Mary Powell and family. As well as keeping the inn they ran a shop here. See Chapter 8.

1838

Samuel and Ann Rees ran the public house but he was also a thatcher.

1841

No longer premises for the consumption of alcohol and occupied by James Lister, a man of independent means, and his wife Jane.

1891

Occupied by widower James Ellis retired bootmaker, who died later in the year, and Thomas, his son, and family.

The Cule family also lived here at some time.

1901

Intriguingly the census gives the house the name Rose & Crown Coffee Tavern and it was occupied by William Mansbridge and family. Why would a teetotal establishment be built as an alternative to an inn-style 'Rose and Crown'? Mr Mansbridge was a colporteur or hawker of books, usually employed by a religious society, as well as a local preacher.

1908–18

John and Kate Jeffery lived here with their daughter Grace Millicent. Originally from Leytonstone in Essex, John was employed as a secretary in Ludgate Hill in London, but being of a somewhat nervous disposition and finding life in the city much too hectic, he opted for a rural existence in Wales. He became secretary to John Cory and was in the employ of the family until the mid-1930s. Initially the job carried with it the responsibility of running the Coffee Tavern, a task undertaken by Kate and Grace, the latter being 17 at the time. The Tavern was one rood and seven perches in extent and included two halls, one with a counter and seating. Grace married Marriott Holland Moore

(1887–1967) of the Post Office and the parents moved to Glyn-Cory until their retirement.

THE POST OFFICE

Formerly two stone-built cottages of considerable age, which were probably thatched judging by the steep roof pitch, contradicting the present slate and render exterior.

1838

The Tithe Map indicates that numbers 296, a house and 317, a garden on the opposite side of the road (both amounting to twelve perches) were rented by Evan Howard. Number 297, extending to 28 perches was lived in by James Pratt Brooks. The latter also rented the Gaer field, number 309 a meadow, number 262 Cae Tre Cefn y Scybwr, adjacent to Pwll Sarn and other lands totalling 24 acres and seven perches.

Evan Howard, who died in 1862, was a man of the parish and married Mary Price (1790–1859), also a local, on 9 September 1811. She was a sister of Llewellyn Price of Caia Farm. Mr Howard was a mason, as were three of his sons: Thomas (died 1843 aged 20), Abraham and David. Other children of the marriage were Samuel (baptised 1827), Matthew Price (baptised 1829) and Elizabeth (baptised 1832). Evan Howard undertook a lot of work on behalf of the parish, including:

£ s d

1824

... for mending the window (in the church) 3s. 6d.

1827

... for repairing the churchyard walls and pointing part of the tower £10 13s. 4d.

1828

... for white washing the church £1 1s. 0d.

1829

paid Evan Howard & Son Masons 1 day at the Church House 3s. 6d.

1831

... for attending meeting to be sworn as constable 2s. 0d.

1833

Paid for a grate for Ann Richard putting it up and white limeing...   3s. 6d.

James Pratt Brooks, who died in 1864 at the age of 75, came from Shipton (Gloucestershire, North Yorkshire or Shropshire) and was village schoolmaster from the 1820s, certainly until 1851. He married Elizabeth, who died in 1879 aged 74, the daughter of William, a tailor, and Mary Rees of St Nicholas. It is likely that Elizabeth was related to Samuel Rees (see Chapter 8), possibly his sister, as he was a witness at her wedding. James, who was 16 years older than his wife, and Elizabeth had the following children: Mary Ann (1826–48) who died in Merthyr; Elizabeth (1828–50); Sarah (1830–64); William Robert who was born in 1832, a tailor, he married Jane Griffiths of Bonvilstone in 1855; James Rees, born in 1834 was a staff boy to the Tylers of Cottrell, 1851; Charlotte (1836–54) a dressmaker; Thomas, born in 1838; Martha, died in 1840 when only one day old and was buried with her grandfather William Rees; John born in 1841 and a tailor; Frederick born in 1844 and George born in 1846.

The parents would have considered themselves deeply unfortunate to have all of their five daughters predecease them. Mr Brooks was Overseer in 1828 and a regular member of the vestry. In 1832 he was paid ten shillings for his trouble in making "the List of Population for the Parish." Although buried in the village churchyard, Mr and Mrs Brooks had lived in Llandaff during their retirement.

From the 1860s right through to the twentieth century, the Moore family occupied the Post Office. William Moore, born in 1827 in Nether Stowey, Somerset came to the Vale of Glamorgan looking for work as a travelling saddler. Here he met his future wife, Elizabeth Thomas, born in 1833, who came from Wenvoe and they married in Twyn-yr-odyn. He also worked as a grocer and village postmaster and, at one time, they lived in a cottage at the top of Duffryn Lane. Their children were: Alexander Marriott, born 1857, a saddler and village

153

postmaster; Sarah Jane (1859–1947), she married William Cole the schoolmaster and assisted as a mistress in the Infants; William Walford, born 1862, a reporter for the *Western Mail* who moved to Swansea; Henry, born 1866, a pupil teacher at the National School and then schoolmaster at Llantrithyd and Llantrisant; Mary Catherine, born 1868, worked in the Post Office before marrying Kempster Harbottle, they farmed in Llancadle.

Mr Moore was Churchwarden for many years between 1881 and 1909 as well as Overseer and Sidesman.

Resident at No. 2 Church Row in 1891, Alexander had married Ellen Holland, who came from Ashted Warwick in Birmingham, in 1884. She had previously been a parlour maid at the rectory. Their children, all of whom had the middle name Holland, were William, born in 1886, a saddler; Marriott (1887–1967), lived in Whitchurch, Cardiff; Gladys born in 1888; Ellen born in 1890; Alexander born in 1891, a First Lieutenant in the 5th South Wales Borderers, he was Killed in World War I; Violet, died aged one month in 1891 and Dorothy Elizabeth (1894–1987).

THE OLD RECTORY

This building was usually, but not always, occupied by the rector during the nineteenth century. The barn was rented out to one of the local farmers.

1806

Baptism of William son of James James by Anne his wife.

1812–14

Occupied by Rev. D Thomas and owned by Rev. Francis Eldridge. In 1818 the Rev. Mr Thomas was paid 10s. 6d. for working on the highways for one-and-a-half days with a cart and horses.

1820

Occupied by Lewis John.

1823–32

In residence was the Rev. Thomas Davies who died 14 July 1832 aged 51.

1838

The Tithe Map lists the Parsonage House, number 312, as being owned by the Rev. James Colquhoun Campbell, comprising three roods, 32 perches, as well as number 311, a barn and yard extending to one rood, 30 perches.

The Rate Book gives a succession of occupants for the years 1838 to 1843 and somewhat contradicts the Tithe Map by listing the Rev. R T Tyler as owner in April, August and December 1838. The tenants respectively were the Rev. M Nicholls, Thomas Jones and a Mrs Sulleven. In July 1839 the Rate Book agrees with the Tithe Map that the Rev. Campbell was owner with W Evans as occupier. The following two years show that James Evans, a 30-year-old surgeon, lived here with his wife Mary, five years his senior, with their daughter Emma (8) and three servants, renting from the Rev. William Bruce.

1842–3

Occupied by Thomas Watts.

1844–72

The owner/occupier was the Rev. William Bruce of Duffryn House, and his wife Mary Elizabeth who died in 1866 at the age of 48. Their children were William Conybeare (baptised 1844), Anna Mary (baptised 1846), Wyndham Lewis (died 1848 aged 18 months), Ernest Knight (baptised 1854), Charles Frederick (1857, died aged one day), Isabel Elinor (baptised 1858) and Charles Rowland Henry (baptised 1860). After Mary's death the Reverend remarried; his second wife was Margaret Harriett and she bore him two more children: Archibald Dacres Austin (baptised 1869) and Mary Agnes (baptised 1871). They kept a household of seven or eight servants including, in 1861, a Swiss governess Lowisa H Grebil and, in 1871, Wilhemina Heckt from Baden in Germany.

1873–93

Rev. Bruce's eldest son, W Conybeare, was rector during this time and kept eleven acres of land. His wife was called Antonia and his children were Montague William John and Mary Rosa. They too had a governess and she came from Tunbridge Wells.

1891–1901

Rev. Miles Whiteside lived here with his wife Jane Isabel and their son Miles Bruce Dalzell who as a First Lieutenant in the Highland Light Infantry. He was killed in World War I.

1920

Occupied by Rev. Armstrong.

BLACKSMITH'S HOUSE & WORKSHOP

The present workshop is a twentieth-century construction, separate from the house. The old shop was demolished, being a northern extension of the house, to allow the widening of the main road.

1817–33

The village blacksmith was Edward David and he lived here with his wife Catherine and daughters Elizabeth, Catherine (who died in infancy), Anne, Margaret, Catherine and Mary. There was no son to carry on the trade. In 1821 the parish paid Edward seven shillings and sixpence for mending unspecified tools and seven years later four shillings and sixpence "for iron for the new Grubber." Mr David made a quarterly payment of one shilling and eleven pence to the Overseer of the Poor.

1838–74

David Hopkins (c.1805–74) from Llanguned was the smith throughout this period and even after his death, his wife Elizabeth (c.1792–1888) remained here to farm, and to run the smithy. They had children, none of whom lived here, but some of their grandchildren did. Mr Hopkins, a noted swing-plough maker, was twice awarded prizes by the Glamorganshire Agricultural Society. There was a second prize of £1 for "best and most useful implements of husbandry" in 1844 and a similar award in 1845.

Churchwardens' Account	£ s d
1839	
Paid David Hopkins Smith for Stai nails as per bill	2s. 2d.
1852	
... for a new Gate etc.	£2 13s. 4d.
Highways Book	
1842	
... for mending the wheelbarrow	1s. 0d.
1848	
... for 28 Yards of Stones as per bill	9s. 4d.
1860	
... for a grate for a culvert by Lanylai	3s. 6d.

Between 1864 and 1867 Mr Hopkins was parish constable.

1878–1901

Abraham Harry from Radyr was the village smith. His wife was Martha and their children were Abraham, Evan Henry, Mary Elizabeth, John and Ann. After his marriage, the eldest son lived at various times at 4 Smith's Row and The Pryce's Arms, as well as the Blacksmith's House.

Abraham Senior was apprenticed to David Hopkin (no 's') in an indenture lasting four years and dated 1 September 1864. During that time there were stipulations about what he could or could not do: "In return for food and lodging he shall not commit fornication nor contract matrimony and shall not play at Cards or Dice Tables and shall not haunt Taverns or Playhouses." For these privileges he had to pay David Hopkin £15 and in return he received £2 10s. during years two and three and £5 during his final year.

HOUSE

Now demolished, but number 315 on the Tithe Map occupying the site of the Church Hall.

1824–38

The house and land were owned by the Hon. W B Grey and rented by William Edmonds. The latter undertook a considerable amount of work on the parish highways and died some time between 1845 and 1851, leaving a destitute widow, Elizabeth, and a son who was a blacksmith.

Highways Book	£ s d
1828	
Paid William Edmund per job carrying earth over John Thomas field £4 10s. 0d.	
1834	
... for 76½ yards 3½d. per yard on Doghill Road	£1 3s. 2½d.
1841	
... for 15 yards of stones at 6d. per yard	7s. 6d.
1845	
... for 10 days work on Witton Road at 1/8	16s. 8d.

THE MANOR HOUSE aka GREAT HOUSE FARM

The origins of the manor house remain unclear, as beneath the present exterior are reputed to be portions of a much older construction. Presumably this was the centre for the administration of the Pembroke-third of the St Nicholas manor, the other thirds being Cottrell and Duffryn. When the Pembroke share was bought out, the house changed its role, becoming a base for gentlemen farmers and businessmen. Its occupation in the last century by the Bruce family, some of whom also lived in the rectory in preference to Duffryn House, probably led to a change and consequent rise in the standard of its architecture. From the early nineteenth century until the 1850s, the building was called Great House Farm reflecting its use. With the coming of the Bruces it reverted to its original name, as Mr Bruce was a gentleman not given to husbandry as a means of earning a living. Confusion was caused by the name when Broadway farmhouse was built in the 1850s as it too, until the 1870s, was known by the alternative name of Great House Farm. One reason for this may be that a considerable portion of Broadway Farm was originally part of the Manor House lands which L K Bruce ceded to John Evans.

1816

Occupant James Howard was buried on 3 October at the age of 73.

1819

Richard, a farmer, and Catherine Jones lived here with their daughter Mary Anne.

1824

Henry Douglas Donovan lived here and the house had a rateable value of £76 3s. 0d. Mr Donovan's wife Emily bore him three children: Alfred Douglas (baptised in 1825), Henrietta Maria (baptised 1827) and Henry Douglas (baptised in 1828). Mr Donovan, seemingly exercising some form of droit du seigneur, also fathered an illegitimate son, Frederick Granby, by Catherine Butler who was, unsurprisingly, a vulnerable servant girl. The year was 1830 and the poor child died, having lived for only one week. Mr Donovan was active elsewhere in the parish helping to maintain the highways including:

	£ s d
… 45 load of stones to the Well Road	£1 1s. 6d.
… and hauling 12 load at 4d. per haul	4s. 0d.

Mrs Donovan died in 1832 at the age of 39 and her husband left the village, probably soon afterwards, and died in St John's parish Cardiff in 1863 at the age of 69.

1834

Occupied by Rees Powell, a farmer, his wife Jane and their children William Llewellyn (baptised 1834), Elizabeth Jane (baptised 1836) and Ellen Maria (baptised 1837). Mr Powell was an Overseer in 1834 and hauled stones for the highways with his cart and two horses.

1838

Occupied by William Jonas Watson from Ireland, a merchant in timber and lately a farmer of 151 or 112 acres (depending on the source of information). In the village he also rented numbers 318, 379 and 506 on the Tithe Map. Mr Watson was churchwarden for two years from 1841 and undertook work for the parish including hauling stones and providing lime, timber, laths and slate. Mrs Martha Watson was also Irish but none of her children were born there, the family having previously lived in St Athan. The children were Thomas (a civil engineer), Anna, Martha, Sarah, Harriet, Louisa, Jonas (a timber merchant like his father), Henry and Florence Colclough. They kept three or four servants and often had house guests including Ferdinand Reeve, an admiralty surveyor from St Helier in Jersey, in 1851. The family was still in the village in 1852.

1857–93

The new tenant was Lewis Knight Bruce Esq., of Aberdare, Pendoylan House and Duffryn House, who died in 1883 at the age of 54. He reduced the manor house to a mere 16 acres of land and was, at various times, a Magistrate, Churchwarden, Overseer and Surveyor. His wife Emelia Caroline bore the following children: Emelia Gertrude (baptised 1856); Jane Isabel (baptised 1857); Lewis Herbert (baptised 1861); Walter Knight (buried in 1863 aged three months); Francis Villiers (baptised 1864); Evelyn Millicent (baptised 1867); Ethel Lilian (baptised 1869) and Gerald Trevor (baptised 1871). After the death of Lewis Knight, Mrs Bruce stayed on there but with other temporary residents including a Mr and Mrs Macdonald and family.

The two eldest children of Emilia Caroline and Lewis Knight Bruce Esq. of the Manor House. On the left Emilia Gertrude and seated Jane Isabel taken in late 1870s or early 1880s. Their uncle William was rector of the parish from 1840 to 1872 and their cousin William Conybeare Bruce likewise from 1872 to 1884.

1919–26

Percy Hill was resident having only eight acres and 27 perches of land.

BROADWAY FARM HOUSE occasionally known as GREAT HOUSE FARM

Although the name Broadway appears in early nineteenth-century documents, the actual farmhouse was built at some time between 1851 and 1856. Prior to this it is the land in this area and the now demolished Broadway Cottages which bore the name.

In the 1820s the Broadway lands were divided between the farmers of Caia, Vian's Hill and Lan y Lay. It was from Caia that Llewellyn Price ran this farm until the building of the house. It is likely that John Evans, formerly of Pwll y Min and the Three Tuns, constructed the homestead here on what the 1838 Tithe Map calls a "hayguard rented by Great House" (or

Manor House) farm. Mr Evans ran the largest farm in the parish, at 340 acres in 1861 and he required eight labourers to help him. He and his wife subsequently left the village and, in 1881, they were running the Market Hotel in Llandaff with their daughters Mary and Louisa, barmaid Eliza Ann Brown and domestic servant Clarinda Brown.

The next occupant in 1864 was Robert Morrish from Broomfield, Somerset farming 268 acres and employing four men and two boys. His wife, Mary Anne, also came from the West Country and they had five children.

After this, c.1879, came William Evans, with his wife and family, a brother of the above-mentioned John Evans and formerly of Pwll y Min and Tinkinswood. The extent of the farm was now 280 acres. Two elder sons, Evan and John, were farmers like their father but Thomas and Edward became clerks (see Chapter 5). Mrs Evans died on Christmas Eve 1912 at Highdene after a long illness and within a few days of her 84th birthday.

1913–26

In residence were G T and S M Williams farming 175 acres.

BROADWAY COTTAGES

Three adjoining cottages, now demolished, but clearly delineated on the Tithe Map. They do not appear on the 1901 census return.

The 1838 Tithe Map shows number 381, a house and garden of 16 perches occupied by William Rees, number 382, of similar description, accommodating Thomas Griffiths and number 383, 24 perches in the possession of Edward Cule. Mr Griffiths was a shoemaker and his aged mother Jane, who lived with him, kept a grocer's shop. Throughout the rest of the century the cottages were invariably occupied by farm labourers and their families. These included:

1851

John and Joanna Collins (née Coghlan) from Cork in Ireland, their four children and various Irish visitors and lodgers. Then, James and Sarah Howard with two young children.

1861

Henry Hooper, a carter from Old Aveton, Somerset, his wife Catherine from Ireland and their daughter who was born locally.

1871

James Penny, who died in 1874 at the age of 37, from Kingston, Somerset, his Irish wife Ellen, a charwoman and their seven children. They had previously lived in the parishes of Cadoxton, Wenvoe and Merthyr Dyfan. Later, Richard and Annie Norman, their son Frank and Mr Norman's mother Elizabeth and his brother Samuel. They were all born in Somerset.

1881

Richard and Hanera or Julia Griffin, from Waterford and Cork respectively, whose son Richard was a farm servant and daughter Mary a dressmaker – both children were born in Kent. Afterwards, John and Margaret Fubbert, who were locals born in Wenvoe and St Georges, and their four children.

1891

Richard and Julia Griffin were still occupying a cottage of just two rooms whereas Robert Norman, his wife and daughter had a three-room cottage. The third cottage of four rooms housed Thomas Yates, his wife and six children.

COTTAGE

Now demolished but formerly situated between the Police Station and Broadway.

1838

This is number 384 on the Tithe Map, a house and garden of 36 perches occupied by William Kent. It is known that in addition Mr Kent rented land totalling three acres and eight perches and then moved elsewhere in the village around 1840. He did a considerable amount of labouring on the parish roads between 1848 and 1850 when he was over 60 years old. In 1841 this cottage and land passed to Thomas Watts, a butcher, his wife Sarah and their daughter Margaret. They left the following year to live in the rectory prior to building Pwll Sarn around 1846.

1861–91

Although conclusive proof does not exist it is likely that the next and probably last tenant was also a butcher farming the same three acres that William Kent had rented. This was Thomas Hopkins, formerly of Kingsland Cottage, with his wife Sarah and their eight children.

POLICE STATION

It was in 1841 that the County of Glamorgan first set up a police force and initially constables were stationed in Cowbridge, Llantwit Major and St Nicholas. The choice of the latter may have been due to the convenient location on the main road between Cardiff and Cowbridge. It is thought to be the first purpose-built police station in the county and it once had an adjacent courthouse which has been demolished.

In the Poor Book dating from the 1820s, the Vestry had appointed parish constables at 10s. 1d. a year, but in 1851 and 1854 there are two instances of policemen being sent to the village for a turn of duty. They were Philip Banner with his wife Elizabeth and children (see Chapter 7) and William Jones and family. They lived elsewhere in the village because the Police Station was not built until 1858. After this date, apart from the occasional local parish appointments, the constabulary lived here and included: Robert Harniman in 1859; John John from

Little Newcastle, Pembrokeshire in 1861; Thomas Griffiths in 1864; James Rutter from Devon in 1871; Phillip Williams from Pembrokeshire in 1881; Sergeant William Brinson in 1884, whose wife gave birth to twin boys both of whom died within six weeks; Sergeant Walter Chorley in 1888; in 1890 Sergeant William James from Carmarthenshire was in residence with his wife and two sons. Also at the station were Police Constables David Jones and Benjamin James. By 1895 it was John Perkins, who died at the age of 33; in 1901 Police Officers Maurice White and Charles Melhuish; in 1903 Sergeant Charles George Lane and in 1904 William Davies. By 1926 it was Sergeant Thomas Hamilton, who was still remembered by village octogenarians in the 1990s, for the way he dispensed instant justice to errant teenagers. This could include a clip around the ear for minor misdemeanours, or even a night in the cells followed by an early morning release for slightly more serious matters.

POUND COTTAGE

Now demolished but formerly the lock-up for stray animals.

Described as number 378 on the Tithe Map with an extent of one rood and occupied between 1818 and 1861 by the Thomas family. The most interesting of them was thrice-married labourer William Thomas (c.1783–1855). In 1805 he married Margaret John who died 13 years later, at the age of only 34, a few months after the death of their infant son. In 1824 he wed Mary David, who died in 1835 at the age of 42. There were at least two sons of this union. His third marriage, in February 1837, was to Catherine Truman, a spinster of the parish. She survived William and earned her living as a dairywoman.

QUARRY HOUSE

Only a heap of rubble remains but that gives some idea of its size and orientation.

During the nineteenth century the house played host to numerous families.

In 1824 William and Mary Thomas lived here receiving 4s. a week in poor relief. Mary was buried on 7 April 1826 aged 80, at a cost to the parish of £1 13s. William continued to be supported with cash, clothes and rent money until his death two years later.

Living here at the same time was the Ford family: John who died in 1830 aged 84, and Sarah who passed away in 1827 having reached 85 years. Also resident among others with the same surname were John, who died in 1929 at 50 years, and Prudence who died in 1833, aged 49. The older couple obtained poor relief and extra money in times of illness and both had a pauper's funeral paid out of the poor rate.

The next occupant was John Howard (c. 1801–70) who rented the house and garden (number 321 on the Tithe Map) extending to three roods and 22 perches. He was a farm labourer but his main claim to fame was that he married four times – one up on his near neighbour William Thomas in Pound Cottage. Firstly to Catherine who was buried on 27 February 1837 aged 35. There are two known children – Morgan and Robert. Secondly to Elizabeth Morgan of St John's, Cardiff. She married John just five months later. There are three known children – Ann, Edward and Sarah. Thirdly to Ann who was buried in November 1858 aged 45. Three known children called Alice, Elizabeth, and Mary. Lastly to a Mary from Cardiganshire, who produced two children – Margaret and Jane.

John was survived by Mary who became a charwoman to provide an income for her family. She still lived here in 1891 aged 63, which suggests that she was about 27 years younger than her deceased husband. She occupied three rooms, as did the other inhabitants (Henry Wilkinson, a groom, and his wife Mary).

In the 1830s, John Thomas, a local pedlar, also lived here and between 1851 and 1861 the widowed and poverty-stricken Elizabeth Griffiths was resident with her four grandchildren, one of whom worked at a local inn.

In 1871 a 25-year-old carpenter from Devon, Thomas Searle, moved in with his young wife Alice, aged 20, and their son John aged seven months, yet tragically within 15 months both mother and son were dead.

Marrying three or four times was seldom a matter of choice but rather a reflection on the uncertainty of life in the nineteenth century and it can be assumed that Thomas Searle moved on likewise.

Quarry House was uninhabited in 1901 and possibly already dilapidated.

CHAPTER 5

Family Trees

CULE

OF THE MANY surnames currently associated with the village it is only that of Cule, also spelt Kule, which can be traced with certainty back to the eighteenth century.

Elizabeth Rees, widow of the parish, made her will on 23 March 1735/36 two days before the new year began noting, "as I now lye upon my death bed" that she would leave a legacy of £5 apiece to her four children namely Elizabeth, Florence, Edward and Henry. Elizabeth was the wife of Edward Kule, innkeeper, comfortably making them the earliest Cules documented in the village.

Edward Cule, a labourer, who died in 1807, married first Mary, who died in 1788 with no apparent issue, and then a Mary Thomas (1750–1823) in 1790. The latter died at the Quarry House. They had two children, Edward (1790–1859), an agricultural labourer, and William (1793–1825). Edward married Susan(ah) Thomas in 1822. She had been born in St Lythans and she died at Rhiw Cochon, St Georges. The couple lived in Broadway Cottages with their four children: William (1828–1902), Anne (c.1830–57/58) who was baptised in 1844, Thomas born c.1834 and Mary born in 1838.

Thomas, who was a carter and agricultural labourer, married Elizabeth, a dressmaker, born c.1840 in Llancarfan. They lived in Trehill Cottage with two children: Ann born in 1864 and William E, born in 1871. William married his cousin Susan Cule in 1898 and they lived in Ely with their son Edward.

William, another agricultural labourer and son of Edward and Susan, had married Margaret Watts (1830–99) of Welsh St Donats in 1855, and they lived at No. 3 Church Cottages with their eight children. They were Anne who was born in 1856 and died aged three years and six months. The second child was Edward (1858–1932), who was an agricultural labourer and farm servant at The Laurels, lived with his wife Minnie (1864–1956) at The Wivern and No. 5 Smith's Row. They had ten children. The third child was Annie 1860–73; fourth came Margaret, born in 1862, who married John James in 1884 and moved to Llantrisant; Susannah, a domestic servant born in 1865; Thomas (1867–1949) who lived at cottage number 272 on the Tithe Map and Trehill Cottage and worked at Cottrell; William, born in 1869, who died aged six weeks; and finally Edwin (1871–1938) who also lived at Trehill Cottage.

The ten children of Edward and Minnie were William a sergeant in the Welsh Guards killed in World War I; Dorothy (1888–1977) who lived at No. 5 Smith's Row; Margaret, born in 1890, married George Reed in 1910; Gladys, born in 1892, married Arthur John in 1915; Georgina (1893–1982) who lived at No. 5 Smith's Row; Dudley George (1896–1982) married Daisy Soat in 1921 and lived at No. 1 Smith's Row with children Kenneth William and Gwyneth. Dudley served in the Horse Guards and worked at Duffryn House; Annie Gwendoline born in 1897; Arthur Edward born in 1900; Mary born in 1902; and Basil Thomas Rudman (1907–62) who lived at North Lodge, Duffryn.

It is not possible to establish their exact relationship to the above but other members of the Cule family in the village included Thomas, a labourer who died in 1775, married Elizabeth Rosser in 1769 and they had two children: Thomas was baptised in 1770 and Lewis baptised in 1772 but died the following year. The widow Cule married Phillip John in 1778; another Elizabeth Cule married William Ellis, a garner (storer/dealer of grain), of Whitchurch in 1771. They had four children: Elizabeth, baptised in 1772, Mary, baptised in

1773, Margaret, baptised in 1775 and Catherine, baptised in 1778.

Richard Cule, a labourer who died in 1810, married Mary John (1747–1813) in 1770. There were four known children of this union: Mary born c.1773, a son baptised in 1775, Mary 1788–9 and Richard who died in 1810. He was a carpenter and possibly fathered an illegitimate daughter, Margaret, who died in 1807; Margaret Cule married a William Thomas of St Nicholas in 1808; Evan Cule buried his illegitimate daughter, Mary, in 1812.

In 1836 Ann Cule and her son Thomas lodged for a while with Edward and Susan Cule before moving to Carmarthen and then Llanelli. For six years Ann received poor relief by post, 2s. 6d. per week plus an occasional clothing allowance for the boy, proving that St Nicholas was her parish.

In 1832 and the following year a total of £4 15s. was paid to a William Cule, his wife and four children as relief and for lodgings, beer, bread and cheese. William had died by 1836 and his widow and children were removed from the parish with relief of 3s. 6d. in their pockets. Hard times indeed.

Parish generosity afforded Edward Cule relief totalling £3 9s. during a long illness in 1834 and the following year. This helped to support his wife and children when he was unable to work.

Margaret Cule born in 1823 was a servant at Duffryn House in 1841.

Another Edward (1827–79) lived in the village with his wife Mary and two sons Edward and Evan, buried in St Andrew's churchyard. He was an agricultural labourer at Pwll y Min Farm in 1841.

Mary Cule married Morgan John of Wenvoe in 1850.

In February 1912, Gwenny, Arthur and Mary Cule were given prizes by Miss Bruce for regular church attendance. Gwenny "did not miss a single one of the 53 Sundays in last year" according to the parish magazine.

Of more recent memory was Dudley Cule, village character and raconteur *sans pareil* of interesting stories and jokes for any and every occasion. One can only wonder if his many village ancestors stretching back at least to the early eighteenth century were of a similar disposition. But, documentation proves that they were not resident in 1673. There was probably more than one branch of the family hereabouts in the late eighteenth and early nineteenth centuries with, as already seen, connections in Carmarthen and Llanelli.

There are two interesting letters written to a Mrs Elizabeth C Bowen of Kenfig Hill, Pyle which tell of other offshoots of the family in Glamorganshire. Her maiden name was Cule and she took her mother's first name. Mrs Bowen had previously written to one Aaron Cule, then an old man, about the family history and origins. His first reply from Dynevor House, Pontypridd is dated 2 July 1887. The spelling and expression are quite original and he begins:

> I don't believe you will find no Cules in England or Wales but our relations you may in Scotland with the word McCule... I have traced the Family of Cules for years and have found most of them agricultar labourers but very Religious Honest and Industrious People... My Father whas [sic] a Carpenter who lived within one mile from here... a Family of eight children six sons & two daughters... all dead except My Brother Moses and Self we had a fair Education and Brought up as tradesmen...

Aaron further relates that he was married at the age of 22 and left his trade to assist his wife in keeping a grocer's shop, then a drapery, before finally becoming the largest merchant in town. They had a large family, seven of whom were still alive, five sons and two daughters. Five of these children were married, "one single" was a minister with "the English Baptist at Ferndale" and "the other single" was a chemist living at home. Four of his married children had become grocers or drapers. He continues:

> I am Retired from business this some years... I must admit I have been successful I have Placed My children, on good Footing, and Built Excelent [sic] shops for them one is 12 Miles up in the Rhondda Valley placed Called Treherbert the next in Pentra the other two eldest have son with a Family at

The Cule Clan pose at the rear door of No. 5 Smith's Row. Minnie Cule surrounded by her nine surviving children, from left to right: Dorothy, Mary, Georgina, Arthur, Gwendoline, Basil, Dudley, Margaret and Gladys.

This group posed on the lawn at The Old Rectory some time between 1914 and 1919 to display the shield. Seated far left is Gwendoline Cule with sister Mary standing in the back row with a white bow in her hair. School headmaster, Tim Jenkins, has the dog on his lap. To the right sits the rector, Henry Southcomb Bunny, and Sister Gwen, the village nurse.

my old shop My daughter married a Draper largest in town... we have a lot of grand children butt [*sic*] I am now getting old I am 70 wife 68 she is not very well this long time butt she is about daily... the Cules are butt few...

The second letter from Aaron is dated 18 August 1887. He states that a cousin of his father, a mason by trade, had gone to live in Carmarthen and also that there were Cules in "Lanelly". Mrs Bowen was related to this last branch of the family. Aaron had known her grandmother from that town, she was called "yr hen Culan" and he used to send her a pound of tea "which pleased her." The old lady's daughter had stayed with Aaron during the 1860s. He remarks: "... we treated her kindly she sleped [*sic*] here with us a night or two she whas fond of a Pipe of Tobacco I wonder whas she your Mother she whas stout with a full face and there whas a Family likeness in her ..." Aaron continues that "... since I wrote you last I burried [*sic*] my first Cousin of the Cules Mrs Ann Rees of Park place Cardiff a wealthy old lady of 81 she whas married twice and had money after each she gave the most of her wealth in her will to her Nephew her Brother son by the name of Llewelin Cule ... the old Cules where born at Saint Nicholas or Shinicalas not far from Cardiff ..."

Of the surname he declares "it's a Scotch name no doubt", presumably passing on a family tradition as to its origin. It also appears as Cull, Culle and Kuhl as early as the thirteenth century. In 1285, Henry Cule and his sister Agnes were hanged and miraculously escaped alive "by a fortunate chance."

ELLIS

Richard Ellis (1779–1845), born in St Georges, was an agricultural labourer and farmer of eleven acres who lived at No. 4 Smith's Row. On 11 May 1802 he married the pregnant Anne John (1782–1867), a local girl and domestic servant. Nine children were born to the couple. Firstly William (1802–60), a shoemaker, married Mary (*c*.1813–87) from St Georges. William had fathered an illegitimate daughter Anne (1830–8) by Anne Lewis when he was in his late twenties but he was in his fifties when Elizabeth

(1852–74) and William (1857–82) were born. He died shortly afterwards and widow Mary lived at Trehill farming 30 acres.

A second child, Anne, was born in 1805. Then Margaret (1807–45) who married David Howard in 1835 and lived in Penllyn with two children Mary, a domestic, born *c.*1836 and John, an errand boy, born *c.*1842.

Then there were Thomas (1808–78), an agricultural labourer, Richard was born in 1811, Mary (1815–23) was baptised in her fifth year with her brother John, who was born in 1817. There was also Edward, an agricultural labourer born in 1825, Richard and Annie's ninth child.

Eighth-born James (1821–91) was also a shoemaker like his brother William, probably farming the same eleven acres as his father and living in the Trehill area. In 1844 he married Sarah Morgan (1821–89) a domestic from Wenvoe. In 1891 the widower James lived at The Wivern with his son Thomas, daughter-in-law Susan, and two of his grandchildren. James and Sarah produced eight offspring: Richard (1845–62) continued the family trade as a shoemaker; Ann, born in 1847, lived for only ten years; Sarah, born in 1849, married Thomas Williams in 1869 and had a daughter Anne in 1871; Edward (1851–72) was yet another shoemaker; James, born in 1856, was an agricultural labourer; Thomas (1858–93), reverting to type, cobbled for a living initially before becoming an agent for the Prudential insurance company. He married Susannah David (1863–1934) from Swansea in 1888 and they lived at Trehill Cottage; later Susannah lived in Taffs Well, having lost her husband and all three children: Rowland Edward (1889–92), Mabel Irene (1891–2) who tragically drowned in a well, and Thomas (1893–1917) who was killed as a private in the Canadian Army.

There were two further sons from the union of James and Sarah: John was born in 1862 and died within three weeks; William was born in 1864 and he survived only for two years and eight months.

EVANS

The Evans family figured greatly in the farming hierarchy of the parish in the nineteenth century and served extensively in executing both civil and ecclesiastical work for the good of the community over four generations.

John Evans Senior was the first of four such-named in this family. He lived in the School House in 1838, renting nine acres of land, and served as a churchwarden for nine years. There is no documentation about him after 1840. His son, John Junior (1782–1841) farmed at Pwll y Min and was Overseer of the Poor and Surveyor of the Highways. He married Esther Powell (1785–1867) of The Wivern on 29 May 1819, and by the 1860s she had moved back to the village to Broadway Farm where she died. They had four sons. The oldest was John, born in 1820, who was variously farmer and publican at Pwll y Min (1841), the Three Tuns (1851) and Broadway (1856–61), which he probably built. He was Surveyor and Overseer like his father but also a Collector of Rates between 1850 and 1855. John's wife Anne (1825–1907) bore him two children, Mary Esther in 1851 and Louisa in 1856. The second son was Evan, born in 1822, who moved from Pwll y Min to the Three Tuns and back again. Unlike the rest of the family he was not into husbandry but was a property dealer and owner and was able to live in receipt of an annual allowance.

Thirdly came William (1824–1906), who left the family farm to live in Llancarfan in the 1850s before returning first to Tinkinswood Farm (1857–78) and then to Broadway (1878–1906). He began his considerable and valuable parish service (over a period of 47 years) first as Surveyor in 1857, then as Overseer, Collector, Lay Elector, Churchwarden, Guardian and also as Manager of St Nicholas School. His wife Catherine (1829–1911) was born in Peterston and there were eight children: Evan, born in 1851, was a farmer at Broadway and also Collector, Sidesman and Census Enumerator in 1881; John, born in 1852, worked with his elder brother and was Collector of Rates; Ann, born in 1857; Jane (1857–9); Thomas, born in 1859, was a railway clerk; Jannett (1861–1945), lived at Highdene; Edward was a shipbroker's clerk born in 1865; and finally came Elizabeth (1868–1946), also resident at Highdene.

The youngest son Thomas (1826–87) farmed at Pwll y Min until 1875, was at Drope Farm in the 1880s, and also served as Surveyor, Overseer and Guardian. He married Ann Yorath (1826–1907), born in Llanharry, who was the daughter of Henry and Ann of Molton Farm, Llancarfan. Their three children were Henry, born in 1860, Thomas (1862–1927) who lived at Ash Hill, Cowbridge, and Mary Anne, born in 1868.

Not surprisingly there were more people around bearing the Evans surname who cannot with certainty be linked to the above.

John Evans farmed at Homri with his wife Margaret (c.1759–1821) and four children: Mary born in 1790; Evan (1793–1816); William baptised on 27 March and died on 2 December 1796; and another William born two years later.

Also farming at Homri and possibly related to the aforementioned was yet another John married to Ann John(s). The family was Nonconformist and part of the congregation at Croes y Parc Chapel where the oldest son, Evan (1824–36) was buried. There were three more children: Ann born in 1825; Thomas who died in 1826 at only two weeks and another, Thomas, born in 1830.

William Evans (1795–1866) was born at Homri but died in St John's parish, Cardiff and his wife Mary (1794–1880) died at 56 Union Street, Cardiff.

Living at the Winch Pit was Thomas Evans (1822–92), a farmer of eight acres, agricultural labourer, haulier and parish constable. Like his wife Ann (1824–90), he died at Llanover and there were three children: Martha Jane (1862–82) who died in Cardiff and John and Ann, both born in 1866.

THOMAS

Essentially a Nonconformist family, some of the Thomases were buried at nearby Twynyrodyn Chapel and others at the more distant Croes y Parc Chapel, although two of them served as churchwardens in St Nicholas. The inclusion of David as a son of Richard and Gwenllian is slightly conjectural. Conclusive proof does not exist but in favour of this arrangement is the use of the Christian name Gwenllian for his eldest daughter and the link with Homri Farm.

Richard Thomas, born c.1759 in Aberdare came to farm at Doghill, with his wife Gwenllian, who was born c.1767, and lived to be over 90 before dying in the 1850s. There were probably seven children to this union, some of whom did not marry until their forties or even fifties, suggesting a strong if not overpowering, parental bond. Of three of their children – Job, William and an unnamed daughter – nothing is known.

The first known quantity was Richard born c.1796 in Llanwono and he shared the farming duties at Doghill with his father in the late 1830s before moving to Homri Farm where he stayed certainly until the early 1860s. He did not marry his wife Rachel, five years his junior and also from Llanwono, until about 1852, shortly before the death of his father in 1854. He worked for the parish as Surveyor, Overseer and Churchwarden.

Another son, David (1802–73), born to Richard and Gwenllian while they were resident in Ystrad Yfoddu, also farmed at Homri at the same time as his elder brother, and held the same parish offices as well as being Collector of Rates. His first wife was Phoebe who produced three children: Gwenllian born c.1837, Morgan born a couple of years later, a farmer and tax clerk who served the parish as Collector and Overseer, and Mary born c.1840. Second wife Jane (1809–52) from Llantrithid had three children, all born at Homri: the first was Mary in 1847, who married John M Morrish and they had three children: Walter, born 1870, John David, born 1872, and Jane Magdolen, born 1874. Two more daughters followed in the form of Julia born in 1849 and Jane (1851–6). David had left Homri by 1866 to live in the village, and seven years later he was resident at Caia Farm.

Except for his birth around 1811 nothing is known of Robert, brother to Richard and David.

Seventh child Rees, born in Ystradowen c.1812, farmed at Doghill in the 1840s and again from the 1860s to the 1880s with an interlude in St Lythans in the 1850s. Like his elder brother Richard he married late, to Ann Thomas in 1851, again suggesting that their father had been something of a stumbling block to their matrimonial ambitions. Ann, about twelve years younger than her husband and from Llantrithid, gave birth to six children. Rees would have been in his mid-fifties when the youngest was born.

The eldest child Gwenllian, taking her grandmother's and cousin's name, was born in St Lythans in 1852 and was followed by her predictably named brother Richard (1855–1940) who, equally predictably, farmed at Homri between 1893 and 1938 and was parish Overseer. In 1878 he married Lydia Evans (1855–1944) born at Beauville, St Andrews and they produced eleven children: Rhys, Annie, David, Ethel, Tudor, Eleanor (1888–1955), Gwilym, Gwendoline, Robert, Gwyne May and John. Gwyne May, who died in 1982, married David Randal Morgan of Caia and Pwll Sarn and they had two children, Nesta and Ann.

Next came William, born in 1860 in the same place as his brother and sister, followed by Mary (1863–1958) who had obviously inherited the family longevity gene. She married John Dunn (c.1857–1936) who farmed at Tinkinswood from 1893 and they had four children: Thomas (c.1887–1971) another octogenarian, Annie, Emrys and Doris.

Their fifth child was Robert born in 1866, who farmed Doghill from 1919 before retiring to Twynyrodyn and Penarth. His wife was Eleanor and there were no children.

The last child, Rees, was born in 1867 and took his father's name.

Gwyne May's daughters still maintained the family farming connection with the parish into the twenty-first century.

CHAPTER 6

The Vestry

Structure

THE ELECTORATE (RATEPAYERS) provided the wherewithal to effect beneficence. This august body was under the control of the Chairman, usually the Rector. Responsible to him were one or two Overseers of the Poor (although notionally replaced in 1836 by a Guardian of the Poor this office is not mentioned in St Nicholas until 1861).

Two Churchwardens: One represented the Rector and the other the Parish.

First mentioned in 1889 were Sidesmen, three assistants to the Churchwarden.

There were one or two Surveyors of Highways (when two, one worked to the north of the Turnpike Road and one to the south, for example, 1829–30 Phillip Davies, Tinkinswood and John Thomas, Lan y Lay).

Next came the Parish Constable and then the Keeper of Parish Accounts (in 1849 John Evans of Pwll y Min held this post at £2 per annum). That was superseded by a Collector of Rates (first appointed in 1853 at £5 per annum) and the Parish Clerk

The Vestry was in essence a form of local government which originally met in the church vestry and at which ratepayers had a say in the running of affairs. The St Nicholas Vestry seems to have conducted itself in a highly responsible manner. The churchwardens and surveyors each levied an annual rate in the pound and the Overseers a quarterly rate in order to provide the money to fulfil their various duties. At times of extra expense a second or third rate might be levied and, occasionally, a voluntary rate was requested. For example in 1867 there were seven rates: Church Rate 1d. in the £; Poor Rate 1s. 2d. in the £ x4; Highways Rate 5d. in the £; Voluntary Rate ¾d. in the £ for the Collector's wage.

In 1869-70 there was also heavy expenditure on the highways requiring two levies. The first in April at 4d. in the pound was estimated to raise £39 16s. 1d. but the second, in October, was a hefty one shilling in the pound to raise a further £119 7s. 6d. Recognition of this burden is evidenced in a note stating that the latter was "to be paid in Instalments as required." It is also clear that by far and away the biggest parish commitment was to the poor and needy.

As early as 1846 the Three Tuns became the venue for meetings, probably because it was too cramped in the small church vestry to accommodate all those wishing to attend. Another requirement at all meetings, beer, was obviously more readily available (presumably the attendees had qualms about drinking alcohol in the house of God) even if it cost five shillings a time to hire the room. The Vestry would meet at least once a year, usually on or near Lady Day, that is, 25 March, one of the quarter days. The account book for the Poor Rate was entered quarterly, with the other days being Midsummer on 24 June, Michaelmas on 29 September and Christmas on 25 December.

The origins of this important body of local worthies goes back a long way. The Settlement Act of 1662 had dealt with the Poor Rate. The Vestry was responsible to the local Justice of the Peace who was usually the local squire or a large landowner, who in turn was selected by the Lord Lieutenant of the county. The JP had, as the title suggests, to dispense justice but was also liable for the upkeep of roads, bridges, workhouses, prisons, relief to the poor and the levying of the rate. Therefore the Vestry, acting on his behalf, nominated and elected a committee to undertake these tasks. Often this body could be ruled by a partnership between the rector and the local squires.

The Rate Books of the parish show that the rector was invariably chairman of the Vestry and that the Tylers of Cottrell and Bruces of Duffryn featured first, as their rank befitted, on the list of signatories reflecting the strong combination of God and the Establishment. Below these gentlemen came the parish officers, nearly all of them substantial local farmers or men of some means. There were two churchwardens to levy the church rate and maintain the fabric of the building, one representing the rector, the other the parish. There could be one or two Overseers of the poor, who, until 1834, were responsible for the employment and support of the poor and destitute of the parish while also trying to keep out or get rid of non-local paupers. Also there were one or two Surveyors of the highways who, as well as maintaining the roads by using pauper labour, could demand up to six days labour per man per year to that end. The parish constable was also elected and paid by the Vestry.

This was the composition of the Vestry but, during the nineteenth century, a number of changes took place resulting in a gradual diminution of power until the time of the early twentieth century when little influence was exerted on the parish by this body. The first change in the Poor Law, which dated back to the sixteenth century, was in 1834 in England, but it did not reach St Nicholas until late in 1836 when the dispensation of relief to the poor was replaced by a national system of Poor Law Guardians. Entitled *An Act for the Amendment and better Administration of the Laws relating to the Poor in England and Wales* it encountered little opposition in Parliament but aroused hostility among the poor. Printed books, replacing the variations and eccentricities of hand-written accounts, were issued specifically to record collection and dispensation of the rates. The tendency around the country was for these guardians to be quite severe in the distribution of their favours, as opposed to the more generous attitudes of their predecessors. The guardian still worked within the Vestry framework and with the Overseers, but strangely the first mention of this post in the parish is not until 1861. Under the Local Government Act of 1888, County Councils were created, which speeded up the decline of the Vestry system. The major blow came with the institution of elected Parish Councils in 1894. This took place in rural civil parishes of more than 300 inhabitants and effectively confined the Vestry to church matters only. The minutes of the St Nicholas highways book state: "On Thursday 18 April 1895... this being the first Meeting since the Parish Councils Act came into operation, the business transacted was entirely in connection with the Church..."

Tithes had long been paid to support the rector and to maintain the church fabric. They constituted one tenth of all wood, milk, eggs, corn and increase of livestock. In 1836 these were commuted to a straight cash payment which continued until 1936. This eased the friction which had often arisen between parish and church as a result of payment in kind and, after 1891, this rent charge was payable only by owners and not by tenants. Many people had taken great pains to hide quantities of their produce in order to avoid some of the tithe payment.

A police force did not exist on a national scale until 1856. Previously law enforcement was a matter for parish constables (complete with staff), appointed by the Vestry on an annual basis. Extra constables could also be sworn in as and when required at Wenvoe, although this happened only occasionally. From time to time one man held an office for a number of years or had more than one office, presumably due to a lack of competition for service in unpopular roles.

The appointment of the first collector of parish rates, John Evans of Pwll y Min, in 1853 suggests that prior to this each officer was responsible for collecting his own dues as and when possible. This new post was created to ensure the efficient gathering of the three different rates as the records show that occasionally there had been problems: "At a parish meeting held at the 3 Tuns the 30th March 1852 it was resolved that a Rate of 4½d. in the £ be made immediately, for the purpose of paying off a debt of £33 which has been long owing / one Rate having been not made in 1849 / to the Board of Guardians."

The debt had owed for three years and one of John Evans'

tasks was to ensure there would be no recurrence. During the previous four years he had kept the parish accounts but now his duties were broadened as follows:

At a Parish Meeting held at the Three Tuns on the 23rd March 1853,

It was resolved, That a Collector be appointed at a salary of Five pounds per ann. for the purpose of Making and collecting Rates & keeping the general accounts as directed from time to time That the Collector do pay to the Parish officers the several sums required by them for their current expences in the discharge of their Parish duties.

The remuneration for the job seems to have posed a problem, for in 1861 the salary rose to six pounds, in 1864 to eight pounds and finally by 1868 to ten pounds.

The Churchwardens

The Church Account Book dates from 1824 to 1877. The accounts were entered annually and included the regular maintenance of the church fabric and churchyard, the purchase of bread, wine, coal and material for church vestments, visits to Llandaff on diocesan business and beer for Vestry meetings.

A typical entry was for the year 1824–5:

An Account of Money Expended Out for Repairs of the Parish Church of St Nicholas from Easter 1824 to Easter 1825 By the Honble W. B. Grey and John Evan Senior Churchwardens.

paid	David William for Tyling	6s. 4½d.
do	To Wm Thomas for mending the Porch	1s. 0d.
	To Benjamin Wright for Repairing the Bells	16s. 0d.
	To Evan Howard for mending the Window	3s. 6d.
	To Mr Vatchel for A wier [wire] for the Window	£2 5s. 0d.
	To Thos Richard Glazier for mending windows	£2 13s. 6d.
	at 2 visitations at Landaff	16s. 0d.
	for Bread and wine for the Sacrament	12s. 8d.
To Thos Price for a Window in the Tower		7s. 0d.
To Edward David Smith		9s. 9d.

To Wm Rees for Being Parish Clerk	£5 5s. 0d.
for washing the Surpless	7s. 0d.
for Bell Ropes	£1 0s. 3d.
for Curtains for the Gallery	3s. 6d.

The total expenditure came to £15 6s. 6½d. to which was added £2 10s. "to the Rev. Thos Davies for Register Parchment for 5 years", nine shillings "for Doing the office and Entering the Same on the Book", four shillings and sixpence for "Beer at the Vestry" and three shillings for an account book, making a grand total of £18 13s. 0½d. The churchwardens had received £21 17s. 10½d. based on a rate of 4d in the pound, leaving a balance due to the parish of £3 4s. 10d.

In 1835 two years are entered as one, possibly to cover unusually high costs: "paid Thos Jones Carpenter for Making two new Windows" which came to £26 2s. 10d. and "paid Willington for Raling the Windows" £2 3s. 10d.

In 1842 extensive repairs to the church fabric and redecoration of the interior were undertaken by a Mr Vaughan and William Earl of Trehill. The latter worked on the painting and carpentry (see Chapter 7) and was paid £17 18s. 0d. The former was a mason:

Mr Vaughans Bill	
Masons rising Gable ends, forming flue & Corbels & lime	£4 13s. 10½d.
Coping on Gables & repairing Stone Mullions in Windows &	
slating Porch & repairing Slating to backs of Coping	£12 0s. 0d.
Transept door Sides & top & Stone Floor including fastenments	£4 18s. 4d.
Total:	£21 12s. 2½d.

May 1847 saw the completion of another big job: "May 11 Paid Daniel Rees as per Contract for Pointing the Tower £21 0s. 0d.", followed by: "April 1848 Excess of pointing Tower £8 0s. 0d.". In May 1859: "It was resolved that a rate of 9d. in the £ be levied for current expences & towards the contemplated restoration of the Parish Church". The nature of this restoration is not mentioned but was obviously carried out as: "Sept 1859 Pd towards the Repairs of the Church £50 0 0."

The rebuilding of the interior woodwork of the church tower and belfry in 1870 is documented in some detail:

Three Tuns 25 March 1869. The dangerous condition of the Belfry was considered, and a report from Parry was read in which he described the woodwork of the Belfry to be rotten and quite untrustworthy. Mr Bruce Pryce promises to provide the wood, and a gift of £20 – The Rev. W Bruce promised £10 – A rate of 7d. in the £ was ordered to defray the possible outlay and foreward expenditure... At a Parish Meeting held at the Three Tuns St Nicholas on the 15th of December 1869, to consider the expediency of replacing the unsound wood of the Church Tower & making all necessary repairs in the Belfry, it was resolved to invite the attendance of Mr Parry of Llandaff & that a Committee consisting of the two Churchwardens, Messrs Wright, Morrish, W & T Evans should accompany him & take the measures they considered advisable... It was resolved that this Committee be authorized to draw up details of specifications etc., & to invite tenders for the works by advertizing in the *Cardiff Times & Merthyr Guardian*... Feb 1870 Paid for advertising for Tenders 18s. 6d... At a Parish meeting... on the 24th of March 1870 to receive tenders & to examine accounts of the preceding year, it was resolved to accept the tender of Mr Lock of Cardiff for the repair of the Bellfry, for the sum of £69 10s. 0d.

1870–1 Paid Locke   £40 0s. 0d.

1871–2 Paid towards Mr Locke's Bill   £4 6s. 6d.

1872–3 Paid Mr Locke as per Bill   14s. 3d.

1875–6 Mr Locks Bill for repairing Church   £7 12s. 9d.

22nd March 1871. A Church rate of 1d. in the £ was ordered to meet the suppressed balance of £1 9s. 7d. due for the Church Bell Tower & for current expences. The remainder due to the Contractor was in great part defrayed by Mr Bruce Pryce who also contributed the wood and paid for the recasting of the Bell.

19th March 1873. A Sum of £4 Annually was offset towards cleaning the church and lighting the stoves etc.

The only note of dissent at any of the many Vestry meetings occurs in 1874, over the issue of the collection of a voluntary church rate. This time the parishioners eventually had their way, not forgetting that the rector W C Bruce had only recently taken office in 1872. The rate must have been abolished soon afterwards and replaced by the offertory in 1876, the first account of which was presented in 1879 showing a balance of £4 5s. 2d. This matter is recorded as follows:

> 23rd March 1874. The expediency of a voluntary church rate was discussed, but it was very strongly the feeling of the meeting that the existence of this rate, even on its present footing [seldom levied], was the sauce [sic] of undue and undesirable irritation on the part of many of the parishioners – who would – it was stated contribute liberally under other conditions. This being the case, it was proposed that the parish generally should be canvassed with a view of ascertaining the probable amount of help that might be obtained in lieu of the Church Rate. The Rector unwillingly concurred in the expediency of the foregoing resolution which after a long discussion was carried.

More work on the church interior is mentioned:

On Thursday 10th September 1874 it was resolved to carry with effect certain changes in the interim arrangement of the Parish Church viz.

1   To remove the pulpit from its present position, to shorten it one foot, and to place it in the corner of the vestry.

2   To remove the present reading desk and to replace part of it in the N. W. corner of the chancel, from which place prayers will be said for the future – to effect necessary alteration.

3   To remove the Duffryn pew from its present position, and to add 2 seats… as a continuation of the seats at present on N. side of Church.

4   To place a lectern at foot of chancel steps.

5   To replace the old Duffryn seats by the substitution of 2 shorter with desk for books in front – said seats to run parallel to remaining seats in nave – and to be assigned to use of Rector.

This plan generally and in detail meets with our approval.

It was signed by the Rector and Churchwardens.

A major event took place on 12 September 1881:

A special meeting of Ratepayers was held in the Three Tuns at 10 o'clock
to signify their formal acceptance on behalf of the Parish of St Nicholas
of a handsome gift of two new bells made to the Parish Church by Mrs
Mackintosh of Mackintosh [of Cottrell House]. In addition to the gift of 2
new bells, Mrs Mackintosh also defrayed the cost of rehanging & reclappering
the old bells, and of repairing and altering the woodwork, also providing a
chiming apparatus.

It was proposed by the Rector, seconded by Mr W Evans, Churchwarden,
& carried, that the following vote of thanks be passed to Mrs Mackintosh,
and that the Rector be requested to convey the same to her on behalf of the
meeting. Resolved 'That the hearty thanks of the Parishioners of St Nicholas
be given to Mrs Mackintosh of Mackintosh for her munificent gift of bells to
the Parish Church'.

It is also recorded that "The two new bells each bear the
inscription 'Presented by Ella Mackintosh of Mackintosh – 1881'.
The smaller of the two bears in addition to the above the legend:
'William Evans, William Moore Churchwardens'." Furthermore,
"The larger has the name of the Rector 'William Conybeare
Bruce – Rector'".

An extraordinary meeting took place "on Friday 23 May 1884
at 11 o'clock in the forenoon" at "the Bps [Bishop's] request
through the Rural Dean for the purpose of electing a Lay
Elector to vote with the Churchwardens in the choice of Two
Lay Delegates who shall represent the Deanery at the Diocesan
Conference, Mr William Earl, Butcher, of the Three Tuns, was
unanimously chosen."

The Poor

The St Nicholas Poor Book, dating from 1824 to 1836, is
a fascinating social document of great interest as the entries
are extremely detailed and indicate quite clearly both the
responsibilities placed upon the Overseers, and the plight of the
paupers of the parish. After this date a regulation printed rate
book was used and amounts of money collected are entered, but
unfortunately no details are given as to the use to which it was
put.

Under the Settlement Act poor relief was available to destitute natives of a parish. Other unfortunates who could not establish a parish might well be moved on, enabling the rate to be kept to a minimum and preventing these potential squatters from occupying any vacant local property.

It was incumbent upon the Overseer or Guardian to find employment, usually menial tasks, for paupers. It was the original job-creation scheme and a typical example occurs in 1870 when "The Guardian was authorised to take steps to apprentice John Penny to some suitable trade."

Working in concert with the highways surveyor, the poor could give service on the roads to reduce their weekly dependence allowance and to allow the Surveyor to avoid the situation of having to commandeer ratepayers of the parish for this punishing and undesirable work. The different rate books reveal the same names time and again, showing that such men and women were completely reliant on the Vestry for their income. A graphic example of this is offered by the plight of the Lewis family.

In 1838 Anthony, his wife Anne and children occupied a small cottage and garden of eight perches, numbered 301 on the Tithe Map. This plot has now disappeared without trace. Prior to this they had lived in the Church/Poor House and the Quarry House in Duffryn Lane. The head of the family was Evan Lewis (c.1758–1830), a labourer and his wife Anne (c.1758–1841), and they had four children: Kate, baptised in 1790, Evan likewise in 1793, the already mentioned Anthony baptised in 1799, and finally Margaret baptised in 1804. Anthony's wife Anne, born about 1803, bore nine children as follows: Evan baptised 1824, a labourer; Catherine, 1827–54; Anne, baptised 1827; John 1830–53, a labourer; Mary, baptised 1836, who gave birth to an illegitimate daughter of the same name in 1853; Eliza, baptised 1836; Thomas 1839–40; Thomas born c.1841 and William born c.1844.

Evan Lewis received relief money totalling ten shillings just before his death in January 1830. His funeral was paid for by the parish: "Jan 13 paid for a Coffin for Evan Lewis 18/– Shroud 5/– Diging the Grave 3/6 £1 6 6."

His wife Anne subsequently entered the poor list and was in receipt of two shillings a week. Meanwhile Anthony and Anne Lewis received an enormous amount of money from the Churchwardens, Surveyors and Overseers, starting in 1826 and continuing for a further twenty-seven years, by which time they had probably left the village. There are more than 350 entries concerning this family alone! These include:

Churchwardens:

1833: Anthy Lewis for White Washing the Back part of Church House and Lime 1s. 6d.; 1839: Paid Anthony Lewis for white washing the Tower inside and Churchyard wall 2s. 0d.

Poor relief:

1828: Paid Ann Thomas for attending Anthony Lewis wife in her childbirth 5s. 0d.

1831: Paid the Midwife for Antony Lewis Wife 5s. 0d.; Paid Anthony Lewis for Hoeing his Mothers Potatoes 2s. 0d.; for Mooving Ann Lewis potatoes to Cardiff 3s 0d.

1835: two pair of Boots for Anthony Lewis children 7s. 0d.

In 1830, for a reason not altogether clear, Anthony Lewis had to be apprehended and returned to the parish by the constable. This is a small selection from hundreds in the Highways book:

1830: Anty Lewis 1 week on Brook 8s. 0d.

1833: Anthony Lewis 10 days at 1/8 p day 16s. 8d.; 7 Perch Picking the Road breaking the stones throughing the Bank at 1/4 p Perch 9s. 4d.

1839: Anthony Lewis for Gathering & Planting Quicks on side of Duffryn Road 4s. 0d.

for Raising Hazards from Tinkinswood to the Lodge 186 per[ches] at 1d. 15s. 6d.

4½ Days Widening Road by Tinkinswood barn at 2/– 9s. 0d.; 2 days filling a fall on doghill road at 2/– 4s 0d.

The poor rate was usually the highest of the three regularly levied rates, being raised four times a year: 1824–25 Recd four Rates at 9d. in the £ each Rate… £205 0s. 10d.

This was set against total disbursements of £190 7s. 11½d., leaving a balance in favour of the parish of £25 11s. 9½d. including £10 18s. 11d. from other sources.

At the front of the Poor Book is a list of house-and-land tenants giving the annual rateable value of the property that they occupied. A typical account names first the people who were to receive regular weekly payments, and then details many other items, including extra money in times of illness, funeral expenses, house rent, money for food, drink, coal, material, clothes and shoes, travelling expenses, legal costs, relief to people passing through the parish, doctors' fees, postage and the usual ale for Vestry members. The Overseers also had to make jury returns and lunatic lists and take these to Cardiff or Wenvoe, usually the latter, to the Justice of the Peace. It was here that the officers received their Orders of Appointment confirming their right to carry out the law.

A quarterly entry states: An account of Money disbursed by Phillip Davies and John Thomas Overseers of the Poor of the Parish of St Nicholas from Christmas 1830 to March 25th 1831 being 13 weeks.

Thirteen weekly payments were made to: 1. Cathn Morgan 3/– 2. Elizth Francis 2/6 3. Jennett Williams 3/– 4. Ann Morgan 2/6 5. Lewis Griffith 2/6 6. Mary Lewis 2/6 7. Margt John 2/– 8. Rachel David 1/– 9. Sarah Richards Child 2/– 10. Thomas Samuel 2/6 11. Thos Rees 2/– 12. Wm Thomas 3/6 13. Peggy David 2/3 14. Elizth Howard 2/– 15. Ann Cule 2/6 16. Ann John 2/6 17. Ann Tyler 2/6 18. Ann Lewis 2/– 19. Jane Harry 1/6 20. Joan Evans 2/–.

	£	s.	d.
Paid Ann David from 19 March to Jany 7th being 42 weeks at 2/6 p Week	5	5	0
for tolling the Bell		1	0

Allowance for Holding Glebe Land		3	6
Coal for Thos Rees 2 Sacks		1	8
Quarterly Payment	5	16	11
Paid John Williams as Relief		5	0
do Rachel David as do		5	0
do Betty Francis as Relief in illness		1	0
do 1 Sack of Coal		1	0
Margt John 1 do		1	0
Thos Rees for 1 do of do		1	0
Paid Betty Francis as Relief in Illness		1	0
For a Blanket to Lewis Griffiths		5	0
Lewis Griffiths as Relief in illness		2	0
Journey to Lanblethian to Visit do		2	6
Mattress for Thos Rees		1	6
Betty Howard as Relief in Illness		2	0
Thos Richards Mending Thos Rees Window		4	1
Peggy David for washing & attending Thos Rees in illness	3	1	0
For keeping Jane Deer's child	1	1	3
Rees Morris's Wife as Relief in illness		1	0
Thos Rees going to Lancarvan		1	0
Jane Harry as Relief in illness		5	0
Thos Price do		5	0
For an Order of Removal to Lewis the Smith		5	0
Attending Meeting with do		2	6
Thos Price as Relief in illness		5	0
Rev. Thos Davies Relieving Ant Lewis at Different Times		9	6
For Shoes to Ant Lewis Children		6	0
For Coffin to Lewis Griffiths		18	0
Shroud for do		6	0
Watching, Candles etc		2	0
Jane Harry as Relief		2	6
Ann Thomas house Rent 52 Weeks at 1/- per week from 31st Dec 1829 to 31st Dec 1830	2	12	0

Joan Evans 38 weeks at 2/6 per week from 2 July 1830 to 25th March 1831	3	16	0
E Francis Coddle at Different Times		1	0
For attending the same in illness		2	0
Omitted in second Quarter E David as Relief	1	0	6
Relief Stephen Williams Wife	1	0	6
do to Edward Davies	1	0	6
do do Antony Lewis		1	4
do do do do 's Wife		3	0
Do 4 Weeks at 6/– per week from 25th Febry to 25th March 1831	1	4	0
Peterstone Saml Rees expences 2 different times		5	0
Self expences to Peterstone 3 times		7	6
Thos Rees Dinner, Supper & Beer By Rev. Thos Davies Order		2	0
do do Expences at Peterstone			6
Wages for do		2	6
John Evans Expences at do		2	6
Beer at Vestry Ommitted in 1st Qr		3	0
4th Qr Disbursment	£57	8	10
By Balance in last Quarter	16	13	10
Collected by Rate at 9d. in the Pound	51	59	¾
Collected By Cash of Jane Powell (towards illeg. child)	1	19	0
do of Peterstone Parish	7	5	0

In total the Overseer collected £77 3 7¾ giving a balance in favour of the parish of £319 4 9¾. The recipient of the coddle, Elizabeth Francis, was not a well woman, for this thin gruel made with wine or ale and then sweetened and spiced was traditionally given to the sick.

The Poor Book contains the only example of a woman reaching the rank of Vestry official as Overseer of the poor from 1832 to 1833. She was Elizabeth Whapham of Trehill Farm, the widow of Richard Whapham.

Money was regularly paid out for house rent or in weekly

instalments, to a number of individuals clearly not living in the parish who presumably were born there. People are mentioned as living in Merthyr, Cardiff, Llancarfan, St Mary Hill, Ely, Llanblethian and Pentyrch. In addition Vestry letters were sent to Carmarthen, London, Bristol, Plymouth, Ludlow, Monmouthshire and Llanelli. Officers and parishioners were sent on parish business to St Mary Church, St Hilary, Bonvilston, Llandough, St Fagans, Cowbridge, Newport, St Mellons, Caerphilly and Swansea.

A Dr Lewis of Cardiff was retained by the Overseers at a salary of five pounds per annum for the treatment of sick paupers, although his main task seems to have been dealing with pregnancies.

The Overseers also took it upon themselves to bring certain men to task for their indiscretions with women of the parish. There are a number of examples in the records, which all follow a similar pattern. A warrant was issued to apprehend the man, and the constable or Overseer, or both, sent to find him. Then he and the pregnant woman were taken to Wenvoe where, before the magistrates, it was attempted to prove paternity or to get the couple to marry. The records show that this was not always successful. In cases where the matter was satisfactorily resolved, the various expenses incurred by the Overseers were repaid over a period of time, in one case by the mother not the father. A good example is that of Margaret Rees and John Davies or David. In the register of baptisms for 29 August 1824 the entry reads: "Ann base daughter of John David, St Hilary, Labourer and Margaret Rees, Trehill, Servant."

The child was baptised on its day of birth and, like its mother, was probably unwell. The Poor Book outlines events beginning on 11 August when Margaret was examined by the doctor and the following day someone went to St Hilary to look for John Davies. By 19 August Margaret was "in Distress" and again on the 23 August before "being Confin'd" on the twenty-ninth. Two days later she was very ill and John Davies was summoned from the aforementioned village. Still ill on 5

September Margaret and her child received weekly payments throughout the month totalling eleven shillings and sixpence. By the first week in October payments cease suggesting that mother and daughter had recovered. On the quarter days in March of 1825 and 1826, John and Margaret repaid the parish "towards a Bastard Child" a total of three pounds and sixpence.

The case of Jane Powell and John Rees took a less satisfactory course. On 18 May 1828 the baptism took place of "Jane daughter of John Rees, Servant and Jane Powell, Servant both of Homri." The story unfolds:

1828 Aug	Paid for John Rees's Child from 19th May to Sept 22nd	
	1828 both inclusive at 3/– per Week being 19 Weeks	2 17 0
	Pd Wm Williams for apprehending John Rees	
	£1 0 0 Marriage Certificate 2/6	1 2 6
	Paid Saml Rees for Bringing Jane Powell to the	
	Meeting at Wenvoe	2 6
	Paid for Order of Filiation etc. for John Rees and	
	Jane Powell	8 0
Oct 11	Paid for a Warrant to Apprehend John Rees	2 0
	Paid Saml Rees for Apprehending John Rees	1 0
	Paid Thos David for John Rees's Child	5 0

In September 1829 the parish paid Thomas Rees to visit Jane who was now living in Llancarfan and the following 29 January she was taken to the magistrate in Wenvoe. The Poor Book account drawn up on 28 March 1830 states that the Overseer had "Recd of Jane Powell £1 13 0." It was quite customary for the fathers of illegitimate children to repay some or all of the parish poor relief as and when circumstances permitted, but Jane is the only single mother to do this. In July of the same year, she again attended at Wenvoe and the last we hear of her is on 23 March 1831, when the sum of £1 19 0 was "Collected by Cash of Jane Powell." Despite the provision of a marriage certificate by the parish and the apprehending, twice, of John Rees, the wedding did not take place. It may have proved impossible to ascertain paternity and certainly John was not eager to be married. Jane then moved to Llancarfan and her repayments to the parish totalled a respectable £3 12 0 against an expenditure of £5 3 0.

The records make clear that the parish maintained a house in which some of the poor lived and this building also served as a village school until the 1850s and was known as either the Church House or the Poor House. In many cases poor houses were originally the residences of the parish priest. When the latter was no longer celibate and larger houses were required for families, these old buildings were used as schools or for the reception of the poor as at St George-super-Ely and Llancarfan. On the Tithe map of 1838 there is only one building in the village which has no occupant. This is a large structure straddling the southern churchyard wall which then was the Church/Poor House. The building was demolished some time after 23 March 1853 when at a Vestry: "It was resolved, That Mr Bruce Pryce having offered the sum of fifty pounds for the Poor House situated in this Parish with the expressed intention of pulling it down, that the Meeting accept this offer."

In a special conveyance the building was transferred to Mr Pryce's ownership ready for its future demolition. The deed dated 25 November 1854 states: "… that the Guardians of the Poor of the Cardiff Union in the Counties of Glamorgan and Monmouth and Thomas Evans and David Thomas the Churchwardens and Llewellyn Price and William Earl the Overseers of the Poor of the Parish of St Nicholas… in consideration of the sum of £50 having been paid by John Bruce Pryce of Duffryn… to the treasurer of the said Union to be placed in the 'St Nicholas Parish Property Account'… Grant and Convey all that Messuage or tenement consisting of a large room above (lately used as a school room for the children of the Parish) and two rooms on the ground floor now unoccupied and the land forming the site … Unto… John Bruce Pryce his heirs and assigns…"

After this date, the Cardiff Union Poor House and Workhouse with a more regimented and severe daily routine, took over previous parish responsibilities. This centralisation process meant that most of the village poor were now cared for in Cardiff away from their families and friends and the parish of their birth. Serving the district from what subsequently became St David's Hospital, the Cardiff Poor Law Union, formed on 13 September 1836, was overseen by an elected Board of Guardians numbering fifty-three for the forty-four constituent parishes, some of which had more than one representative. In its early days annual expenditure exceeded £11,000 per annum or 8s. 10d. per head based on a population of 25,000 and a new workhouse was built at a cost £5,500. The Union provided accommodation, medical care and food for the unfortunate occupants. The cost of running this establishment was met by all the parishes of the Union from the poor rates, and the Guardian represented his parish at meetings of the Union Board. Benjamin Wright of The Laurels is the first-known Guardian for St Nicholas in 1861. The following parishioners died in the Union workhouse:

1853	Llewelyn John	Aged 70
1854	John John	Aged 75
1863	William Young	Aged 60
1873	Edward Thomas	Aged 31
	Thomas Rees	Aged 51
1895	Morgan Thomas	Aged 89

At one time during 1869 the workhouse contained 355 men and women and 270 children.

Below is a selection of entries from the Poor Book relating specifically to the Church/Poor House:

1824 Nov 3	Pd for Lime for the Church house as pr Bill	8 9
1826 Aug 13	Paid Thos Price for Mending Church House door	1 6
1827 March	Paid for Coals for the Poor	10 0

Nov 19	Padlock for Church House door	8
1828 Mar 14	Paid Thomas Price for Mending Church House Door for Thomas Rees [one of the paupers]	1 0
May 26	Funeral Expences of Rachel David's Daughter Coffin 18/–, Grave 3/6, Provisions 3/8, Shroud 5/–	1 10 2
Oct 31	To Repairing the Church House in Rachel Davids Appartment	3 0
1829 April 9	paid Thos Richard Glazr for mending the Church house Window	16 8½
Aug 4	paid Thos Price Carpentr for new casement for Peggy John apartment & Hinges	5 0
Dec 7	paid Thos Price Carpr for Mending Rachl David Door	4 0
1830 Mar 16	paid for coal for the Poor	7 4
May 5	Thos Price for Mending Church House Door	4 6
Oct	Ann Lewis for Cleaning Thos Rees Room	1 0
	Thos Price Repairing Thos Rees Door	3 6
	Paid Edward David for a Grate for Thos Rees	3 0
	For Gin & Ale for Thos Rees in illness	1 6
	To a new Table To Thos Rees 6/–, new boult for the door 6d., mending a Chair 1/–, To Repairing the School Rom floor 1/6	9 0
1832 Jan	Repairing An Lewis windows at the Church House	4 0
1833 March	Paid for Mending Anty Lewis Windows at the Church House	2 0
Dec	paid Evan Howard for Repairs at Church House	6 0
	Do to Thomas Jones for Do	3 7
	Do to Evan Ford for Do	8
1834 Dec	paid Thomas Jones for Repairing Church House	7 0
Dec 16	Paid do do Bill for Repairing Poor House	10 0
1836 Jan 7	Burial of Maria Williams, Poor House Aged six months	

It seems clear that the Church/Poor House was somewhat dilapidated and in constant need of repair.

Among the more interesting and/or unusual entries in the Poor Book are the following. They show the wide range of activities in which the Overseers were involved and both the practical and compassionate nature of their dispensations:

1824 May 4	Pd 3½ yds of flannel at 16d pr yd for Jane Deers Child	4 8
May 19	Pd A pair of shoes for Jane Deers Child	2 3
June 19	Pd John Evan for a Peck of Barley for Thos John	3 0
Dec	Pd Woman & 3 Children in Distress	1 0
	Pd Margaret David for Laying out Mary Davies	6
1825 Jan	Pd John Thomas Shoemaker Pendoylum for teaching Richard Jenkins the trade	5 5 0
April 1	Pd Thos Bowen having a sore Thigh	6 0
	Pd Ann Jenkin to set her Garden	2 0
April 3	Relieved a Man with a Pass★	6

[★ An Order issued by a Justice of the Peace allowing a pauper to reach his or her parish without having to pay tolls and to receive poor money or relief *en route*.]

May 25	Lod[g]ing A poor Woman	3
Oct 6	Blankett for Mary Lewis	4 0
	Pd Ann Richard making a Peticoat for Betty Hopkin	7
Dec 3	Cart Load of Coal for Ann Jenkin	8 6
1826 April 21	Elizabeth Francis Flannel Petticoat 4 yds at 1/6	6 0
	Betty Hopkins Bedgown & Apron 5¼ yds at 1/6	7 10½
	To making of do	1 0
Aug 8	Relieved 2 Women & 9 Children by Pass	18 0
	pr Shoes 5/– pr of Stockings 15d. for Betty Hopkins	6 3
Nov	Paid Ann Jenkins to get up her Potatoes	3 0
1827 May 18	Paid for Sweeping Betty Francis Chimney	1 0
Dec 1	Relieved 3 Irish Women in distress	6
	Paid for Meat for Thos Ford as per Bill	1 9 10
	Paid Mrs Powell [of The Wivern] for Beer for Thos Ford as per Bill	1 16 9
1828 Feb 12	Relief to Betty Howard Very Ill 1/– Rum 6d.	1 6

May	Paid for a Bonnet for Jane Deer's Child	8
July	Paid David Howard for Removing John John and	
	his wife to Newport	1 0 0
Aug	Relief to John Williams to pay a Doctor & Funeral	
	Expences of his Wife	1 11 6
	Paid Mr Sealy for Lunatics Returns	1 0
	Paid for 9 yards of Flannel for Elzth Hopkins for a	
	Bedgown Petticoat & Apron at 14d. per yd	10 6
	Paid for Making Betty Hopkins Bedgown, Petticoat	
	& Apron, with Tape etc.	1 9
Oct 31	Paid for Thos Ford 3 Asses	3 16 6
1829 Feb 20	Paid for a Counterpane and Blanket for Lewis	
	Griffith & Wife at 4/− and 3/6	7 6
1830 Jan 12	paid Ann Lewis for attending and washing Thos	
	Rees clothes	1 6
	Do ½lb of Soap	4½
Feb 20	To 3½ yards of Dowlas [coarse linen cloth] for a	
	Shirt for Thos Rees	3 0
	Do for Making the same & thread and Buttons	9
Feb 26	paid Peggy David Towards E Hopkins Funeral	4 0
	Do for keeping the Corp[se], 2 days and 2 nights	2 0
Sept	A Widow & 6 Children as Relief in distress	2 0
	Relieving a Pregnant Woman in do	1 1½
	Relieving a prisoner by pass	6
1831 March	Paid for 9¼ yds of flannel for the poor at 1/−	9 3
Dec	paid Wm Williams Thos Minnett for Waiting on a	
	Woman out of her mind	10 0
1832 July	Paid David Williams & wife & children for Six	
	Miles [on the turnpike road] at 4d. per Mile	2 0
Sept	Richd David as Relief	1 0
	Do for Order of Removal for him	5 0
1833 Feb	Gave Husband & Wife for going out of the Parish	1 0
March	Trouble with a Vagarand and other expences	1 3 0

May	Expences of removeing Margt Richards to Birdgend,	
	Journey to Wenvoe for Orders and eatables and	
	lodgins three days	18 0
Oct	Stephen Williams for a pair of Trousers	5 0
1834 June 23	Attending meeting with Anthony Ford to make his	
	parish [in order that he could receive poor money]	3 0
Dec 16	Wooden leg for Anthony Ford	12 0
1835	Carpenter for taking down bedsteade	1 0
1836 June	Paid the Bill of expences of Antony Fords funeral	2 13 0
Sept 27	paid Davies and Llewellyn Surgeons for attending	
	Rees Morgan wife in confinement	2 2 0

The final Poor Book entry is for the seven weeks from 11 September to 30 October 1836. From then on the entries are made in a printed rate book detailing only the amounts of money collected and not how it was spent. It is known that this new system was much less generous to the poor and may in some way have contributed to the social unrest of the 1840s.

The parish burial book dating from 1785 to 1812 records the interment of ten paupers, six of whom were male. The 1841 Census lists only eight paupers living locally, whereas in the 1820s and 1830s, the number receiving weekly assistance never went below twelve, and once went as high as twenty-two. Two of the eight people on the Census had received poor relief twenty years before. The difficulties involved in finding employment meant that there were nearly always more women than men on the poor lists, with old widows being particularly vulnerable.

The 1841 Census list of paupers were: Margaret John, aged 74; Mary Webb, aged 34; Joan David, aged 82; Margaret David, aged 46; Ann John, aged 94; Mary Jenkins, aged 75; John Thomas, aged 91; Anne Thomas, aged 83.

The Highways

In the nineteenth century the parish roads south of the turnpike were: Duffryn Road, Doghill Road, Whitton Road and Brook Road. North of the turnpike were: Caia/St Georges Road, Well Road, Mill Road now known as Chapel Lane, Moor Lane presumably leading from Mill Road to Moor Mill and Logwood or Lygod Road.

Other places mentioned in the highways book include: Peterstone Road, Peterstone Bridge, Homri Quarry, The Green by Lan y Lay and Pwll y Min, Kinnett which were fields south of Kingsland and Trehedin, a small hamlet of Pendoylan parish and birthplace of Thomas William (1761–1844) a Welsh hymn writer of repute.

In 1827 there is mention of an unnamed new road and some distances are given with a linear perch being five and a half yards:

Tinkinswood Barn to Duffryn Lodge	186 perches
Peterstone Bridge to Pwll y Min	74 perches
Croes y Parc to Kinnett	234 perches
Doghill Road	423 perches
Duffryn Road	586/584 perches

The jobs and rates of pay for working the highways make for interesting reading. For team labour, local farmers and craftsmen, such as masons and carpenters, could hire out their carts and horses to do the fetching and carrying of stone and lime. In 1820, supplying a cart and one horse for one day commanded four shillings, with an extra shilling for each additional horse. By 1859 the rate was five shillings a day, seven shillings for two horses and twelve shillings for three. In 1820, hauling stones and lime was charged at six shillings a day, with a cart-load of stones being worth between fourpence and sixpence. By 1860 supplying a man, cart and horse for parish use worked out at seven shillings a day, stones were fourpence per yard and hauling the same could cost just over a shilling a yard. With possibly more being paid to younger men, labour worked out at about a shilling a day in 1820 and between one shilling and eightpence and two shillings in 1855. For example, in 1859, the ageing William Earl was paid one shilling and threepence a day, but the younger William Thomas earned two shillings and twopence.

The supplier of quicks or hawthorn hedging for the roadside was paid one shilling and sixpence per one hundred plants. "Quick" is an old word meaning living and it was used originally to contrast this plant, noted for its early spring growth, with the dead and inferior species used in earlier types of hedge.

The hard graft and labour on the highways might involve digging, rising, breaking, picking or spreading stones. Payment was made by the yard, the perch, the day or even by an obscure measure called a crannock. Other tasks included levelling and scraping the road, scouring and cleaning water courses and rising hazards or any kind of bad ground. Rates of pay varied considerably from as little as a halfpenny a perch for scraping, to up to twopence a yard for spreading stones. The best-paid work, at two shillings a yard, was for the rising and breaking of stone.

The declining power of the Surveyor is clearly mirrored in the highways books. From the 1820s through to the 1850s the accounts were made in great detail but the financial year 1860–1 was the last for specific itemised parish entries and Surveyor nominations. The latter post was no longer necessary because responsibility had by then been handed over to the District Highway Board in Dinas Powis, and it was to the Treasurer of this Board or the District Surveyor that regular payments were made. Prior to this, the Surveyor of highways had been responsible for the upkeep and maintenance of all the parish roads except the turnpike road that is the main road through the village. An Act of Parliament had ensured that any stretch of main road could be taken out of the control of the parish in which it had been vested in 1555, and placed in the hands of a private Turnpike Trust. This made them extremely unpopular with the local farmers who had to pay tolls to go to market. These tolls were essential for the upkeep of the highway, but in the 1840s a Royal Commission was appointed to inquire into the state of the roads in south Wales. The result, in 1844, saw the abolition of many tollgates and the handing over of administration of the roads to County Road Boards. This was not apparent in St Nicholas until 1856 when the first payments, totalling forty-five pounds over a period of twelve months, were made to the District Surveyor. The last highway account detailing payments is for the half year ending 29 September 1877, and from then on, there is no mention of the highways or a road rate.

Expenses on adjoining parish boundary roads seem always to have been shared; for example on Logwood Road where it fronted with Pendoylan parish, or as in 1823 when fourteen pounds ten shillings was paid towards repairs on Peterston bridge.

The period between 1 April 1843 and 1 April 1845 saw considerable activity on all parish roads with large groups of labourers, sometimes as many as fifteen, working for weeks without a break, and the farmers hauling many loads of stones. This may have been due to the Royal Commission investigation, or more, simply to the fact that the roads were in a very poor state of repair. Either way, expenditure for the two years amounted to £68 0 0½ and £40 5 3¼, compared to previous outlays of just over eleven, thirteen and seventeen pounds.

The following entries from the 1858–9 rate book detail the large sums of money that were raised for the construction of a new bridge over the River Ely at Peterston. This included repairing the road from Croes y Parc Chapel to the bridge. A conscientious ratepayer at this time was faced with an unbelievable seventeen varying demands: such as for the relief of the poor, the maintenance of the highways and the upkeep of the church, all in just over two years. Starting in March 1858 came the first of four poor rates at one shilling and one penny in the pound, and in the following month a demand for a voluntary road rate was made at threepence in the pound which would raise just over twenty-three pounds. July and December saw two more rates for the bridge, at sixpence and threepence, and another voluntary one for the roads. Unrelentingly, in February 1859, another road rate was levied to bring in a grand total of £146 for the year against an expenditure of £159. To this could be added two church rates at fourpence and ninepence in the pound for restoration of the fabric, four more levies for the poor and two more road rates to bring in £73 to match expenditure. The final "voluntary" road rate of eightpence in the pound was for stones raised to complete the approach to Peterston bridge. In a more typical year the Surveyor of highways would be looking to generate about £35 of income from one rate demand, rather than the large sum mentioned above. From the total expenditure of £159, seventy pounds was put in a bridge fund, which was presumably matched by a similar amount from Peterston parish; £59 was spent on the new approach road; and £29 pounds was disbursed on the rest of the roads. Such was the activity generated by this building programme that William Evans of Tinkinswood, the Surveyor, was given an assistant named Thomas Williams of Trehill Farm. Nearby Homri quarry was re-opened to provide stone and/or lime, and the approach road alone involved more than 150 days of labour including such tasks as "rising & breaking 47 Yards of Stones at 2/– p yard" and "140 Yards of Large Stones 9d. p yard". The labour force was not all local and some of the names have an unfamiliar ring: John Fitz, Patrick Fitzgerald, John Potter, James Shee, Charles Paddington and William Combs. Team labour was undertaken by the farmers:

William Thomas	Lan y Lay	2 Horses & Cart	17 days at 7/–	5 19 0
		1 Horse & Cart	4 days at 5/–	1 0 0
David Thomas	Homri	2 Horses & Cart	9 days at 7/–	3 3 0
Thomas Evans	Pwll y Min	1 Horse & Cart	1 day at 5/–	5 0
David Morgan	Mill	1 Horse & Cart	4 days at 5/–	1 0 0
William Evans	Tinkinswood	2 Horses & Cart	6 days at 7/–	2 2 0
		1 do Cart	2½ days at 5/–	12 6
4 Horses, Waggon & Cart hauling Draining Pipes from Cardiff				15 0
Benjamin Wright	Laurels	2 Horses & Cart	6 days at 7/–	2 2 0
Thomas John	Brook	2 Horses & Cart	1 day at 7/–	7 0

John Evans	Broadway	2 Horses & Cart	14 days at 7/–	4 18 0
		1 Horse & Cart	2 days at 5/–	10 0
		1 Horse & Cart	1 day at 5/–	5 0

The bridge still bears two stone plaques giving the date, 1859, the name of the contractor, Thomas Miller, and of the surveyor, David Vaughn.

As can be seen the farmers more than recovered their extra rate expenditure by providing the wherewithal to facilitate this project, but it is not difficult to imagine what the village shoemaker or tailor thought about it all. The *vox populi* was not recorded.

Below is a small selection of the many hundreds of entries in the two highway books:

1817	To pd Charles Griffiths for 49 days work 1/–	2 9 0
	To pd E Griffith for Haling Stones on the doghill Road	14 0
1827	Thos Miles 2 day fencing be the new Road	3 8
	Thos John for Measuring the S[ame]	2 0
1829	paid Wm John for 550 of Quicks ar 1/6 per Hundred	8 3
1833	paid the Mason for Making the culvart by Cross Park field	3 0
1834	paid David Davies Raising 176 Perches of Hazards by	
	Meeting House at ¾d. p Per	11 0
1837	To Repairing 2 Sinks by Winch Pit	2 0
1838	Pd 10 Men for clearing snow on Duffryn Road	16 8
	To 28 Perches Picking on Duffryn Road at 2/6 per perch	3 10 0
	To Job filling Routs etc.	4 0
1839	Pd ½ the Expences of New foot Bridge at Peterstone	1 15 6
1840	16 Day to Wm Rees on Mill Road for Collecting Breaking &	
	Spreading Stones and Levelling Road 2/– per day	1 12 0
1841	Pd Henery Kempster for raising 92 pr at 1d. from the meting Hous	
	oposite Howerd feld`	7 8
	Do Raising 276 per at 1d. from J Thomas barn to Peterston bridge	1 3 0
	Do 2 days for to Mend the Rood	3 4
	Paid Wm Bennett for Repairing the Bridge at Peterston	12 4

	Pd for the Reparation of Peterston Bridge being the one Half as per bill	2	2 5
1845	To repairing the road leading from St Nicholas Village to Duffryn the Half paid by the Trust for the use of Mr Pryces stones	5	3 0
1846	J B Pryce Esq. for lime for Dog hill Road		2 0
	Paid David David 45 Weeks Viz from May 2nd 46 to March 6th 1847 at 7/– per Week as per bill	15	15 0
1848	Paid Thomas Harry for putting Kerb Stones on Witton		1 6
	For Cutting foundation for a Wall on Doghill road		1 6
	for Cleansing 341 Perches of Water Courses on Doghill Road at ¾ p Perch	1	1 3
1849	Paid for 2 Crannocks of Lime		5 0
1854	Pd a Moiety of the expences of Making a New Bridge by the Peterstone Bridge	5	3 9
1858	Saml Griffiths, hauling 2 loads of Gravel & spreading do		2 0
	John Thomas for repairing the Road by the New Cottages 4 days		8 0
1859	Moiety of Expences with the Parish of Bonvilstone in repairing and Draining part of Lygod road	1	8 0
	John Thomas 1 days hire for making a Gate by Homry Quarry		2 0
	Edward Thomas for clearing surface of Quarry		4 0
1860	J Evans for hauling of 4 Horses 2 Carts one day on Croes y park road		14 0
	Paid Vachell for Draining Pipes		2 0

Travel on the highways and the delivery of post assumed a greater prominence in the daily lives of nineteenth-century parishioners than had been the case previously. In 1789 the coaching roads were considered important enough for a local group of worthies termed 'Gentlemen' to set up an association for the improvement of the roads in south Wales. This group pressurised the Turnpike Trusts into the building of the Newport, Rumney and Canton bridges between 1794 and 1810 as an aid to better communications.

Although The Three Tuns public house had many uses over the years, it never was a coaching inn. It is certain, however, that it, and The Wivern and Pryce's Arms, were visited by weary travellers, on foot or horseback, in distress or in need of food, drink and a roof over their heads. All three were situated near the road and with easily accessible yards. The majority of coaches however, having passed Ely bridge and finding themselves in deep open countryside before toiling slowly up the Tumble hill, used the more horse-friendly terrain from St Nicholas through Bonvilston and on to Cowbridge to pick up speed and save valuable time. St Nicholas was not a stopping place for the mail coach; the first halt after Cardiff was The Dusty Forge in Ely, and the next The Bear at Cowbridge.

Post-coaching was a competitive business and one can imagine the villagers fronting the main road being very much in awe of this fast-flying traffic. The hair-raising journey from London to Milford Haven was frequently completed in a day and a half. Not a comfortable experience, considering that stones up to eight inches in diameter were often encountered on these roads.

The diaries of Victorian travellers can be very revealing. One such lady on a visit to Cardiff stated that the houses were limewashed, "even the roofs", a practice still seen in west Wales to this day. Noting also that the houses in Neath were whitened inside and out every Saturday, it is reasonable to assume that St Nicholas too would have presented a similar appearance. Lime quarries were liberally distributed around the Vale.

The coach road continued to carry most of its users fleetingly, busily, noisily and sometimes dangerously through St Nicholas with little relief until 19 June 1850, when the South Wales Railway was opened relieving the road of its monopoly before the later onslaught of the motor car in the twentieth century.

CHAPTER 7

The Earl Family

THE HISTORY OF the Earl family in St Nicholas is certainly a success story if the yardsticks of social status and income are our guide. There are records of Earls in the Vale at Llantrithyd as early as 1602 but this story begins in Peterston super Ely where Morgan Earl lived with his wife Mary. Morgan had married Mary Rowland of Pendoylan, the servant maid of a Mr Williams, on 6 November 1778 in Peterston and there are five known children: Mary, baptised in 1780, William of whom more later, Anne (1785–90?), Gwenllian, baptised 1792 and Jane, baptised 1794. Mother Mary was buried on 4 August 1831 aged seventy-eight, and it seems likely that the rector of Wenvoe parish recorded that "Morgan Arle" was buried on 9 January 1836 aged eighty-eight. At the time he was living at "Jiacklau" which can be taken as Yackla.

Morgan and another member of the family held ninety-nine year leases determinable on three lives on property belonging to Sir John Aubrey:

Thomas Earle	House and Land	11a 12p
Morgan Earle	Cottage and Garden	3r 27p

Also living in the parish were William and Joan Earle, who had possibly married in St Nicholas on 6 May 1745, and their son William. There is mention of Thomas a "natural son of Thomas Earle by Mary Thomas" leading to speculation that they are one and the same Thomas and Mary who married in Cowbridge on 1 August 1830. In addition, a Cecil Earl married William Ares.

At some stage William Earl, baptised in 1781 and son of Morgan and Mary, came to live in St Nicholas and is first encountered in the marriage register: "Wm Earle Batchelor and Elizabeth Rees Spinster both of this Parish were Married in this Church by Banns this third day of May in the Year One Thousand Eight Hundred and Six by me David Thomas Curate." They signed the register with their mark X and the ceremony was witnessed by Thomas Rees, parish clerk and John Rees who were quite likely related to the bride. Later on the register of baptisms records that William was a labourer when his five children were born and, indeed, he remained so throughout his life. Two of his children died in infancy, with Thomas being buried in 1820, aged three months followed by Ann, aged nine months, five years later. The three who survived were William, born in 1808, Susan, baptised in 1814 and Mary, baptised on 4 August 1822, who subsequently married Robert Thomas on 5 September 1846. Susan married Edward Jenkins and they had three children: Thomas, baptised in 1840, Francis Lindsay born c.1841 and John born c.1854.

Although William was mainly an agricultural labourer, he did other work for the parish in the church and on the roads. As early as 1824 William Earl Senior rented a tenement in the village from the Honourable W B Grey of Duffryn, paying a rate of 3s. 4d. levied at ninepence in the pound on property of annual value £3 10s. 9d. Although only a labourer, he had enough money to pay this rate to support the poor of the parish. On 15 March 1838, it can be proved through reference to the Tithe Map, that William and Elizabeth lived at No 5 Smith's Row:

Landowner	No	Name	Description	A	R	P
J B Pryce	303	Elizabeth Earl	House, Garden			34
do	256	William Earl	Erw Madwls Cum	1	21	
do	258	do	Erw	2	31	
do	326	do	Close	1	1	6

The total area was given as three acres and eighteen perches. Contradicting this, the rate book of 1838 states that William Earl

Senior occupied a house and land totalling one acre, two roods and twenty-nine perches. These two entries are at variance over the amount of land rented, but confirm that William cultivated a small acreage for his own use as well as selling his labour. The Tithe Map shows that this land consisted of three small irregular fields which flanked Brook Road and which were probably used as vegetable gardens and for grazing.

The 1841 Census return for No 5 Smith's Row reads:

William Earl	61	Agricultural Labourer
Elizabeth Earl	61	
Mary Earl	19	
Edward Jenkins	27	J[ourneyman] Carpenter
Susan Jenkins	27	
Thomas Jenkins	1	
Francis Lindsay Jenkins	3 months	

On 13 July 1846 Elizabeth Earl was laid to rest, aged sixty-six years. On 24 September 1850, William married again, this time to Catherine Snook, a widow of Trehill and subsequently moved to that part of the parish nearer to his only son. Catherine was, according to the census, twenty-six years his junior and this was her third marriage. Five years earlier, in April 1845, Charles Snook, widower, had married Catherine or Kitty Price, widow, both of St Nicholas parish. Charles had been buried on 19 June 1850, aged fifty-six years, which meant that Kitty remarried within three months. On the census return of 1851 they are listed as:

William Earl	Head M 70	Farm Labourer	Peterston
Catherine Earl	Wife M 44	Wife	Llangynwd
Ann John	Sister U 94	Pauper	

If Ann was William's unmarried sister, albeit twenty-four years his senior, they should have had the same surname. Ann could be William's sister-in-law but most likely there is an error here by the enumerator.

From the 1840s onwards William undertook a considerable amount of work on behalf of the parish:

1844	Paid Wm Earl and Wm Wild for rising 223¾ Yards of Stones	
	on Witton Road at 5d. per Yd	4 3 1½
	To Wm Earl 5 days Hire at 1/8	8 4
1849	Paid William Earl for rising 30 Perches Hazards at 1d.	2 6
	Do 1 Day breaking Stones	1 8
	Paid W Earl for breaking 20½ Yds of Stones at 8 p Perch	13 8
	Do rising the said stones at 6d. p Yard	10 3
1853	Paid W Earl for rising and breaking 11 Yards of Stones at 1/3	13 9
	W Earl for rising 7 ½ Perches of Drains at 1/6 p Perch	11 3
	Do 4 days hire on Doghill Road at 1/8 p Day	6 8
	Do for rising 66 perches of hazards on the Well Road at 1d.	5 6
	Do 94 Perches on Brook Road at 1d. p Perch	7 10
	Do for breaking 14 Yards of Stones at 10d p Yard	11 8
	W Earl for filling & spreading	1 8
	Do for rising 165 Perches of hazards on Mill Road at 1d.	13 9

This work continues into 1854 and then there is a gap of five years until 1859–60, when there are twenty-six entries mainly for spreading and breaking stones, scraping the road etc. and forty-six and a half days' hire. As an octogenarian, he was now paid only one shilling and threepence a day, a drop of five pence, but he would have counted himself fortunate to find any employment at his age. William died in the village on 21 December 1874 aged ninety-six years, but was not buried in the churchyard. If the given age on the death certificate is correct, then he was born c.1778, but not baptised until 1781 and had always underestimated his years. It describes him as a general labourer and the causes of death are given as "Old Age" and "No Medical Attendant" although Barbara Rees was "Present at Death." His widow appears on the 1881 Census:

Kitty Earl	Head	Widow	78	Labourers Widow	Llangnowd
Hannah Howard	Border	Widow	84	Formerly Cook	Marshfield
William Vaughan	Border	U	45	Woodcutter	Herefordshire

Catherine was buried on 16 December 1885, aged 82 years.

Although Susan Earl had married the carpenter Edward Jenkins in the late 1830s, they were still living with her parents at Smith's Row in 1841. This was not the case with her older brother William. He had married Elizabeth Gibbon by Licence on 15 May 1832. She had been his next-door-neighbour-but-one living at No 3 Smith's Row. Her father, Richard, and Richard Whapham of Trehill Farm were witnesses at the ceremony. William and Elizabeth's eldest child James was born when they were temporarily living at St Nicholas rectory. Then, already with two children and another nine still to come, they moved to The Beeches, Trehill, by March of 1838. William rented the house and a block of fields estimated at twenty to twenty-one acres from Sir George Tyler of Cottrell. The Tithe Map lists them as numbers 54 and 55 and numbers 68 to 76. Of healthy stock, the family grew in size and, unusually, of the eleven children only one, Jane, died in infancy at the age of five weeks. There was also one grandchild living with them.

Unlike his father, William was not an unskilled labourer. He had at some stage been apprenticed and had learned the carpentry trade. Typically for this time he rented enough land to call himself a farmer as well, and this activity reached a peak in the 1870s when he rented forty-eight acres. This must have given the family a degree of self-sufficiency and, seemingly, he was not short of labour as his sons seemed to be in no hurry to get married. Four of them learned a trade, with James, baptised in 1834, and Thomas, baptised in 1838, following in their father's footsteps as carpenters, while Richard (1840–1926) became a tailor and William (1836–1911), after an inauspicious start as a labourer, worked as a butcher. Edward was baptised in 1842, and Samuel (1845–1935) aspired to higher things as a Calvinistic

Methodist preacher of some reputation, despite the fact that his father served the established church. There is a pleasing regularity about William and Elizabeth's offspring, most of whom appeared at intervals of two years, but the sex ratio was less well planned, with six boys before the first girl Elizabeth (1848–1938) who was followed by Henry, baptised in 1851, Jane in 1852, Mary Ann (1854–1932) and finally Alfred, baptised in 1858, a full twenty-four years after his eldest sibling.

The Churchwardens' accounts reveal that William worked for the church for more than thirty years, usually in the role of parish clerk but occasionally as a carpenter or undertaker. The latter was a natural extension of the woodworking profession:

1834	To Six Months Salary to Wm Earl Parish Clerk	2 12 6
1835–6	William Earl Parish Clerk one Year Salary and Bills	6 4 2
	Paid Thomas Jones & Wm Earl for repairing the Bells	6 2 4
1836–7	To Wm Earl as per Bill	9 4
1838–9	Painting two gates and other thing by Wm Earl as per Bill	18 6
1841–2	Wm Earls Bill for Painting:	
	Painting Church 3 Coats	£5 10 0
	Graining Oak & Varnishing	£10 5 0
	White washing & Colouring	£1 0 0
	Pd Margt David Washing Church	5 0
	2 Ship ladders for Tower	12 0
	Repairing Seats & Church door	6 0
	Total	17 18 0
1842	Clerks Salary as usual	5 5 0
	Sundry Payments for Wm Earl	2 9 10

These payments continue until 1866 and in addition to this William was elected Overseer of the poor for the years 1854–5 and 1864–5. There are two further entries in the Poor Book:

1834 Aug 25	Paid Wm Earl for burying Thos Rees	3 6
1834 Dec 16	paid William Earl for burying Jane Clackson	3 6

It is not clear if this is William the carpenter or his father William the labourer. Burying the poor was not a pleasant task, and as no bill was presented; the job was probably done by the illiterate William Senior from Smith's Row.

The fourth son Richard, who eventually became a master tailor, married Joanna Symons Townsend on 13 February 1872 and they had three children: Alice Ann, Arthur Richard and Reginald Townsend. Alice never married but gave birth to Theobald Checchi Earl, the father reputedly being in the Italian army.

The fifth boy Edward and his wife Margaret Jane had two daughters, Florence Mary and Isobel Margaret, and he worked in the 1890s at Edward Earl & Co Shipbrokers in Bute Street, Cardiff.

Samuel Earl comes within living memory. He was apparently an impressive man, both in terms of physique and in the volume of his voice, which it is said could clearly be heard in St Nicholas when he was preaching in Pentyrch! Further proof of his size and strength is evidenced in a story told by Mrs G M Morgan of Pwll Sarn, then a young girl living at Homri Farm. 'Old Sam' had agreed to buy seven weaners from Mr Thomas of Homri and duly arrived to collect them. The family was puzzled however by the fact that he did not bring a cart or anything suitable in which to transport the pigs. When Mr Earl was questioned about this matter, he produced a large sack and announced his intention of conveying the pigs home, in the same, on his shoulder. To the utter amazement of the Thomases, he proceeded to do so. They watched him stride away over the field known as Cae Ofal and on towards the Gaer, from which point the journey downhill to the village would have proved very easy.

Another story relating to Samuel Earl tells how one day he took a black pony to St Mary Hill fair. This pony he sold for a small amount to a rather dubious dealer. Later that day, having spent some hours taking refreshment, he bought a replacement pony of the same colour, but with a white blaze. This animal proved very costly – for not only did he have to pay more for it, but on returning home its white blaze rapidly began to disappear revealing the same black pony he had left home with that morning.

The churchyard gravestones reveal the final resting places of some of the large Trehill section of the family. The father William died on 7 June 1883, aged seventy-five, and his wife Elizabeth on 21 March 1906, aged ninety-two. Daughter Mary Ann died in 1932 aged seventy-six, preacher Samuel in 1935 aged ninety and his sister Elizabeth in 1938, aged eighty-nine years. At the time of their deaths Mary Ann and Samuel lived at Gwern y Steeple, Peterston, and Elizabeth at 25 Moore Road, Ely. This was truly a family noted for longevity.

The Earls of Trehill were said to have kept as full a table as another branch of the family resident at The Three Tuns. Blackcurrant tart with cream was a favourite offering of both. Samuel's two sisters, Elizabeth and Mary Ann, spent most of their time in the home, fully occupied in caring for the abundant needs of their large, outgoing brother. At some time between 1861 and 1864 second son William, the butcher, had left Trehill, married and moved to The Three Tuns to carry on his trade and to farm. This was his wife's home where she and her mother ran the public house. The new Mrs Earl was formerly Hannah Maria Banner and in 1851 her family is recorded:

Phillip Banner	Head	M	50	Policeman
Elizabeth Banner	Wife	M	45	
Arthur Henry Banner	Son	U	14	Scholar

It is not known where they lived, as the police station was not built until 1858. Hannah, at this time aged only fifteen, was in service as a scullery maid at Duffryn House. The family had come to St Nicholas from Bristol and, although the census does not say, it could be that Elizabeth was Hannah's stepmother. In 1843 one Esther Banner, wife of Phillip, had been buried aged forty-four years. If her father had remarried then it was not in the village church.

Circumstances quickly changed for they moved into The Three Tuns inn, only for Phillip to die on 27 September 1854 aged fifty-five years. His trustees and executors William, his brother, and David Thomas of Homry, were to divide his money equally between Hannah and Arthur which they were to receive at the age of twenty-one, or before if they married. Phillip's widow Elizabeth was the recipient of all his interests in The Three Tuns public house and the goodwill thereof and business debts plus stock, utensils, provisions, furniture, horses, carts, implements and "anything else in or about The Three Tuns for carrying on the business of a publican." Arthur was to be funded to advance himself in the world. William Bruce, the rector, and William Moore the village saddler were witnesses to Phillip's will. The inventory of the pub's contents is of great interest and far exceeds that of the average village tradesman. Taken room by room, it includes the parlour, kitchen, bar, dairy, brewhouse, back room, cellar and four bedrooms. Chairs numbered more than twenty and there were at least a dozen tables and nine beds including stump, chaff and two French bedsteads with palliasses. The long list included: an eight-day clock, elbow chairs, china, eight pictures, a knife case, rugs and carpets, brass fenders, extensive cooking paraphernalia, bells, scales, candle snuffers, bottles, jugs, glasses, spirits, milk pans, cheese vats and a press, a furnace, corn bin, barrels, bedding, a commode, wash stands, book shelves, a bureau, a towel horse, pigs, sheep, a horse, cow and cart. The estate was valued at £90 13 shillings.

In 1861 the family comprised:

Elizabeth Banner	Head	Widow	55	Innkeeper	Dumfries, Scotland
Hannah M Banner	Dau	U	25	Assistant	Bristol, Bedminster
Martha Banner	Sist'n law	M	57	Builder's Wife	Pennely, Pembs
Richard Bailey	Servant	Widwr	50	Ostler	Minehead, Somerset.

The unfortunate Arthur was consigned to Bridgend Lunatic Asylum where he died in November 1876 aged thirty-nine years, leaving a wife, Anne Danson. The widowed Elizabeth ran the inn well into the 1880s, lived to be eighty-two and was buried on 16 April 1888.

This was the family into which William married and he and Hannah spent the rest of their lives at The Three Tuns. The census return of 1871 confirms:

William Earl	Head	M	35	Butcher, Farmer of 19 Acres
Hannah M Earl	Wife	M	35	
Phillip Earl	Son	U	3	
Elizabeth Earl	Daughter	U	4	
Phillip W Banner	Nephew	U	9	Scholar
Ann Jenkins	Servant	U	18	General Servant
Robert Carlass	Servant	U	19	Butchers Servant.

William and Hannah Earl outside The Tuns

The eldest son, yet another William, aged six, lived with his grandparents at The Beeches and unlike his brother and sister was not baptised in church. William the butcher's parish involvement was not as extensive as his father's, being limited to churchwarden and lay elector.

William and Hannah, like Samuel, seem to have been impressive in appearance. William was a large man weighing a good twenty-two stone, much of this expanding outwards. This created mobility problems for, according to Mrs Morgan of Pwll Sarn, he spent a great deal of his time on a day-bed when home at The Three Tuns. He did, however, go about the village on business now and again. This exercise involved a considerable amount of assistance from the one man then in William's employ, Mr Albert Ford. William would be carefully helped into a dray-cart which had been specially fitted with a seat made from a beer barrel. This seat moulded itself comfortably around William's body and there he would stay until the return journey. Mrs Morgan's memories of the Earls relate to the latter parts of their lives and it is to be assumed that William was much more mobile in his youth.

Hannah Earl is clearly remembered as remaining a very good-looking woman well into her old age. Her hair apparently retained its fine golden colour right to the time of her death in 1923. She dressed immaculately, usually in a mauve-coloured frock printed with sprigs of white flowers and a basque-like bodice buttoned from neck to waist and decorated with a brooch. The skirt of the dress was full and reached to the ground. In her eighties, Mrs Earl began to suffer from bad feet, and so when Mrs Morgan and her sister paid their regular Saturday evening visit, Mrs Morgan would sit and crochet red wool slippers while her sister bathed the elderly lady's feet. The cold and uneven flagstone floors in most old buildings must have been responsible for causing similar suffering in the population at large.

Miss Elizabeth Earl, the last member of the family to act as hostess at The Three Tuns, was well known for her excellent cooking. She provided cakes on many occasions for the functions held by the church and they appear to be the last contribution made by the Earls to that establishment. It seems that Elizabeth's hospitality was so appreciated that when some farm workers from Homri were helping with the hay at nearby Village Farm and were offered a cow's udder for lunch, they tactfully made their excuses and paid an expectant visit to The Three Tuns. They were duly rewarded with roast lamb, peas and mint sauce, followed by the usual blackcurrant tart and cream and a jug of cider. Needless to say they returned to work well satisfied, if a little reluctant to resume their labours. What happened to the cow's udder is not known and probably best forgotten.

After William's death, Elizabeth took over as official tenant of The Three Tuns in the rate books, even though her mother lived for another twelve years. William had died on 9 May 1911 aged seventy-four, and Hannah in November 1923, aged eighty-seven years. Their son, sadly not to be yet another octogenarian, had predeceased them and had continued to live at The Beeches. The gravestone reads simply:

William Earl
Died 7th December 1898
Aged 34 Years

Miss Elizabeth lived at The Three Tuns until her death and burial on 3 March 1949, aged eighty-two years. She has an unmarked grave.

CHAPTER 8

Samuel Rees and the Powell Family

IN THE ST Nicholas register of baptisms is the following entry: "Samuel son of Edd Rees was born 30th Jany 1787." Of Edward (c.1743–1833) and his wife Susan (c.1748–1814) little is known except for the approximate dates of their births and deaths. At some time before 1820, Samuel had married, and his wife Margaret (c.1796–1821) was ten years his junior. By this date he was well into his first occupation, that of thatcher. On 12 July 1820, the couple baptised a daughter Mary, but tragedy quickly followed. On 23 December 1821 Margaret died, and she was only in her twenties when she was buried on Christmas Day, but what became of the baby is uncertain.

Samuel is next encountered renting a tenement in the village in April 1824. The rateable value was £6 6s. 9d., meaning a payment of 4s. 9d. per quarter to the Overseers of the poor, levied at 9d. in the pound. By 14 March 1830 there were other things on Samuel's mind as the register of baptisms shows: "Anne base daughter of Samuel Rees Thatcher and Anne Powell, Barmaid."

On 8 July 1831, Samuel and Anne (1791–1864), the fourth Powell daughter, were married in plenty of time to celebrate the birth of their second, and this time legitimate, daughter Jane in March 1832. The significance of this alliance was that the Powell family rented from the Hon. W B Grey a thatched public house called The Wivern, which stood on the site of Westways. The Powells were certainly living there in April 1824 and the property was valued at five pounds. Roger Powell (c.1752–1826) was head of the household and had spent a good part, if not all, of his life in St Nicholas. In 1785 he was a churchwarden, making the first entries in a new book of baptisms and burials, and in 1815 and 1821 he was a Vestry signatory where he is styled shopkeeper, indicating that the public house served a dual purpose. His wife Mary (c.1758–1832) née Griffiths bore six children to certain knowledge and possibly more. The only boy, William, born in 1799, was a skilled man as the Poor Book states: "1824 July 21 Pd Wm Powell Carpenter as pr Bill 7 6."

Of the eldest daughter Mary, born in 1783, little is known except that her married name was David. The second daughter Esther (1785–1867) did not leave home until she was thirty-four when she finally wed John Evans of Pwll y Min Farm on 29 May 1819 (see Chapter 5). The marriage was witnessed by her brother William and brother-in-law James Lister.

Elizabeth, born in 1789, was Roger and Mary's third daughter and she married Richard Gibbon, bachelor of the parish of Bonvilston, by Licence on 15 May 1812. There are two known children of this marriage: Elizabeth, born in 1814 who married into the Earl family (see Chapter 7) and James born c.1823, who was a carpenter. Richard seems to have died by 1824 as Mrs Gibbon only is mentioned in subsequent rate books, census returns and on the Tithe Map. Elizabeth lived with her son James at No. 3 Smith's Row, first renting the house and ten acres of land and then in 1839, following in her father's footsteps, she relinquished the land and ran at the same premises a grocer's shop instead. She contributed parish service as follows:

1825	Mrs Gibbon for A Shift for Kate John	2 2
1826	Elizabeth Gibbon for 10 cart load of stones 3d p load	2 6
1828	paid Elizabeth Gibbon for 12 Cart load of Stones	3 0
1834	Pd by Mrs Gibbon towards the funeral (of Thomas Rees)	4 1

The fifth daughter Jane (1796–1847) married James Lister, a widower nearly twenty years her senior, on 14 November 1818.

His previous wife Elizabeth had been buried a year earlier, aged thirty-nine years.

In Roger's will, dated 18 July 1826, he states that he has an income from a share of a freehold lease and a stable and court in the parish of St John, Cardiff as well as the lease on a house in St Nicholas. After his wife's death all possessions are to revert to daughter Anne. After Roger Powell's burial on 1 August 1826 at seventy-four years, his wife still continued the victualler's trade: "1827 Paid Mrs Powell for Beer for Thos Ford 12 9 and £1 16 9."

At some stage, possibly on their marriage or on the death of Mary Powell in 1832, Ann and Samuel Rees moved into The Wivern and took over the business even though Samuel's first job was as a thatcher. The Tithe Map of 1838 shows that Samuel rented:

251	Cae Trehill	2 2 3
253	Garden	1
254	Pedwar erw Trehill	2 1 28
255	Mwddwlls Cwm	2 2 3
261	Garden	32
302	Inn, Garden	35
316	Stable, Garden	14
320	Erw Harry	1 16
	Total	9a 2r 1p

Alternatively, the rate book of the same year states that "Samuel Rees of the Wivern Public House rented eight acres one rood and twenty-five perches." Although he was quite new to the publican's life, Samuel, for some considerable time but certainly from 1825 to 1836, had been a parish constable retained at a salary of ten shillings and sixpence a year. He performed many duties on behalf of the parish during this period, some of which are detailed below:

1825	Saml Rees Constable Attending Licences Meeting	1 0
	Attending Militia Meeting	1 0
	for taking Swansea Man to Bridewell	1 6

Memorandum that Samuel Rees Thatcher is indepted [*sic*] to the Parish... £1 for Spars recd by him from Wm Williams [Three Tuns]. Samuel Rees has paid the above £1 to Dd Jenkins Overseer

	Saml Rees going to Merthyr 5/– pd in 3 Meetings 3/–	8 0
	do 1 Day to St Hillary & Wenvoe 2/6 forgot last year 1/6	4 0
1830	... for Cleaning Thos Rees House & Chimney Whitewashing	3 0
	... executing warrant & Expence For Warrant [see Chapter 6]	3 0
1831	... expences 2 different times at Peterstone	5 0

The Churchwardens' and Surveyors' accounts between 1836 and 1840 show that Samuel was paid a shilling for mending the church roof and one shilling and fourpence for four loads of stones. Ann was paid three shillings and ninepence for washing the church seats.

Samuel and Ann were still living at The Wivern on 12 January 1841 but would have been much more concerned about the progress being made on their new house. Whether The Wivern had outlived its usefulness as a public house is difficult to say, for its next occupants were none other than Samuel's sister-in-law and husband, and the latter did not have to work. It is also possible that they had been living here all along:

The Wyvern	James Lister	64	Independent
	Jane Lister	45	
	Sarah Morgan	15	Female Servant

By April 1841 Mr Lister had dispensed with most of the land that Samuel had rented, leaving only one acre and two roods. Jane died six years later aged fifty-two years, and husband James lasted a little longer, until 1849 when he was seventy-three. He was buried in St Nicholas even though he had moved to Cowbridge after his wife's death.

For some years Samuel Rees had rented land at Trehill and it was here that he chose to build a new public house called The Pryces' Arms, named after the Pryces of Duffryn who owned the site. The Rees family had moved in by 15 April 1841 and, in addition, rented another seven acres of land. Samuel, now fifty-four years of age, was described as "Thatcher and Publican" and unless appearances are deceptive, this building has always been slated – not too appropriate for such a craftsman. A lease dated 14 August 1841 gives more detail concerning the "Lease of a piece of ground with a Dwelling House thereon," the term of which was ninety-nine years from 1 May 1841 at a rent of one pound per annum. It states further that "to Samuel Rees, Victualler be leased on rent the part of land, whereon Samuel Rees hath lately erected and built a messuage or dwelling house and out buildings." The extent of the house was given as five perches and twelve yards and the following conditions applied. It was to be exempt from the land tax and kept in good repair, and Mr Rees was not allowed to erect any other buildings or houses, or carry out the work of beer retailer or alehouse man without written permission. To this end there was to be a cooling-off period of forty days from when payment was due for the owners to consider the application for beer-retailing, during which time Samuel could not sell ale. A plan of the new house was attached to the document.

Ann and Samuel Rees lived here until their respective deaths more than twenty years later. Their elder daughter was a house servant and Jane became a dressmaker. By 1861 Samuel, not surprisingly given his age, was no longer able to clamber on rooftops, but he was still an innkeeper. Gravestone inscriptions poignantly tell the rest of the tale. Samuel was buried in 1870 aged eighty-four, reunited with his first wife Margaret after nearly fifty years. Ann, who had died six years earlier aged seventy-two, had been buried with Samuel's parents.

By 1871 The Pryces' Arms was no more and had become an agricultural labourer's cottage, housing William and Hannah David and their two daughters Emma and Hannah.

CHAPTER 9

The Wright Family

"Be not the first by whom the new is tried,
Nor yet the last to lay the old aside."

WHEN ALEXANDER POPE penned these lines in 'An Essay on Criticism' he was comparing fashions in dress and manners with fashions in language. Keep up with the new and keep track of the old. In matters of agricultural implement manufacture, the Wright family did just that, so while they were never at the absolute cutting edge of innovation, neither were they Luddites.

The story begins with William (c.1770–1822) and Betty (c.1758–1837) Wright who originally came from the village or parish of Rishangles in the county of Suffolk. Today it is a hamlet comprising a cluster of houses including a shop and church. Of similar size to its counterpart in St Nicholas, and with a squat battlemented tower with angled buttresses, the old church, having stood empty and derelict for many years, has now been converted into holiday accommodation.

Mr and Mrs Wright first settled in Wenvoe parish at White Hall Farm, somewhere around the turn of the eighteenth century, with their two sons Benjamin (c.1799–1882) and William Twaits (c.1802–22) the last appellation being a surname not uncommon in Suffolk. What caused them to move across the country can only be a matter of speculation and it is a possibility that William worked on the Wenvoe estate. Not in doubt though are the skills that led him, his son and grandson to be mentioned in agricultural circles throughout most of the century.

Rishangles Church, Suffolk – unused for many years. William Wright was born in this parish, *c.*1770

The Glamorganshire Agricultural Society had for some decades been intent on improving farming practice. It had introduced the "four-course system" and then with the sum of £50 had bought "new and improved farm implements best suited to the county". These included "a Northampton plow" worked by two horses, and they were deposited in a warehouse in Cowbridge for the inspection of members. William Wright made his first contribution to the new agriculture in 1809 when, on 14 March, the Society awarded him a premium of five guineas "for having constructed two machines for thrashing by water and horse power (one for Mr Wm Evans, Fairwater and one for Mr Davies, Wenvoe)". The Society was well pleased, commenting that "Mr Wright thus stands out as the first practical machine manufacturer in the county." High praise indeed. Presumably there had been quite a few impractical contributions to improved husbandry techniques and possibly William had taken advantage of their mistakes.

Tragically and mysteriously, in 1822, William and his younger son of the same name died within twelve days of each other.

Shortly afterwards, some time between 1824 and 1828, the widowed Betty and bachelor Benjamin moved to Village Farm in St Nicholas. Benjamin, who had been born in Bedgrave, also in Suffolk, took a wife in his new parish in 1828. She was Elizabeth Williams, a spinster from Cardiff.

Wenvoe was held dear in family affections and fifteen years after her husband's death Betty was buried with William and her son. Benjamin and Eliza baptised their four children in the parish church and interred their first-born with his grandparents.

A double and symmetrical gravestone reads:

In Memory	Likewise
of William Wright	Betty Wife of the
of this Parish	said Wm Wright
native of	she died March
Rishangles in	30th 1837 Aged 79
the county of	Also
SUFFOLK	Wm Twaits Wright
who died Feby 9th	their Son died Feb 21st
1822 Aged 52	1822 Aged 20

Also William Twaits
Son of Benjamin and Eliza Wright
he died May 16th 1837 Aged 4 Years

In St Nicholas, the original Village Farm lay at right-angles to the present building and has been described as "a pretty thatched cottage with thatched porch". Benjamin was a carpenter by trade and no doubt, inspired by his father's success, he was also ambitious. This would ultimately make him one of the most important members of the village community. In 1838 he rented just two acres of land but then this increased as the Tithe Map shows.

294	House, Garden			1
333	Cwrt y wheod	1	2	37
334	do		1	36
335	do		2	21

Total 4a 2r 14p

The rate book of 1838–40 also indicates that he rented a carpenter's shop. By January 1841 Benjamin's interests had expanded again. He was still renting a "House, Land & Shop" but its extent was seven acres and seventeen perches. In the same year the census tells of Benjamin's young family and the beginnings of a workforce which was to grow considerably over the next three decades. There were two sons, William and Benjamin, one female servant and two apprentices in the household as well as the mother and father. In 1840 the couple had lost their only daughter Mary, and Benjamin would follow in 1845, leaving just the one son, William. This information is given on a gravestone in the churchyard but is not in accord with the register of burials, which reads:

Mary Wright, buried April 1st 1839

Benjamin Wright, buried February 7th 1844

The dates may vary but their early deaths cannot be disputed, as Mary had been born *c.*1835 and Benjamin *c.*1840.

It is at around this time that Benjamin first comes to notice as a manufacturer of agricultural machinery, including threshing machines and seed drills. In September 1844 his name figures on the prize list of the Glamorganshire Agricultural Society; he was awarded four pounds for the "best and most useful implements of husbandry." A similar award was made the following year and, on 26 September, 1848 Mr Wright was commended for a horse rake and scarifier.

Inspired by this success, Benjamin's plans for expansion took a new turn in 1846; he decided to move house and build afresh, extending the business in the process. Part of the site which attracted his attention had previously been rented by Joan David and comprised a house, garden and orchard. Mrs David, who was eighty-two in 1841 and a pauper, was the widow of William David, a carpenter who had died in 1826 aged sixty-seven years. It was in 1840 that Benjamin Wright had first rented a carpenter's shop in addition to that at Village Farm. It is a reasonable assumption that this was Mr David's old workshop and that through these circumstances, Benjamin first came to see the potential of the site and then, within six years, to occupy it himself. The original house here was a two-part structure, possibly a tenement and workshop, built onto Smith's Row. Then the end section was demolished and the remaining half used by the Wright family as a showroom for the products of their fast-developing village industry. This showroom has since been converted into or replaced by Nos 1 and 2 Smith's Row. The rest of the site that was earmarked was a large meadow where Llaneinydd now stands. Mr Wright was therefore responsible for building The Laurels (Pikel House) and other related barns/workshops, shortly after Joan David's death in 1845, slightly to the west of the previous, but now demolished, house. The following extracts from a lease state: "Register of Freehold Land. February 2nd 1887. Lease dated 1st January 1864 by John Bruce Pryce to Benjamin Wright from 1st January 1846 for 99 years of so much of the hereditaments numbered 307, 309 and 310 on the Tithe Map… of St Nicholas…"

From the time of his arrival in the village, Benjamin Wright gave valuable service to the parish in many roles. He was churchwarden for four years, Surveyor and Overseer for one year each, Guardian for two years and a Vestry signatory many times between 1844 and 1863.

The highways' book:

1828	paid Benjn Wright for Wilbr [wheelbarrow]	12 0
1835	Paid Benjamin Wright for 6 Cart loads of Stones at 4d. per cart load	2 0
1855	Benjamin Wright for a new handle etc. to a Rake	1 3
1860	Paid B Wright for a new Wheelbarrow	17 0

1861	Pd Benj Wright 2 days hire for Man, Horse & Cart		14 0

1864 It was agreed that Mr b Wright should undertake the supervision of the repairs contemplated on the Brook Lane – which would probably amount to £10 more or less.

The Poor Book:

1830	paid Benjamin Wright for a Coffin for Elizabeth Hopkin		16	0

The Churchwardens' book:

1831	Wright Carpenter Constables Staves mending door, gate	6	0
1848	Mr Wrights Bill	6 7	8
1849	B Wright, balance of last year	5 5	11½

Mr Wright was no longer just a village carpenter, for in 1851 at the age fifty-one he was able to style himself as "agricultural implement maker, farmer of forty-eight acres and employer of seven labourers". At the time of the census his household comprised of his wife, but not William his only surviving child, plus Elizabeth Gibbon, a twenty-one-year-old house servant. Also resident were six young men listed as an ironmonger-blacksmith, apprentice carpenters and farm servants, two of whom came from Suffolk. Benjamin was obviously importing English labour from the county of his birth as well as training a locally-born workforce. They are not men of his own generation but possibly sons of his childhood contemporaries.

Living elsewhere in the village in 1851 was a blacksmith called Mr Leggett. At first glance there seems to be no connection, but his birthplace of Rishangles is obviously significant, reinforcing the fact that the Wrights still kept close contact with friends and relatives back in Suffolk. There were certainly some good job opportunities in south Wales at this time and the assumption must be that Leggett was working for Benjamin.

William Leggett was thirty-six, his wife Matilda eight years his junior, and they had two daughters, Emma aged three, and a baby Harriet. They had two lodgers David Leggett, a farm labourer and Richard Baily, a gardener aged forty-two. The Leggett family was in the village as early as 1846 when, in January, a son William was baptised but he died on 26 September 1847, aged one year and ten months. After Emma and Harriet, a third daughter, Mary, was baptised on 29 February 1852. She was the last child of this marriage, for on 5 November of the same year Matilda died, aged thirty-two years. She and her son William are buried, appropriately for a smith, beneath a splendid cast-iron gravehead, the only one in the churchyard. The fate of the head of the family and his surviving children is not known. In 1861 there were still two of William's brothers in the village. Ephraim Leggett, farm labourer of Wickham, Suffolk, aged forty-seven, had married local girl Jane Evans in 1856; and David, the youngest of the three at thirty-seven, had previously lived with William. Also in this family unit was Thomas Evans, Jane's father, a widower of eighty-eight from Merthyr Dyfan.

Mr Wright's implement business seems to have been highly successful with, it is rumoured, more than twenty hands being employed particularly during the period 1860 to 1880, when the influence of son William was felt. By 1861 the latter also styled himself "implement maker" as did five other live-in apprentices. Of these, one came from Suffolk, one from Ireland, and there were three locals. Benjamin had laid the foundations of the business for his son and seems to have retired more and more into the background, eventually preferring to call himself a private resident. Meanwhile, William came quickly to the fore in both business and parish affairs. He was a member of the Vestry in his early twenties and served in this capacity until his relatively early death only one year after his father's. He was rector's Churchwarden from 1867 to 1873, Overseer of the poor 1876–8 and Guardian on four occasions. There are four known children from his marriage to Betsy Wride, but the first son, Francis William, born in 1861 died before he was a one year-old. Whereas, the second child, Harriet Amelia, was baptised soon after birth in 1863, William waited until 9 March 1873, when he was churchwarden, to christen Francis William aged eight, and George Ernest aged four.

In the 1870s, William employed four men and one boy on

a permanent basis but there must have been a larger temporary workforce, because the farm had now grown to 144 acres. Like his father and grandfather before him, William devoted much of his time to the design and manufacture of agricultural implements producing among other things mechanical pitchforks and pikels or hayloaders. Some of these devices were patented and exhibited.

On 9 June 1870 "William Twaites Wright, of St Nicholas, … Agricultural and Implement Maker, and Evan Yorath, of Molton, near Cowbridge, … Farmer" deposited a provisional specification and detailed drawing "for the Invention of 'Improved Apparatus or Machinery for Lifting, Lowering, Loading, and Unloading Hay, Corn, Straw, and other Materials'". The patent was granted on 26 November of the same year and consisted of four pages of description.

The vertical pole, which was likened to a ship's mast, was about forty feet long, let into the ground three or four feet deep, and secured by four stay ropes. A double boom stood out from the mast in opposite directions and could be raised or lowered by a man turning a ratchet wheel and handle fixed to a system of double and single pulley blocks and stay rods. A waggon or hoisting rope passed through pulleys attached to the booms "to one end of each of which is fastened a fork (of quite a new description)." The disengaged end of the first rope passed along the boom, down the mast, under a pulley and carried on to the anchor pulley which was set horizontally, allowing the rope to pass round and be attached to a horse. The anchor pulley was placed at a distance from the mast equal to the height to which the hay had to be raised. A second rope with fork followed a similar course, but having passed under the bottom mast pulley was attached directly to the horse missing out the anchor pulley. This contrivance caused "the same action of the horse" to ascend one fork and descend the other "at one and the same time", or if desired, by detaching one rope the other fork worked independently.

For unloading a waggon, the ropes were adjusted to have one fork close up to the boom, the other one being right down on

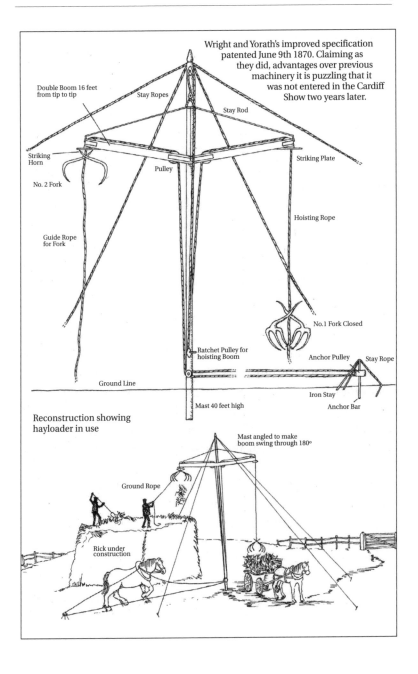

Wright and Yorath's improved specification patented June 9th 1870. Claiming as they did, advantages over previous machinery it is puzzling that it was not entered in the Cardiff Show two years later.

Double Boom 16 feet from tip to tip

Stay Ropes

Stay Rod

Striking Horn

No. 2 Fork

Pulley

Striking Plate

Hoisting Rope

Guide Rope for Fork

No.1 Fork Closed

Ratchet Pulley for hoisting Boom

Anchor Pulley

Stay Rope

Ground Line

Iron Stay

Anchor Bar

Mast 40 feet high

Reconstruction showing hayloader in use

Mast angled to make boom swing through 180°

Ground Rope

Rick under construction

the hay itself. This latter fork or pikel was pushed into the hay, the lifting action causing it to close by its own weight, when the horse moved from mast to anchor pulley. The fork then ascended, and as the mast was fixed leaning slightly towards the rick, the loaded pikel swung the boom around until the end was over the centre of the stack. The horns of the fork hit the striking plate and the load was automatically shed, at which time No 2 fork was loaded, the horse turned round and started in the opposite direction repeating the process.

Alternatively the two ropes could be spliced to form an endless rope passing round the anchor pulley. A horse or other motive power could be attached by a bar at right angles to the anchor bar, but attached to the base of the anchor pulley, so that the horse could turn the pulley and by so doing wind the endless rope round it.

The double action pitching fork could be worked "by any ordinary lad and will elevate as much as many men", and it could be made to deposit materials in two different places up to fifteen feet apart. Messrs Wright and Yorath wished it to be "distinctly understood that we claim as new: First; fixing the peculiar construction of boom and mast so as to revolve or move up and down by means of the pulleys, ropes and ratchet. Secondly; the application and action of the self-acting double action forks by closing when down and opening when coming into contact with plates on the boom. Thirdly; the application of the pulleys and wheels together with the anchor pulley so as to cause an opposite and continuous action at one and the same time at each end of the boom on both of the said forks respectively, causing one to revolve, ascend, and open, the other to revolve, descend, and close."

This was the most famous product of the flourishing Wright/Yorath partnership, but how many were made and sold is not known. It is very difficult to assess the efficiency of the apparatus but the following points are of interest: the horse had to move an equivalent distance to the hay; there was a surplus of motive power with the horse being capable of raising a far greater amount of hay than the fork could hold; attaching a steam engine to the apparatus would have increased its efficiency.

The folklore of hay-raising equipment further suggests that there were dangers involved in working swinging booms with related rope-and-pulley systems, as any yachtsman would testify. That the efficacy of this kind of machinery was in some doubt was confirmed two years later, in 1872, when for the first time the Royal Agricultural Society of England held its annual show in Cathays Park, Cardiff. William Wright was a member of the Society and used the show for exhibition purposes. On the forty-acre site there were on display and trial a total of 5,843 implements. Strangely William entered not his improved pikel mentioned above, but a previous and less sophisticated version.

This machine was entered in the "Trials of Implements, Class V, For the best Straw or Hay Elevator to be worked by horse power" for a first prize of ten pounds and a second prize of five pounds. The design differences of this pitchfork were that the vertical pole was held by three, not four, guy ropes, there was only one boom which was swung by a man pulling a guide rope and not by the inclination of the pole and the fork unloaded itself when the ring struck the tappet. There were ten entries in Class V of the competition with seven being machine-powered elevators. The other three smaller implements that acted as pitchforks were raised by ropes and drawn by horses and included Mr Wright's invention and one by H Yorath, presumably one of Evan's relations. The trial for these machines took place on Friday, 12 June 1872, the task being to elevate the loose haulm (stems) obtained in threshing-out clover. This material which was "short, dry and loose was best done by the double pitchfork shown by W T Wright while the Yorath single fork was not much inferior in its performance". Mr Yorath submitted a pitchfork of gigantic proportions, with sharp tines three feet long, and this was considered by the judges to be dangerous to the men on the stack. Mr Wright incurred criticism of his design for the jar which occurred when the ring struck the tappet as this was thought to be "very severe and objectionable when raising a large and heavy

235

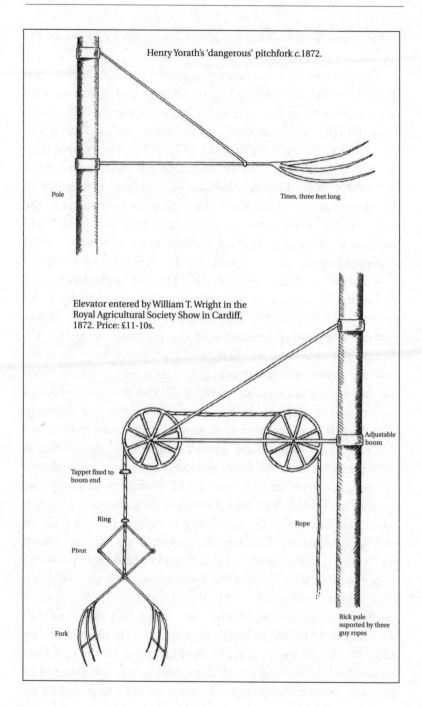

Henry Yorath's 'dangerous' pitchfork *c.*1872.

Pole

Tines, three feet long

Elevator entered by William T. Wright in the
Royal Agricultural Society Show in Cardiff,
1872. Price: £11-10s.

Adjustable
boom

Tappet fixed to
boom end

Ring

Rope

Pivot

Rick pole
suported by three
guy ropes

Fork

pitch of hay." It was also considered better suited to straw than hay. Significantly the judges commented that there was no chance of a prize when "competing against machines which dispensed with manual assistance" suggesting that "on future occasions, it will be well to enter them in a class by themselves". Also "when pitted against the more effective and expensive machines they had no chance of succeeding, although on small holdings and under special circumstances they may be found of great use where the other machines cannot be obtained". The working life of such contraptions was limited to ricking hay and corn at harvest time, and there was "inconvenience" in erecting poles and ropes, whereas the new improved stackers, elevators and rickers were mobile on wheels.

The catalogue of the Cardiff show gives the prices of the two loaders:

| H Yorath | £8 15 0 | Weight 3¼ cwt |
| W T Wright | £11 10 0 | Weight 4 cwt (not including poles and ropes) |

These two exhibitors were not to be discouraged, for two years after William's death there is the following note at the Royal Show at Preston in 1885: "Mr Henry Yorath exhibited a new clip-fork elevator No 5228 which is an improvement upon the implement that was exhibited by Mr W T Wright in 1872 at Cardiff." The jarring of the ring striking the tappet had now been rectified "by adding 3 small pulleys to the upper frame of the clip forks and passing through them a check cord in such a manner that when the cord is pulled the fork is opened and unloaded at any point of the sweep of the boom."

The Wright enterprise was sold in the 1880s, and in 1881 Benjamin, who had been a widower since 1864, and a hitherto-unknown brother Robert, aged sixty-six, lived at 48 Llandaff Road, Cardiff with a servant, Emily Eyles aged twenty to assist them. Benjamin died the following year and William the year after that. The widowed Betsy was still living at the "Wrights" and "living on her own means" in 1891 with her three children, of whom Francis was variously described as a commercial clerk in "steam coal" and an accountant. At some point she moved to Abergavenny but was brought back to St Nicholas for burial in 1916. By 1901 The Laurels was occupied by Thomas and Alice James and he is described as running a dealer's shop.

It is likely that one of the Yorath family was instrumental in setting up Yorath, Grieves and Co. of Pitman Lane, Ryder Street, Cardiff. In 1919, at the Royal Agricultural Society show in Cardiff this firm exhibited a machine-powered hay and corn elevator priced at twenty-four pounds and ten shillings. The Wright/Yorath era of horse power was over.

Benjamin Wright's epitaph reads: "The Memory of the Just is Blessed."

CHAPTER 10

Lay Subsidy Returns / Hearth Tax Returns

Lay Subsidy Returns

The "parysshe of Saynt Nicholas" 1543–45.

Levied from the twelfth to the seventeenth century, the lay subsidy was a rate payable at one penny in the pound for all householders who were not paupers and whose lands or personal effects such as goods, crops or wages were valued at not less than one pound. The lay subsidy was so-called because clerical property was exempt, although there were separate clerical subsidies. From these returns it is possible to make some assessment of the population and prosperity of the parish. Of interest is the frequent use in the names of 'ap' and 'verch' perpetuating the Welsh custom of patronymy. By the time of the 1670 Hearth Tax Return, there is only one 'ap' but this does not necessarily prevent the taking of a father's Christian name by his offspring. This custom has frequently caused problems for compilers of early Welsh genealogies.

First on the list in 1543 is James Button, resident at Doghill Grange and by far and away the largest landowner. He is followed by thirty-seven other people, eleven of whom had property valued at or more than twenty pounds:

Jamys Button for hys lands	26s. 0d.
Gwenlhean Dyo lands	3s. 4d.
Matho John Duy g(oods)	6s. 8d.
John Richerde g(oods)	2s. 0d.
William Robert g	2s. 0d.
Kateryn Jeynkyn g	2s. 0d.
John Smyth g	8d.
John Harry g	1s. 8d.
Thomas John Duy g	1s. 8d
Hoell? Beasts g	1s. 8d.
Thomas ap Jevan Lloyde g	6d.
Hoell ap John Hoell g	6d.
David ap Morgan g	2s. 0d.
John ap Jeynkyn Hoell g	4d.
Jevan ap Jevan g	6d.
Dyo Hullyn g	2s. 0d.
John Hoell g	1s. 8d.
Hoell Dyo Thomas g	6d.
Llewelyn Hoell g	4d.
Morgan ap Hoell g	4d.
Marget ap Hoell g	6d.
Dyo ap Jevan g	6d.
Dyo Thomas David g	6d.
Nicholas Hoell g	2d.
Jenet verch Hoell	2d.
Thomas ap Hoell	2d.
Allson?	2d.
John Robert	2d.
John Evan?	2d.
Llewelyn Dyo	2d.
John Dyo	2d.
Thomas Phelip Lewys g	4d.
John ap David	2d.

John Rosser g	4d.
Morgan John Duy g	4d.
?Robart (?Barbbyst) Grono	2d.
Jene ap John	4d.
Jenet verch Richerde	2d.

The list for the following year 1544 contains twenty-eight names, with these people paying between them a total of thirty-five shillings and ten pence, and the following year thirty-five people were eligible to pay the rate.

Hearth Tax Returns

Introduced by Charles II who was facing serious financial problems, the hearth tax was in effect a tax on chimneys, charged at a rate of two shillings per fireplace, hearth or stove, and payable between the years 1662 and 1688, at which time it was abolished. Strictly speaking it was a half-yearly rate of one shilling for each hearth of every person whose house was worth more than twenty shillings. The two transcriptions for St Nicholas date from 1670–1 and 1673. It is the first of these which is the most accurate and comprehensive. It lists the great majority, if not all, of the households in St Nicholas at the time of the assessment, including those who were discharged from payment through poverty or having an income of less than £100. Charitable institutions with an annual income of less than £100 were also exempt as were industrial hearths such as furnaces or kilns, but not smithies or bakeries. The 1673 return has fewer names and some of those originally classed as "chargeable" or liable to pay the tax were later discharged for no given reason.

In 1670–1, out of eighty-seven householders, a total of fifty-six had exemption from payment. All of these were "Discharged by legall Certificatt" and listed as having one hearth only. Of the thirty-one people paying the tax, only two can be identified in their own houses, namely Martin Button at Duffryn and Thomas Button at Cottrell. It is possible that William Williams with ten hearths lived at the Manor House, as this would have been a building to rank with Cottrell. The eastern half of Smith's Row had two hearths back-to-back in No 5 and The Three Tuns would have had two or more fireplaces. A total of twenty-four of the eighty-seven householders were women, widowed or single, a proportion not out of keeping with other parishes in the Vale of Glamorgan.

The Hearth Tax Returns of 1670–1 show that Martin Button Esquire had twelve hearths and Thomas Button Esquire and William Williams had ten each. George Morgan and Harry Miles each had five hearths, Widdow Williams four, John Rosser and Morice Williams three. Householders with two hearths: Rees John, Lewis Jones, Thomas Griffith, William Lewis, Anne Adam, Richard Morice, Thomas Rosser, another Widdow Williams, John Morgan, William Thomas in two houses and John Griffith. Householders with one hearth only: Thomas John, Roger Howell, John Alexander, Rees Williams, William Francis, Thomas Williams, Widdow Richard, Roger Richard, Robert Watkin, Margaret Morgan, Phillip Dart, William Rosser and Gwillim Rosser. Discharged with one hearth: Maud Gwillim, William Phillip, Katherine Llewelyn widow, Jenkin Richard, Lewis Gibbon, William Morgan Taylor, Evan ap Rees, Edward John, Edward Griffith, John Morice, John Gibbon, William Phillip, David Morgan, Rees Edward, Lewis Robert, Thomas Richard, Robert David, Johan Meyrick widow, William Robbert, Samuell William, Friswith Edward, Johan John widdow, John Evan, Harry John, Miles William, William Morgan, Evan John, Mary Paine widow, Anne William, Walter Morgan, Alice David, Richard Morice, John Rosser, Thomas Rosser, Margarett Gwillim, William Thomas, Margarett Phillip, George Elliott, Reinold Evan, Maude John, Richard Miles, Jenkin Morgan, Mary William, Katherine Howell widow, Cecill John, Anne William, Gwenllian Griffith, Cecill William, Johan John, Leyson Jenkin, Thomas William, Elizabeth John, James Morgan, Thomas Gervis, Rees Robert and Evan David.

The 1673 return lists fifty-nine householders of whom it

seems only twelve eventually paid the tax. A third member of the Button family, Robert, is listed as occupying a house with four hearths.

It is not easy to estimate a parish population from the number of households. In the Neath area it has been calculated that there were 975 houses at this time giving an estimated 5,200 people or 5.33 persons per house. Applied to St Nicholas eighty-seven houses could have held a hypothetical population of 464, a figure higher than at any time during the ninetenth century. Further research has suggested that an average of 4.75 persons per household would be a more accurate assessment and this would reduce the projected population to a more acceptable 413 which is in line with later proven statistics.

CHAPTER 11

Smith's Row
*c.*1620–1980

(BLACK)SMITH'S ROW OCCUPIES a central position in the village of St Nicholas, on the north side of the main road. Built of the local limestone, it fronts this road with a long southern elevation and turns its back on the village green and church emphasising, yet again, the long-standing importance of this means of communication. The Row, now divided into three cottages (four, at one time) was originally two houses with a working unit in between, sharing a gable with the western house. The earliest surviving architectural details are at the eastern end of the Row, and later lean-to units at the rear of each cottage are of mid- to late-Victorian origin.

The eastern house has two rooms with a large central back-to-back chimney with timber bressummers over the fireplaces. In the late nineteenth century, it was divided into two cottages, with a straight flight timber stair inserted in each room, the spiral stair blocked and the large window made smaller. The original south doorway to this house, now partially blocked and containing a window, opened into the narrower central room which has a ceiling of roughly adzed, lateral joist-beams. When the cottage was sub-divided a lobby entrance was formed by inserting a new doorway in line with the central chimney. This gave a common entrance to each of the housing units. A new rear door to the eastern room may also have been inserted at this time. This room once had a large, and possibly three-light, dressed stone window

Smith's Row 1908

Smith's Row 1930s

under a relieving arch. The ceiling over is supported on lateral quarter-round moulded beams, with thirteen reed-moulded joists in each bay.

In the eastern gable wall at first-floor level is a small blocked dressed stone window combining sunk-chamfered jambs with a hollow-chamfered head under a stone hood. This feature allows

245

Smith's Row 1950s

Smith's Row 1960s

the cottage to be quite accurately dated. Similar mouldings at Beaupré castle and Llantrithyd church suggest a date for the eastern half of cottage and workshop of c.1625.

Apart from the thick walls, the central cottage dates from about 1900 in style but originally was some form of workshop open to the roof. By 1838 it had been converted to a dwelling.

The situation of the cottage and workshop suggests that it might have been the original smithy, as the present village blacksmith's shop is directly opposite. In the first half of the nineteenth century the occupants were shoemakers. The stonework of the south wall confirms at least two raisings of the roof, with old thatching material remaining in the previous levels. This accords with the straight joint at first-floor level between the eastern house and the workshop, indicating that the latter was once of single-storey height. In 1981, just at the top of this storey and within the thickness of the wall, a woman's shoe was found. Dating from the nineteenth century it has a stacked heel, cross-over latchet fastening and a chisel toe with punched decoration, once painted blue and white. It is not uncommon for shoes to be found under house walls but quite unusual at the height of the eaves. The roof timbers over the whole of the eastern part of the Row are sawn and have late butt-purlins.

The western house has two main rooms with a cross-passage now within the western section. The walls of this house are somewhat thinner and all the openings have wooden lintels. The ceiling beams in the eastern room are narrow chamfered with curved stops and probably date from about 1700. The fireplace in the eastern wall of this room has a voussoir stone arch. From the back of this chimney is a flue which leads through the wall into the old workshop or central house. This flue is faced with industrial bricks and was once connected to an oven or boiler.

This type of housing is of a standard of construction which suggests that the original occupants could have been yeomen farmers or village craftsmen, and not labourers. In the nineteenth century the occupants tended to be tradesmen/women and labourers who rented smallholdings scattered throughout the parish in order to supplement their incomes.

Within living memory the cottages had larger front gardens surrounded by a high stone wall. As late as 1930 the western half was painted a deep cream and had once been yellow ochre as successive layers of limewash testify. This latter colour had enjoyed some popularity throughout the area. In 1835 the churchwardens

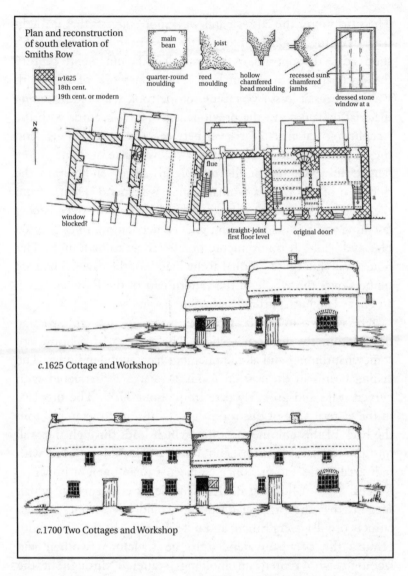

Plan and reconstruction of south elevation of Smiths Row

*w*1625
18th cent.
19th cent. or modern

main bean

joist

quarter-round moulding

reed moulding

hollow chamfered head moulding

recessed sunk chamfered jambs

dressed stone window at a

N

flue

window blocked?

straight-joint first floor level

original door?

a

*c.*1625 Cottage and Workshop

*c.*1700 Two Cottages and Workshop

of the parish purchased a "liming brush" and "yellow oka" for two shillings and nine pence for washing the church, church house and churchyard wall, showing that not all buildings were in the traditional white lime of the Vale.

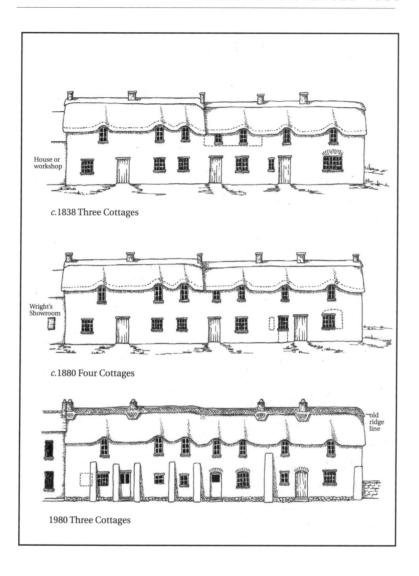

*c.*1838 Three Cottages

*c.*1880 Four Cottages

1980 Three Cottages

Traditional Recipes

Faggots

(as made by Mrs G M Morgan of Pwll Sarn)

Ingredients:
1 pig's liver
1 pig's heart
1 piece of lights (lungs) – optional
1 lb of suet (or gribbles)
2–3 cups of breadcrumbs
2–3 cups of porridge oats
1 pig's apron (belly skin) well soaked in salt water
4 big onions
2 apples, minced – optional
4 chopped sage leaves
1 teaspoon of nutmeg
handful of salt and pepper

Method:
Scald the liver, heart and lights in a large pan half-filled with water. Bring to heat and boil for three minutes. Remove contents from the pan, allow to cool and mince with the onions. Add all the other ingredients including the chopped sage. Mix in a large bowl with a wooden spoon.

Cut enough apron to cover the top of a good-sized breakfast cup. Place this in the left hand and fill with one dessertspoon of the mixture. Squeeze together to close.

Put the faggots in a large pan and half immerse them in water. Cook in a slow oven for one hour. Cool and then grill or fry as desired.

Fruit Cake

(as made by Miss Elizabeth Earl of The Three Tuns)

The following is a recipe for a rich fruit cake made by Miss Earl. The superb quality of the cake comes from the method rather than the ingredients and probably the use of fire heat influenced the taste as it was cooked on an old range.

Ingredients:

1 lb flour	teaspoon of salt
¾ lb butter	rind of two lemons
¾ lb caster sugar	juice of one lemon
4 oz raisins	cup of brandy
4 oz currants	½ cup of cherries
4 oz sultanas	6 eggs
4 oz ground almonds	½ cup of milk

Time: one day

Method:

Place the butter in a large bowl to warm slowly by the fire. Add the sugar and leave to dissolve while occupied with other chores. When completely dissolved, beat well with a wooden spoon. Then beat in the eggs and add the milk and lemon juice. Add one cup of brandy and the rest of the dry ingredients. The cake tin is lined in the usual way with brown paper inside and out, and after placing the mixture therein place greased brown paper lightly on

251

top. The tin is then put on a large meat tray and surrounded by salt, some of which is allowed to lie under the tin itself. The cake is cooked at an even temperature (which is unspecified as it is fire heat) for at least four hours and without looking at it.

The finished cake, if decorated, was covered liberally with rose water, marzipanned three-quarters of an inch thick, covered with royal icing and finally dotted with sweet violets.

Afterthought

THERE IS VERY little information in this book concerning the twentieth and twenty-first centuries, and most of what there is stops at around the time of the Great War. Many interesting themes suggest themselves and I mention a few below, anticipating that they will encourage someone else to research and write another episode in the life of this fascinating parish, as I, in my turn, was inspired by reading Mr Shepherd's book.

Subsidised farming courtesy of the European Community and the demarcation of the so-called Green Belt and village envelope have had a marked effect on the use and development of land. The protection of listed buildings, alien architectural designs for new housing and a lack of provision of affordable housing for the young have all had their adherents and opponents. The role of a commuter village, the mobility of the individual and changing nature of employment have affected the social and demographic make-up of the parish. The two big estates of the parish have become amenities, with the ailing Duffryn Gardens finally being restored to something like its former glory through large inputs of cash, and the neglected Cottrell reinventing itself as a thriving and successful golf course. The thwarted plans of would-be developers would make for interesting reading. Another golf course, a large hotel, a new village with racecourse and extensive housing on green-field sites have all been proposed and thankfully rejected. The story moves on…

Sources

Books

George Borrow, *Wild Wales* (Humphrey Milford, 1920).

R L Brown, *The Population of the Hamlet of Glyncorrwg* (Tongwynlais, Cardiff, 1982).

C Burgess, *The Age of Stonehenge* (J M Dent & Sons Ltd., 1980).

Nicholas Carlisle, *A Topographical Dictionary of the Dominion of Wales* (1811).

Julian Cope, *The Modern Antiquarian* (Thorsons, 1998).

Dewi Davies, *Welsh Place-Names and their meanings* (The Cambrian News).

Sir Cyril Fox, *Ancient Monuments Vol. IV South Wales & Monmouthshire* (HMSO, 1954).

Giraldus Cambrensis, *The Itinerary through Wales* (J M Dent & Sons Ltd., 1908).

Matthew Griffiths, *Penmark and Porthkerry Families and farms in the 17th century Vale of Glamorgan*.

B E Gully, *Some Norman Links in the Vale of Glamorgan Fence* (Gully Publishing, 1997).

D W Harding (ed.), *Hillforts*.

W G Hoskins, *The Making of the English Landscape* (Penguin, 1991).

W R Lambert, *Drink and Sobriety in Victorian Wales c.1820–c.1895*.

Rice Merrick, *Morganiae Archaiographia* (South Wales Record Society, 1983).

A Morris, *Glamorgan* (J E Southall, Newport, 1907).

Richard Muir, *The English Village* (Thames & Hudson, 1981).

Richard Muir, *Riddles in the British Landscape* (Thames & Hudson, 1981).

Dr F J North, *The Geological History of the Vale.*

Francis Pryor, *Britain BC* (Harper Perrenial, 2004).

John Richards, *Cottrell* (Cottrell Park, 1999).

Edward Royle, *Modern Britain A Social History 1750–1985* (Hodder Arnold, 1997).

C F Shepherd, *St George-super-Ely.*

C F Shepherd, *St Nicholas* (1934).

C F Shepherd, *The Winding Trail.*

M R Spencer, *Annals of South Glamorgan.*

C J Spurgeon, *Glamorgan's First Castles (Glamorgan, Vol. III Part 1a)* (Royal Commission on Ancient and Historical Monuments in Wales).

Roy Strong, *The Story of Britain* (Hutchinson, 1996).

C Taylor, *Roads and Tracks of Britain* (J M Dent & Sons Ltd., 1979).

Charles Wesley, *First Visit to Wales,* (10th November 1740).

Professor G J Williams, *The Vale of Glamorgan.*

W G Wrenche, *Wrenche and Radcliffe of Glamorgan.*

Archives, Articles, Documents and Directories:

St Nicholas registers of:

banns, marriages 1755–1812, 1825–1970

baptisms, burials 1780–1812

burials 1812–1966

marriages 1813–37

baptisms 1813–1915

Registers of baptisms, burials and marriages for Peterston-super-Ely, Wenvoe, St George-super-Ely, Bonvilston, Llantrithyd, Llancarfan and St Lythans

Nonconformist Baptist Register, Trehill 1823–36

St Nicholas Churchwardens book 1820–80

St Nicholas Highways book 1820–80

St Nicholas Poor Book 1824–36

St Nicholas Rate books 1838–43, 1879–83, 1919, 1926

Exchequer receipts St Nicholas/Malefant 1541

Lay Subsidy Returns 1543–45

Manorial Survey, Earl of Pembroke 1570

Hearth Tax Returns 1670–1, 1673

St Nicholas Census Returns 1841, 1851, 1861, 1871, 1881, 1891, 1901

Land Tax Returns

St Nicholas Tithe Map 1838

Tithe Maps of Wales, The National Library of Wales

St Nicholas Wills, The National Library of Wales

The Patent Office, London

Survey of Wenvoe Estate 1762–3

Duffryn Estate Sale Catalogue 1937

Glyn Cory Brochure *The Garden Village of South Wales*

Journal, Royal Agricultural Society of England 1872, 1885

Records of Glamorgan Agricultural Society

The Welsh Revival 1904–05 Edith Blumhofer

A Topographical Dictionary of Wales, Samuel Lewis (1833)

The Parish Magazine (1912)

Worrells Directory (1875)

Slaters Commercial Directory (1880)

Kellys Directory 1895, 1926

Literary Connections with Swanbridge John Hicks GFHS Journal No. 75

The Diary of William Thomas (1762–95)

Bishop of Llandaff's *Ecclesiastical Questionnaire* 1946

Apprenticeship Indenture of Abraham Harry

Gravestones

The parish churches and graveyards of St Nicholas, Peterston-super-Ely, Wenvoe, St George-super-Ely, St Lythans, Bonvilston, Pendoylan and Croes y Parc Chapel.

Acknowledgements

I WOULD PARTICULARLY like to thank Anne Walklate for her encouragement, assistance and support during the early stages of research, fieldwork and information gathering and also for the traditional recipes and the illustration of the Earls at The Three Tuns.

My thanks also to Edward Angell-Parsons, Mrs D Cule, Miss Georgina Cule, Miss Gwyneth Cule, Lionel Cull, Paula Embley, Dr M Griffiths, Mrs P Harry, Mr & Mrs R Harry, Mr P Haynes, Peter Jones, Miss A Morgan, Mrs G M Morgan, Mrs D Penny, Rector G Rees, Mr H Brooksby from the Royal Commission on Ancient & Historical Monuments in Wales, Mr E Scourfield from the Department of Farming and Rural Life, The Librarian – Museum of Welsh Life St Fagans, Mrs Gwendoline Prosser, Daphne West, Glamorgan Record Office, Bridgend Library and Information Service.

Inevitably in a work of this nature there will be unintentional errors of fact, transcription or interpretation and for these I apologise.

Also from Y Lolfa:

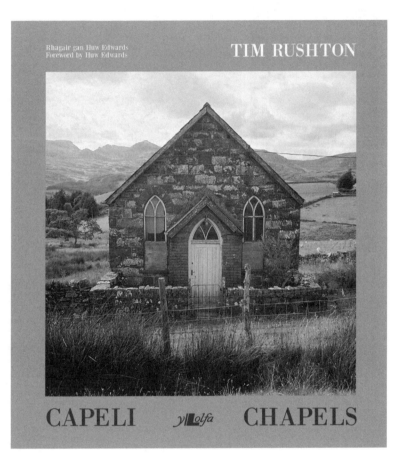

£14.95

cyflwyno **cartrefi** cefn gwlad cymru
introducing **houses** of the welsh countryside

RICHARD SUGGETT & GREG STEVENSON

£14.95

Wales

the **100** places to see before you die

John Davies
and Marian Delyth

Y Lolfa

2010 Welsh Book of the Year winner

£19.95